Praise For

Thermostat Cultures

"Culture is not a side priority on high-performing teams. It is EVERYTHING. Jason Barger is right on in his approach to people, alignment and values. His spirit and work is infectious and highly valuable. *Thermostat Cultures* is a must read."

> - Howard Behar, Former President, **Starbucks Coffee**,
> author of *It's Not About The Coffee* and *The Magic Cup*

"There is a common desire to be part of something larger than ourselves. In a team setting, culture is the glue that brings together like minded individuals, for better or worse. Perennial losing cultures have indifference to communication, accountability, and grit. Strong winning cultures promote these values as the lifeblood of their journey. Jason Barger's proactive spirit and message is foundational."

> - Shane Battier, **2-Time NBA World Champion**,
> 2001 NCAA Men's Basketball National Champion

"Organizations love posters with words about values. That's always good. But thankfully Jason Barger takes the next steps to help you live the culture you want with intentional action. *Thermostat Cultures* gives permission to lead and to care."

> - Terry Hershey, **author** of *The Power of Pause*

JasonVBarger.com

Thermostat Cultures

How Proactive People Create Inspired & Engaged Teams

FIRST EDITION

© Copyright 2016

by Jason V. Barger

This book may be purchased for personal, educational, business, or sales promotional use. To obtain discounted bulk copies for your organization, please contact Info@JasonVBarger.com. For other information regarding additional resources, books, speaking engagements, or consulting for your team, please visit www.JasonVBarger.com

ISBN: 978-0-692-79121-9

One Love Publishers

PRINTED IN THE UNITED STATES OF AMERICA

Cover Design: Adam Emery

THERMOSTAT
CULTURES

How Proactive People Create

Inspired & Engaged Teams

By Jason V. Barger

ISBN: 978-0-692-79121-9

One Love Publishers

Dedicated to every leader, friend, coach, teammate, and business relationship who has engaged my mind and heart and therefore ignited positive work in the world. I am especially grateful to my parents, who created a family culture that valued adventure, purpose, possibility, and consistency. I know the temperature you set has had a lasting and meaningful impact on me and many others. Thank you.

CONTENTS

The ROI on Culture & Engagement
We're in A Metrics World and Some Need Statistics
to Begin the Journey

If you are someone who seeks data to affirm the return on investment for your efforts, consider these:

"Organizations with a high level of engagement do report 22% higher productivity, according to a new meta-analysis of 1.4 million employees conducted by the Gallup Organization." (Harvard Business Review)

"The most-engaged workplaces experience the following performance metrics: 2 times higher customer loyalty, higher productivity, and lower turnover." (Pont, Decision-Wise)

"Engaged companies grow profits as much as 3 times faster than their competitors." (Corp. Leadership Council)

"A disengaged employee costs an organization approximately $3,400 for every $10,000 in annual salary." (McLean & Company)

According to a recent national survey, the most common reason couples divorce is a "lack of commitment"(73%). Not far behind is "unrealistic expectations" (45%). Lack of a shared vision.

When the coaches of the last two College Football National Championships were asked why they won, the word "culture" led the way.

Preface: WHY READ THIS?

Why do some teams with basically the same level of talent as their competitors succeed while others fall short?

Why do some businesses seem to capture the minds and hearts of their employees while other similar organizations simply sputter along?

Why do some marriages or families seem to thrive in the midst of busy schedules and challenging situations while others become scattered and splintered?

Culture.

No matter what they are doing, *HOW* they do it is different. They have clarity and alignment that allow them to adapt, grow, and develop.

This book is written for those who want to lead or be a part of creating compelling cultures in their life and work.

It is written for anyone who leads or contributes to a team of any kind and has a desire to raise the level of joy, passion, clarity, and success with those people. And by *team* I mean...

11

Business teams working together to accomplish identified results.

Parents or soon-to-be parents who want to set the temperature for the kind of family they hope to design or still have time to create.

The sports team who has now figured out that *HOW* they work together is critical to *WHAT* they actually accomplish.

The church, club or organization you serve that is aiming to mobilize people to come together for a mission greater than themselves.

The teachers and educators who know that the learning environment they create determines whether the curriculum they teach moves from a compilation of transactional information into a transformational experience.

And it is for those people who are part of a company or entity and who desire to ignite the minds and hearts of its people. It is for those people who wake up every day and strive to accomplish great things in a fast-changing world.

I wrote this book because I have studied, experienced, and witnessed the power of creating compelling cultures that elevate people and performance. From Little League sports to Fortune 100 companies, the culture we create with those around us is everything.

I hope you'll read this book because:

You want to play a role in creating compelling cultures in your life and work.

You want to bring out the best in yourself and others.

You know deep down that everything will be better because of the culture you create.

You know it's easier not to care, to disengage, to go back into autopilot mode in your life and career. But in your most honest moments, you know you desire more.

So let's begin setting the temperature in your life.

Introduction:
THE THERMOMETER
VS.
THE THERMOSTAT

You know the difference between a thermometer and a thermostat, right?

A thermometer *reads* the temperature. If there were a giant thermometer on your wall right now, it would tell you only the temperature in the room. If it got cold in the room, the thermometer would indicate the change. If the temperature went up, the little red line on the thermometer would go up and tell you the temperature. A thermometer *reacts* to the external conditions and reads the temperature.

A thermostat *sets* the temperature. It controls the temperature. It regulates the temperature. You set the temperature you desire and the thermostat *proactively* responds by regulating the temperature moment by moment. If it gets too cold in the room, the thermostat adjusts and allows the room to return to the desired state. If it's too warm, the thermostat responds to create the environment you desire.

Too many leaders, teams, and organizations are stuck in thermometer mode. Their culture is trapped and reactionary. Every day vacillates up and down depending on who is in the room, what the external conditions are, and what the mood of the day is. Without any clarity or precision about what culture they are trying to create, the culture becomes a roller coaster of emotions and scattered responses to outside conditions. One day these folks are fired up about one thing, and the next day they're fired up about another. Up and down the thermometer goes. When we're mired in the reactionary thermometer mode we often blame others, worry about ourselves rather than the team, and lose sight of the bigger picture.

The best teams and organizations operate in thermostat mode. Those who achieve massive success in all the obvious ways—championships, awards, best-in-class, and market share—are those that people want to be a part of, are inspired by, and aim to be. They set the temperature they desire and have the discipline to bring it to life. They operate in thermostat mode. In this mode, we work from clear values, take personal ownership for our actions, and see the bigger picture of what the team is trying to accomplish.

The *Best Places To Work* lists that come out everywhere from Forbes to Fortune, Inc., Glassdoor, and Fast Company, to name just a few, highlight companies around the world. Within the first few words that describe why the companies they've chosen are rated so highly is the word *culture*. Listen to the way Nick Saban, legendary football coach at the University of Alabama, or Urban Meyer, The Ohio State University football coach, speak about the defining elements of their teams who have won College Football National Championships. They speak first and foremost about *culture*. Listen to the way life coach and motivational coach, Tony Robbins speaks about the keys to successful relationships, and you'll hear him talk about the proactive culture a couple has created to pursue their love for one another. Some intentional actions were put in place long before any of these teams or partnerships ended up being successful. They had proactively set a temperature. They were in thermostat mode.

Any team or organization is simply a collection of human beings. Imperfect and different. And the

17

culture among these human beings is dynamic, which means that it is always changing, whether they want it to or not. So the question isn't "Will the culture change?" because it already is. The real questions is, "Do you want to play any role in determining what it becomes?"

Culture is shaped every day by the way we *think, act,* and *interact.* The people we work with every day, we wake up with in our families, and we compete with on our teams are all contributing to the culture we are creating together.

This book will dive into more of what I mean about how the way we *think, act,* and *interact* shapes the culture we create. We all have the opportunity to set the temperature (the thermostat) every day, and it is our clarity as a team that allows us to regulate that temperature.

For those of you who have been with me on my professional journey, you may recall that many of these formal discussions began back in 2008 in an airport terminal. In 2008, I was the guy who quit his job and spent seven straight days flying to seven different cities—and stayed in the airports the entire time. That profound journey was part of the creation of the book *Step Back from the Baggage Claim: Change the World, Start at the Airport* that spread all around the world.

It came at a pivotal and vulnerable point in my life when I was stepping back and examining my life to determine the next steps along my path. The message of that book was the culmination of ten beautiful years of serving others: building homes for the homeless, directing a large nonprofit summer camp for kids, and leading programs that encouraged us all to think about our core beliefs and the impact we have in the world. The book uses air travel as a metaphor to discuss the ways we travel through life. It is a passionate call to action to bring a spirit of patience, compassion, and generosity to the way we move throughout the world. In doing so, we can have a strong impact on the culture of the places we move in and out of. We can, one person at a time, name a new way to lead throughout the world. The Movement began (and it continues)!

I was blown away by the response to the first book and had no idea the metaphor of the baggage claim was going to resonate with so many people, be celebrated all around the globe, and lead to three other editions of the book: the Business Leader Edition (2010), the Healthcare Leader Edition (2011), and the Education Edition (2012). Since then I have been tremendously grateful to share the Step Back message with teams and organizations around the world. Across all sectors—business, healthcare, education, nonprofits, and communities of faith—a dialogue has begun about the kind of people, culture, and vision we have for the future. I have been blessed with the opportunity to give countless keynote speeches and workshops for groups. I founded Step Back Leadership Consulting LLC and now collaborate and partner with organizations to support the development of their people, shape their culture, and help them gain clarity on the mission and vision they have for the road ahead. It is amazing to see this spirit spreading and contributing in so many ways.

Stepping Back continues to be a powerful and contagious mindset for me and many others. And then came the next message along the journey. After we *Step Back* we enter the process of *ReMembering*. This process resulted in the creation of the highly celebrated book **ReMember**: *renewing our* *memberships, relationships and focus in a distracting world* (2013), which spells out that process in detail.

We've never lived in a more distracting, cluttered, and busy time than today. We are bombarded by more than 3000 marketing messages every single day and we shift our focus hundreds of times in a twelve-hour day. It has never been harder (and more important) to stay focused on the things that matter most to us individually, to our team, or to our work in the world. *ReMembering* is about what we choose to give our hearts, time, minds, and focus to every day. It's about coming alive and cutting through the distractions.

I share this background information with you because this story continues to build from the previous messages and aims to add further value to your journey. After you *Step Back* to see things from new perspectives as an individual leader and then *ReMember* and name the priorities that need your eyes and your heart in your life and work, you are poised to develop the team around you.

Whether you've been along for the journey the entire time or are jumping into the conversation at this point, thank you for considering how your leadership actions will help create a compelling culture in your life and work.

The rest of this book will highlight the *6 A Process For Leading Change*™ (Assess, Align, Aspire, Articulate, Act, Anchor) that I use when working with teams and companies to design, reinvigorate, and strengthen their culture. Many people say they want to shift the culture of their team, their family, church or organization, or their entire company, but don't know where to start. This book will plant the initial seeds to begin this journey. It will steer you through the interactive process of leading change with stories that will resonate with your mind and heart, as well as questions and a framework to help guide your next actions.

Leadership development and culture-shaping are not drive-through experiences. I know we live in a world where we can ask Google any question and in less than one second have four million answers. I know we can go through a drive-through window and in four minutes have a sandwich exactly the way we want it. I know that we live in a world where Amazon will be able to use a drone to drop us whatever we want to buy with amazing accuracy.

22

However, developing people and culture is not like that.

It takes discipline, vision, and persistence to see it through. You can't be reactionary like a thermometer. You must be proactive like a thermostat. We can't wait for someone else to begin these conversations for our life or with our team at work; we have to be willing to be the best ambassadors for the cultures we want to be a part of.

The only question now is *what temperature do you want to set with the teams in your life and career?*

Disclaimer: Nothing about changing the culture of a group of people is easy. Quick solutions do not exist. What you are about to read might seem simple, but is achievable only with dedicated leadership, practice, commitment, and persistence.

Warning: Courageously committing to the process laid out in this book actually will change the culture of your relationships and teams. Enter at your own risk.

Dare to begin.

ASSESS

"The only man I know who behaves sensibly is my tailor;
he takes my measurements anew each time he sees me.
The rest go on with their old measurements
and expect me to fit them."
—George Bernard Shaw

Chapter 1

Assess: WHERE'S POINT A?

It was a long day in the Adirondack Mountains in upper New York State. There were eleven of us in our patrol, and we were on day five of a ten-day backpacking voyage. The summer heat was beating down on us, and the heavy packs with all the necessary items for the expedition were beginning to get on a few people's nerves.

We paused for a quick break on the trail to rest our shoulders, grab some water, and look at the map. Our plan for the day was to reach the summit of Whiteface Mountain, one of the largest peaks in the Adirondacks. We already had been hiking for a good two hours that morning, and it was time to stop and get our bearings.

"Where are we?" was a common question that would be lobbed into the discussion from someone in the group whenever our sherpas, the two guides for this patrol, pulled out the trail map and looked at the compass.

"I think we're right here," said one of the sherpas as he pointed his finger at a tiny squiggly line on the map. Then the two of them began to talk out loud as they tried to make sense of the path we had just walked.

"Remember when the trail curved around to the right about thirty minutes ago and we passed that area that was a bit more sparse?" one continued to the group. "I think that was right here, which means we are standing right about this point."

His voice was confident. The group trusted the leader and nodded in acceptance. We had enjoyed the brief pit stop, but knew we had to keep moving to accomplish all that was ahead of us. He pointed us down the path curving to the left and off we went.

It wasn't until about another two hours into our ascent up the mountain that we stopped for a little huddle. We were beginning to have some gorgeous views from the trees at various spots along the trail and the group was getting into a nice groove.

This time, though, the sherpas dropped their packs and quietly walked away from the group for their secret meeting with the map. A few minutes later they approached the group with devilish smiles, like a kid caught with his hand in the cookie jar cleverly trying to deliver some not-great news in a more appealing way.

"Hey guys, remember a while back when we thought we were at this point on the map?" they said as they directed everyone's attention to the previous spot on the map. "Well, it turns out we made a little mistake and have gotten a tad off course."

"How far off course?" a very astute group member questioned.

"Quite a bit," the guide responded with a slight quiver in his voice. "You see, we thought we were a bit further down the trail than we actually were, and we ended up taking the wrong path."

After a moment of silence, a few giggles broke the tension in the group. I may or may not have made a wisecrack about the helicopter coming any moment.

"You see, we're not even on the right mountain," the sherpa said as he pointed his finger through the trees and directly at the peak through the trees to our right. "This is Mckenzie Mountain and over there is Whiteface Mountain."

Now giggles really kicked in, mostly as a coping mechanism for many in the group who were now doing the math in their head and realizing that their long day had just gotten longer. We had a decision before us, either to backtrack all the way back to that fork in the road and essentially start our day over or take the more direct route, which was to continue up and over Mckenzie Mountain and then tackle Mountain #2.

We decided to embrace the challenge and to take it as an opportunity to summit two peaks in one day and see some breathtaking views. We accomplished the task (although it was a long and grueling day), and when we finally got to our resting spot to set up our tents, it was pitch black and we were exhausted. It was in that moment that we relearned this valuable lesson — *Always Know Where Point A Is!*

I think back on that moment when we conferred with the sherpas earlier in the day and they pointed to the map to show us where we were (our Point A). Not one of us spoke up to say, "Are we sure that is actually where we are?" or "Hold on a second. Let's take another look to see if we truly have gone that far already." Nobody questioned or engaged in the process of identifying where we were. We just blindly trusted and fell in line.

We knew our Point Z (our destination, Whiteface Mountain), but we weren't accurate about where we currently were on the map. We didn't know our true starting point. Our assessment was off.

Whenever I am begin a new leadership development program or culture-shaping initiative with a company or organization, the first step is always to *Assess*. We have to figure out where the individuals and the group currently are. And if we know where Point A really is. Assessing; that is, knowing the starting point is critical.

It is all too common to walk into a room with any team and for them to be confused about where they actually are. They might be very excited to talk about where they're going and what Point Z is going to look like, but they aren't totally honest about where Point A is. When I ask them the state of their team or their company, I might get five or ten different descriptions of where they are on the map.

So it's critical to allow time for these simple but foundational questions:

- *Where are we as a team, partnership, or company right now?*
- *What do we do well right now?*
- *What are our current strengths and where are we winning?*
- *What are the largest obstacles and challenges we face?*
- *What is the baggage we are carrying and what is it keeping us from accomplishing?*
- *What are the opportunities that are before us, based on where we stand right now?*

Before we know where we are, we can't chart an effective course for where we're trying to go. The first step in setting the temperature for the culture you want to create is assessing the current temperature right where you are.

Culture change doesn't start "out there." It isn't someone else's problem to solve. Culture change starts "in here" with all involved. It begins with calibrating our own thermostats (collectively and personally) to make sure we know where Point A truly is.

Leveraging Strengths

Part of the assessment process is not only to assess the team or the organization as a whole in order to determine where Point A is, but also to assess the individuals who make up the team or group. As Jim Collins so eloquently put it in his game-changing book *Good to Great*, you've got to have the "right people on the bus" and then also "in the right seats."

For individual team members, I use what I call the *Step Back 360* assessment process to help them understand where they are on their leadership

31

journey. The best teams are continually assessing the talent on their teams and are committed to the development process.

Countless assessment tools are available in the marketplace to help teams and organizations assess their current talent and wade through that important discussion about the "right people" and the "right seats." Many organizations I've collaborated with have had tremendous success with leadership 360s, the Myers-Briggs Type Indicator (MBTI), the Enneagram, and the DISC, to name just a few. They all have merit and I have experience using many of them to help clients with their assessments. I often remind clients that no test can tell every single thing about a human being, but they are indicators that help reveal our most natural modes of self-expression.

One of the assessment tools I am particularly fond of is the StrengthsFinder assessment by the Gallup Organization. Their mission is to help us all move beyond the common human instinct to point out what is wrong with a person and to shift the conversation toward leveraging the strengths of an individual. We all have *strengths*, plural. But, we spend so much time focused on our weaknesses that many people do not have a good sense of what they naturally do well. They do not understand how they are uniquely oriented to be an incredible asset to the team they serve.

It doesn't mean that we don't identify the opportunities we have for improvement (believe me, this is pivotal for the assessment phase), but we must shift our eyes to understand how we are uniquely positioned, to know what we do well, and to bring awareness to those strengths.

Beyond the countless numbers of teams and companies I have helped assess, discuss, and create actions around their strengths, I also have used this tool with my wife, Amy. The easily accessible language from StrengthsFinder opened up rich discussion between us about how our strengths play a role in decisions we make, how we respond to family situations, and how our strengths might serve us as we create the family life we desire. For example, I learned that she is most effective in her decision making when she has time and space to process the situation. We discovered that I am a "maximizer" who brings a mindset (joyfully, of course) to each situation focused on maximizing each moment and experience. I think about this often when I am anticipating the way she will think about or react to a particular situation. Sometimes teams just need language that helps explain what we intuitively know about the people we interact with.

If we want to gain clarity on the temperature we wish to set in the future, we must first know where we stand currently as a relationship or a team.

Your Ecosystem

This past summer, my family had the great opportunity to visit the Galapagos Islands, which are nearly six hundred miles off the coast of Ecuador and the northwest corner of South America. The Galapagos are an archipelago of volcanic islands that sit on either side of the Equator in the Pacific Ocean. It is one of the most preserved and treasured parts of our world.

Beauty surrounds the islands, whether it be crystal clear waters, volcanic rock, and the tremendous wildlife and biodiversity. We spent much of our time traveling throughout the islands and learning from naturalists of the area. In addition to snorkeling right next to sharks, standing feet away from sea lions that would crawl right up to you, and observing giant 200-year-old tortoises, it was particularly interesting to learn about their ecosystem as a whole.

Our naturalists spoke about the three types of species they have in the Galapagos:

Native Species: The species of plants and wildlife that are native to that area and have been there from the beginning. Native species are common and are often found in other parts of the world. Examples of these would be the mangrove trees, flamingos, and other wildlife that you can find in other locations around the world.

Endemic Species: The species that are unique only to this spot in the world. These species have adapted over time to be able to live solely in this location and cannot be found anywhere else. Examples in the Galapagos are marine iguanas, blue-footed boobies, and Galapagos penguins.

Introduced Species: The species that are not native to the island, and can be found in other parts of the world, and only became "introduced" to the ecosystem by coming to the islands with travelers or somehow on their own. Examples include species such as ants, rats and goats.

The ecosystem is continuing to grow and adapt based on how each of these species affect each other and the changing elements in the world, such as the climate, pollution, and visitors.

No, this is not a science lesson, but I love this image because every team on the planet experiences these three elements as they grow and mature their own cultural ecosystem: native, endemic, and introduced species.

The natives are the people who might have been on the team from the beginning or some of the first employees to jump onboard. They are familiar with the way of life on your island and they play a role that is probably very similar to roles that you can find on other islands (companies). They hold an important place in the infrastructure and provide a nice foundation to keeping the ecosystem balanced.

The endemic species are the unique players or members who have adapted to the very specific ways in which things get done on your island. These are specialized contributors who have learned how to grow, develop, and adapt in your climate, but are not found elsewhere. They are unique to your team, your company, and your group and might not be nearly as effective and adaptable somewhere else.

And last, the introduced species. As every team or organization grows and matures over time, new people are introduced to the ecosystem. Outsiders jump aboard and make their way into living within the ecosystem. The ecosystem must adjust and react to these new species, and together, they create a new normal.

Each of the different species within every team ecosystem has an impact on the others. All play a particular role and see things from a unique perspective. They all belong to the culture, but need leadership to help them work together to maximize the environment.

After you *Step Back* and assess where you are, you also assess what "species" you have in your organization.

Then you're ready to take the next proactive step to set the temperature for your group, relationship, or team: alignment of the members.

Where's
Your
Point A?

ASSESS

TEMPERATURE GAUGE

+ HOW WOULD YOU ASSESS WHERE YOU ARE CURRENTLY WITH THE TEAMS IN YOUR LIFE AND CAREER?

+ WHAT ARE THE STRENGTHS AND CHALLENGES THE TEAMS IN YOUR LIFE AND WORK ARE CURRENTLY FACING?

+ WHO ARE THE NATIVE, ENDEMIC AND INTRODUCED SPECIES IN YOUR ECOSYSTEM? HOW ARE THEY CURRENTLY WORKING TOGETHER?

+ DESCRIBE THE CURRENT CULTURE OF THE TEAMS IN YOUR LIFE—NOT WHAT YOU WANT THEM TO BE, BUT THE WAY YOU SEE THEM NOW.

NOTES

ALIGN

"The task of leadership is to create an alignment of strengths so strong that it makes the system's weaknesses irrelevant."
—Peter Drucker

Chapter 2

Align: **THE CURRENCY FOR CHANGE**

Conversations are the currency for change. If we want anything to change within our relationships and the people we count on every day, then we better be willing to talk about important stuff. An ethic of the best teams is the ability to have real, meaningful, and engaging conversations. These conversations are the beginning building blocks to achieving alignment.

But, they can't just be conversations for the sake of conversing. People want meaning. They are thirsty to contribute. They want to know that they are valuable and what they are doing is making a difference to someone else. They want to be connected to a greater mission than themselves. This is why I say that the real work I am doing with teams and organizations is aimed at *engaging minds and hearts.* We need and want both.

Simon Sinek, national bestselling author of *Start With Why*, has been an inspiring voice on this subject and continues to remind us all of what he refers to as "The Golden Circle." He draws a ring of three circles: an inner circle, middle, and outer ring. The inner circle has the word "why." The middle ring reads "how." And the outer ring says "what."

His simple diagram has had a tremendous impact on so many people globally because it reveals what they intuitively already knew. They knew that we often have our focus backwards in our own lives and certainly within the teams and organizations we serve. How many meetings have you gone to when the first question on the table was, "What are we going to do?"

42

I'm guessing many of you have your hands up right now. I've watched this in companies across the country and around the globe, especially in the midst of the highly distracted and scattered culture I talk about in *ReMember*. We are running so quickly that our first interactions with each other are often focused on "what we're going to go do" which races us directly past the more important and engaging conversations.

We get stuck working from the outside of the circle in, instead of beginning from our core and *Starting With Why*. It's a common sense thing but when we're in reactionary thermometer mode, we tend to jump to the *WHAT* rather than return to *WHY* we're even doing it in the first place.

Aligning the temperature we are trying to set begins with getting clear on why we are doing what we're doing. Why are we in business? Why did we come together as a team? Why did you or I decide even to play this game? Why are we actively choosing to be here today? Why do we want to have an impact on people or in this world? Why are we committed to this relationship?

As we begin traveling the 6 A's (*Assess, Align, Aspire, Articulate, Act, Anchor*) to create a compelling Thermostat Culture, we begin with why. To properly align as a team, we have to be willing to have conversations that lead us into why are we doing what we're doing. We have to touch the meaning, the engagement, the mind, and the heart.

Adam Grant, the very talented Wharton professor as well as bestselling author, shares research in his book *Give and Take* that highlights how powerful purpose and meaning is to those on our teams. He tells about a university call center that is set up to call alumni for donations to the school. The workers in this call center are not shy about talking about the challenges of the job and the fact that ninety percent of their asks are rejected. It's a tough and constant job, and the call center employees were often unaware of where the money they raised was even going.

However, Grant highlights a turning point in this case study. One day, the call center employees were able to spend time face to face with someone who had received a scholarship to the school thanks to their efforts. Immediately, the call center team was

44

more energized. Almost overnight the results also followed: 144 percent more alumni donated each week and the average caller donation rate jumped from a $412 average to more than $2,000 afterward.

What happened?

The members in the call center became aligned around the purpose and the meaning of their work. They found motivation in the faces and stories of the people they were trying to serve. They returned their focus to the why of their work. It was a conversation which was the currency for change. They remembered the temperature they were trying to set for the future.

The Metrics of Feelings

We live in a time of metric mania. We know it is important to measure how we are doing and that metrics can lead us to better decision making. It matters for a sales team to better understand the metrics behind how many touch points with a customer generate a typical sale. It matters for a basketball team to know the analytics that reveal where on the floor they shoot a higher percentage. It matters for a church or nonprofit organization to understand the giving patterns of their membership and where their mission is resonating.

But we've got to make sure we're measuring the right things and also know that some elements are tricky to measure. For example, how someone "feels" on your team or within your organization isn't always the easiest thing to measure when it relates to wins and losses.

However, ask anyone who has ever been on a winning or losing team whether how they feel matters and watch them light up. Everyone who has experienced the top-of-the-mountain euphoria of achieving, winning, or accomplishing a goal, knows that the feeling, the mojo, the momentum, the attitude and spirit of the group is like fuel for the engine.

At the other end of the spectrum, ask any individual or any team that has been living in the cellar for the last few years and experiencing very little success about whether feelings matter. They will talk about the constant drain of negativity, the hopelessness of attitudes, and the extreme pressure from all over. You don't think that has a negative impact on their performance? Teams or departments, entire businesses, marriages, families, churches, schools, or organizations of any kind all run on the fuel of the feelings and attitudes of their people. And some fuel is cleaner than others.

Don't take my word for it. Barsade and O'Neill, in an article published in the January/February 2016 issue of *The Harvard Business Review* commented:

"Countless empirical studies show the significant impact of emotions on how people perform on tasks, how engaged and creative they are, how committed they are to their organizations, and how they make decisions. Positive emotions are consistently associated with better performance, quality, and customer service... On the flip side (with certain short-term exceptions), negative emotions such as group anger, sadness, fear, and the like usually lead to negative outcomes, including poor performance and high turnover."

Setting the temperature in your team starts with conversations that allow you to align human beings, make sure all are on the same page about where Point A is, and manage the collective emotions. When emotions are left unattended to and there is no clear temperature you're trying to set, you'll slip back into thermometer mode. And that little red line will just go up and down depending on the moods of the day and the external forces against you.

A couple of years ago I was approached by a large organization and asked to help strengthen their leadership at the senior level, revitalize the core values for the company, and begin to impact their culture after a less-than-favorable employee engagement survey had come back from their few thousand employees. We charted a course and launched into the process and conversations that were going to lead change. Part of the worry from some on the senior leadership team was, "How can we measure our effectiveness? How would we know we were making a difference?" Good questions.

Less than one year later, following months of development sessions, company focus groups, and many conversations that were the currency for change, that twenty-person senior leadership team sat in an offsite conference room. We had just wrapped up a full-day retreat to bring their year to a close.

Based on reports from the team, there were certainly metrics they could point to that would indicate the improvement in performance over the last year (engagement scores that had risen between 16-32 percent in many areas), but that alone would not have been significant. One at a time however, person after person chimed in about how they *felt* differently about the team. They spoke openly about increased levels of trust, better collaboration, and clarity on vision and alignment. They spoke with passion about the temperature they were trying to set and how they saw the culture changing.

The last comment was the perfect exclamation point on the day.

"In all my years at this organization, I have never felt better about this team and what we're trying to accomplish together. I finally feel like we are a real team for the first time. We are now moving in the right direction, together."

What's Your Vibe?

We all have a presence when we come into a room and that presence sends vibrations to those around us. We can't control everything about what people feel about us, but we can become more mindful about how we enter and what is the focal point of our vibrations.

When a boss rushes hurriedly into her office while on a phone call and doesn't make eye contact with the staff members along her path, vibrations are felt. When a spouse tunes out their partner during a dinner conversation or shuns a gesture of personal touch and intimacy, vibrations are felt. When a coach looks deeply into a player's eyes and says, "I believe in you," vibrations are felt. When a teacher expresses care and empathy for a student who is experiencing struggles at home, vibrations are felt.

In her enlightening book *Contagious Culture,* Anese Cavanaugh refers to this as vibrational energy. Moment by moment each day our presence is sending energy (good and sometimes bad) to those around us. She encourages all of us to ask ourselves these three questions as we enter situations:

- *Is my presence hurting or helping the impact I want to have?*
- *Is my presence adding to or detracting from the quality of the energy in the room?*

- *Will my presence make others—and myself—feel better or worse?*

If we know that our spirit and vibrations are contagious, what are you spreading? Are your vibrations aligned with the mission of your team and bringing out the best in those around you? Is your vibe enhancing the culture or detracting from it? Aligning with other people begins with our willingness to take ownership for the presence we bring to the relationship and the energy we contribute. How we feel and the energy we share with those around us creates powerful momentum that is often hard to explain or identify. But the vibrations absolutely impact the outcome.

Common Goals

In 1999, Marc Benioff, Parker Harris, Dave Moellenhoff, and Frank Dominguez founded salesforce.com, a cloud computing company that has grown into one of the most highly valued American companies in its market. From the very beginning, they specialized in delivering "software as a service" and Benioff, as chairman and CEO, has been committed to creating an open, transparent culture.

Salesforce has consistently shown up over the last few years with a Top 25 ranking on Fortune's *100 Best Companies To Work For* list. Although known for a high-pressure and fast-paced environment that isn't suitable for everyone, they are clear on what works for them. Walking through their office in Chicago, I could feel the focus that fuels them. They have been celebrated for many elements of their culture. For example, their integrated philanthropy model allows each employee to have six paid days off each year to volunteer for a cause they care about.

From the beginning, Benioff wanted to align his people around common goals. He began by writing what he called his V2MOM, a method that refers to the Vision, Values, Methods, Obstacles and Measures he set for the company. He knew he needed to have language for the company so that he could align other people around it. But, it couldn't stop there. To to this day, every employee has their own V2MOM for their work that rolls up to the CEO's V2MOM, creating a framework for aligning their work and their vision.

The entity needed to not only bring people together in spirit and vibration, but also align human beings with structure for their work together. So, what are the common goals you and your team are working toward? Are you aligned?

Opt In

With the proliferation of spam emails and junk solicitations in the world today, the word "unsubscribe" unfortunately has become quite common. Because we are enrolled so often in things we do not actually want and that clutter our lives and work, we have had to exercise the practice of "opting out." We follow the trail of messages and buttons to say "get me out of here."

Opting out has become necessary in a world that is shooting us in the face with a firehose of more and more information. It has become such an emphasis that sometimes we become focused on what we're opting out of rather than the important places we are actively choosing to opt in.

Opting in is intentional. It takes energy. It takes action. It takes ownership. When alignment occurs within the most successful teams, marriages, schools, or companies, the root of that alignment is actively choosing to participate. Team members opt in with their mind and their hearts and align themselves with those on either side of them around common goals.

Alignment matters. Alignment begins with conversations that are the currency for change. Alignment allows the next conversations to be possible. Alignment is critical to reach your desired culture.

ALIGN

TEMPERATURE GAUGE

+ WHAT ARE THE CONVERSATIONS THAT THE TEAMS IN YOUR LIFE AND WORK NEED TO HAVE IN ORDER TO LEAD CHANGE?

+ WHY ARE YOU COMMITTED TO THE MISSION OF THE TEAMS IN YOUR LIFE AND WORK TODAY? NOT YESTERDAY OR IN THE PAST. WHY ARE YOU COMMITTED NOW?

+ DESCRIBE THE FEELING YOU HAVE ABOUT BEING A PART OF THE TEAMS IN YOUR LIFE AND WORK? WHAT VIBRATIONS ARE YOU SENDING?

+ WHAT CAN YOU DO TO CREATE BETTER ALIGNMENT WITH THE PEOPLE IN YOUR LIFE AND CAREER?

NOTES

ASPIRE

"Your aspirations are your possibilities."
— Samuel Johnson

Chapter 3

Aspire: WHAT THE BLEEP DO WE WANT?

My kids love going to Dave & Buster's—the giant arcade with life-size video games and blinking lights everywhere you turn. The company has eighty-three locations across the United States and one in Canada. Even as they get older, my kids run from game to game with infectious smiles on their faces.

My children still enjoy the games, but at this stage in their life (ranging between ages seven and twelve) the games aren't what captures their

57

imaginations the most. It's the tickets. Each game has a certain number of tickets that spit out at the end of the game (depending on how well you do) and then they are quickly off and racing to the next one.

Without fail, every single trip to Dave & Buster's ends with their three faces pressed against the front of that all-too-familiar glass case. Up against the glass, they can see what seems like an endless supply of little plastic toys, candy, and various other knick-knacks. They slide from one end of the case clear to the other side scouring their possibilities. Other kids also are plastered all around the glass case gazing at their glorious options.

Inevitably, we always reach the moment where I need to intervene to ask, "What the bleep do you want?" I don't really ask it that way and I don't advise that you do either, but parents can attest that the thought races through their minds. I give them a two-minute warning to put a clock on their decision-making process and what seems like endless possibilities. There is always a moment where they freeze because they don't really know what they want.

58

It is great fun, and they do end up walking away with some tiny plastic item and some candy, but none of it was what they truly "wanted." They wanted the chase, the experience, and the items they ultimately get are certainly things they won't turn away.

In our life and work, it's easy to get caught up in a very similar chase from one task to the next and repeat the same patterns from yesterday. So, I've asked a similar question to many teams and organizations around the world: What the bleep do you want? I don't really ask it that way, but when it comes to culture-shaping and setting the temperature in their organization, after we assess and align, it's time to ask the aspirational questions.

- *What is your desired culture?*
- *What do you want to be different in the future?*
- *What do you aspire to be?*

Setting the temperature requires each team or entity to push beyond what they currently are experiencing toward the vision of what they hope to be. When I'm guiding teams through this process, I often urge them to shift their line of sight from looking out the rearview mirror (where they've been and what they've experienced lately) to looking out the windshield (where they desire to go). Fixing your eyes as a team out the windshield puts you into a state that is yet to be created. It shifts your mind from describing the culture that currently exists and moves you into a state of mind that requires you to name what you ultimately want. The process itself pulls people in and provides an opportunity for them to share their voice for what they want to create.

Standards

Last year I was honored to speak in Las Vegas at the largest HR Conference in the world, the Society for Human Resource Management (SHRM) Annual Conference. My topic was *Growing An Engaged Culture* and thousands upon thousands of people from all around the globe gathered to discuss honoring and improving the human element of organizations.

On the same day that I spoke, legendary Duke Men's Basketball Coach and Olympic Team USA Coach Mike Krzyzewski spoke. The five-time NCAA National Champion and three-time Olympic Gold

Medal Coach entered the stage in front of more than 15,000 excited leaders. He was everything you would expect: poised, thought-provoking, and steady.

His sixty minute keynote speech was very well done, but there was one element in particular that got my attention immediately and fit beautifully with all I had shared at the conference earlier. He spoke passionately about how he begins each new season with a team.

Whether it is with the next Duke team in line to carry on their winning tradition or a gathering with some of the best basketball players in the world who have been selected for Team USA, he starts each new adventure the same way. He gathers the group together to gain alignment and start the conversation about who they aspire to be. He is always very aware that some of them may be back for another year on the team, but it's a new year and they need to experience this team as if it's the first time.

He explained how he stands in front of the group to mark the beginning of a new season and he poses one question: "What do you want the standards of this team to be?"

And then he steps back and listens.

61

One by one, the players on the team stand and voice their thoughts about the type of team they want to have. They talk about the standards they think are important. Each one brings his voice to the team. They put their name behind their comments and make subtle requests of their teammates. The conversation goes on for as long as it needs to in order for each voice to have a say, but also to honor the other voices.

When it is time to wrap it up, Coach K then steps in and explains to them that there are no rules on this team. He pauses for effect. He explains that rules are someone else's expectations that are placed upon you. "We don't have rules. We have standards we decide on together."

Even in his position as the Olympic coach, he has stood in front of LeBron James, Kobe Bryant, and others who have won NBA championships in their own careers and calls them into a process to create this new team. It's a new year and will necessitate new focus, spirit, and commitment.

Participatory

Stop for a second and think about what is popular in the world today. What are the popular restaurants? Experiences? Trends? How are most people moving through the world today? Consider the fact that we now live in a participatory world.

Years ago, it was Starbucks who taught us that we didn't just want a cup of coffee, we wanted to share in the creation of our own cup of coffee. Howard Behar, the former President of Starbucks, is a good friend and has been a wonderful mentor to me. His stories about Starbucks taking off are a fascinating study in connecting with people. Starbucks didn't want you to just order a "coffee." They wanted you to participate in the process of making the coffee. So you and billions of others now have walked into a Starbucks to tell the barista that you would like a double of this with extra of that.

Think about Chipotle. They practically created the new "fast casual" restaurant market. When you walk into a Chipotle, you participate in the creation of your own meal. You walk down the line and pick your unique combination of the items they have to design your special meal. You don't just order a burrito, you actively choose what you would like to put into your unique burrito. Did you know that the fast casual restaurant market has now reached more than $21 billion in size? Evidently we like the cost, the freshness and, I would add, our ability to participate in the process.

Forbes estimates Fantasy Football to be a $70 billion market. I'm in a loyal and committed (and the best) Fantasy Football league in the world, and I can tell you that we are not alone in our fascination with picking the players and competing with those around us. We don't want to just watch the game; we want to participate in the experience.

And, of course, the greatest example in today's participatory world is social media. According to a 2015 Daze Info study, there are an estimated 2.03 billion active social media users in the world with a high percentage of people spending 2-3 hours daily interacting on social networks. We want to share things, tell what we like, comment, and be part of the discussion. We are a participatory culture.

This is extremely important to remember as you begin to engage with the people in your teams and organizations. They don't want things handed down from above. They don't want a memo or email with news about their job. They want to participate.

This is the day we live in, and I would argue that we always have wanted to participate. Coach K is engaging participation with his basketball teams. And whether it's Tony Hsieh at Zappos, Brian Chesky at Airbnb, Sheryl Sandberg at Facebook, Blake Mycoskie with Toms Shoes, or the leadership team at Kiva, they all are collaborating with partners to create a great future together. They actively involve their people in the visioning, dreaming, and the aspiring for their future.

Why is this important beyond your team members desiring a voice in your visioning process? Your people, or the other members on your team, cannot possibly see what's going on in your head. Everyone on the team lives only within their own heads. It takes work to align the group and get them sharing in the vision they want to design.

This does not mean that everything on your team or in your company needs to be by consensus or discussed by all, but these trends do reveal to us that your people want to participate. They don't want everything dictated from above or delivered in a cookie-cutter sound bite. Where appropriate, they want to have a voice, a buy-in, ownership in the direction you're heading. They want to participate in the creation of the culture.

Generationally speaking, Millennials (those 18-34 year-olds in 2015) are now the largest generation in the American workforce, and Millennials want to participate. They want to be aligned with each other and the direction you're heading.

She who aims at nothing hits it every time. If you do not have clarity about the culture you desire or what your people would like to create, then anything goes. Remember, the culture is changing already. It's changing as we speak. It is dynamic. It will continue to change. The question is, will you actively participate in the creation of what you want it to become?

Authentic for You

Although it is interesting to know what has resonated in other places, the important question is what is authentic for you and your people? Your opportunity is not to be someone else. Your opportunity is to figure out what is authentic for you.

PayPal, one of the world's largest online payment companies, was one of a handful of companies in 2015 to rank one hundred percent on the Corporate Equality Index (CEI), a national benchmarking study on corporate policies and practices related to LGBT workplace equality, administered by the Human Rights Campaign Foundation.

Not only was this a terrific honor for the company to receive and for employees to take great pride in, but they also ranked one hundred percent because it was authentic for them. At the heart of PayPal's culture is collaboration, innovation, wellness, and inclusion. Those are descriptors for the culture they've been committed to building.

As they say, "Inclusion and equality are values at the center of everything we believe in and endeavor to achieve...we must always strive for an environment of involvement, respect, collaboration and connection—where the richness of ideas, backgrounds, and perspectives are cultivated and celebrated every day."

The recognition they received from the Human Rights Campaign Foundation was just an outcome of the shared vision of their core values and their commitment to live them each day. They weren't trying to be someone else. They were striving to set the temperature for who they want to be in the world. They were clear on what was authentic for them and who they aspired to be, and the recognition followed, not the other way around.

Your opportunity is not to duplicate the culture of the New England Patriots football team or the San Antonio Spurs basketball team. Your opportunity is not to replicate zappos.com or Chick-fil-A. Your opportunity is not to pretend to be Greenpeace or any other organization you admire. Those organizations have been successful because their culture is authentic for them and each person within their culture knows the temperature they are trying to set. Your job is not to duplicate them, but to become you. Your job is to find your unique temperature.

The best leaders help set the temperature within their team by inviting the team's participation in the design of their desired culture. You can't assume anyone gets it or understands what you've been thinking about for years. They must participate. It's more effective when they join the conversation and bring their voice to the aspirations.

So, ask yourselves, what the bleep do you want to create?

ASPIRE

TEMPERATURE GAUGE

+ HOW WOULD YOU DESCRIBE THE CULTURE YOU DESIRE?

+ WHAT DO YOU WANT THE "STANDARDS" FOR THE TEAMS IN YOUR LIFE OR WORK TO BE?

+ WHAT DO YOU WANT TO BE DIFFERENT IN THE NEXT YEAR OF YOUR JOURNEY? 3 YEARS? 5 YEARS?

+ HOW COULD YOU INVOLVE OTHERS TO PARTICIPATE IN THE CREATION OF THE CULTURE OR VISION?

NOTES

What

Temperature

Do

You

Desire?

ARTICULATE

"The single biggest problem in communication is the illusion that it has taken place."
— George Bernard Shaw

Chapter 4

Articulate: **WHAT'S YOUR STORY?**

You and your people tell stories all day long. You tell a story by the way you dress. You tell a story by the way you greet your family members or friends in the morning. The way you sit in meetings. The way you interact with clients. And every time you hit that send button on social media that blasts out into the world. We are a storytelling culture.

The messages we send and the stories we tell shape the environment and experience we live. The cultures we help create in our lives and work are cultivated by the way we *think, act* and *interact*. How we think about ourselves, the people around us, and the culture we aim to create has a massive impact, in positive and negative ways.

People who have told themselves for years that they are inadequate, unlovable, or somehow less than those around them, see that play out in how they live in the world. Each negative event reinforces that story. A person who tells a story of possibilities often sees opportunities in areas where most others see only roadblocks. A couple who constantly tell the story about the "glory days" of when they first started dating or their first years of marriage often get stuck living in the rearview mirror of their life rather than out the windshield of the life they want to create now.

In companies and organizations, the way you think and the stories you tell permeate the culture. Teams who live into the story that "it's all about the numbers" eventually erode relationships and generally dehumanize the people around them. Teams who tell the story that "success is tied to the authenticity of the relationships we make" tend to have people who appreciate the others around them. Teams that tell themselves "it is possible" tend to take risks, find optimism in the midst of failures, and discover solutions others might miss.

The thoughts we tell ourselves, the stories we perpetuate, and the messages we share with those around us set the temperature for the culture we experience. What stories do you tell yourself? What stories does your team tell? What messages are you spreading in the world?

Language Drives Behavior

Audience members at one of my keynote speeches or members of teams and clients I work with hear my passionate belief that *language drives behavior*. The words we choose have a significant impact on the temperature we set, which is why the next step in the *6 A Process for Leading Change*™ on your team is to Articulate. Once you've *assessed* where you are at Point A, have *aligned* the human beings around the purpose and mission of your team, have entered with them into participatory conversations about their *aspirations* for the culture they desire, then it is time to *articulate* the story.

If you are beginning to understand the culture you desire, then what are the values that will help guide that culture? How would you describe your core values as a team in order to bring to life the culture you want? How would you articulate the values of your team inside and outside of these walls?

It's Not a Poster, It's a Tool

If you just winced or rolled your eyes when you heard the phrase "core values" then hang with me. Unfortunately, some of your reaction is for good reason. You see, the exercise to determine your Mission/Vision/Values has not always been handled well by teams and organizations. Many have just gone through the motions to create them and then they slap them up on the wall with a fancy poster. They put them up there because every organization "has to have them."

Let's be clear. I'm not talking about doing these

> **Defining Terms**
> Mission = *Why we exist*
> Vision = *Where we're going*
> Values = *How we will travel*
> Strategy = *What we'll go do*

things out of some sort of obligation in order to look more like a team or legitimate operation. When I talk about the language that drives behavior and creating core values or guiding principles, I'm not talking about a poster. I'm talking about a tool.

When I lead teams through this exercise, it is to unearth the values that are meaningful and significant to them. It doesn't matter what I think their values should be or what some other outside consultant thinks they should be. Our job is not to give you your values, but to unlock your thinking and guide you through the process to discover your values. Your values are *YOUR* values. The best teams engage their people to participate by identifying and owning their values. And what I mean by the values being a tool and not merely a poster on the wall is that you and your team begin to leverage the language to drive the behavior you want.

We articulate core values to get us all looking in the same direction—a compass to guide not *WHAT* we do, but *HOW* we do it. How do you and your teammates want to commit to showing up at work? How are you committed to traveling together?

The best teams gain clarity on their core values and articulate them with precision. They don't just say "Integrity" or "Innovation" or "Excellence." They take the next step to link the value to specific behavior and action so that it's clear what integrity, innovation, or excellence look like on their team. The precise language is a compass to guide the *thinking, acting* and *interacting* they want to foster in their culture.

And when the language is not clear, anything goes. When you haven't gained clarity around your values and how they come to life on an everyday basis, then you can't be surprised when the values don't exist in action. You're stuck in thermometer mode.

This exercise has been equally effective with the conversations that are the currency for change in my family life. Amy and I have been able to talk about the type of marriage culture we want to create. We're nearly fifteen years in, and we know that the culture between us is dynamic and always changing. So we need to be proactive about what we want it to become. With our three wonderful and quirky children, we have come up with five family values to guide the family culture we want to create. They weren't "Mom & Dad's Values" dictated from above. They weren't another family's values. They are our values and everyone had a voice in what we want to create.

Our family worked hard to identify and define what it was going to look like in action for us to be grateful, loving, healthy, respectful, and positive. Those are our words and they aren't carved in stone.

We revisit them, adjust them, and continue to return to them each year.

We are not perfect by any stretch of the imagination. We have our bad days, our disagreements, and moments when the world throws challenging curve balls that are out of our control. We aren't perfect nor is any other family, team, or organization on the planet. Obstacles and events will undoubtedly continue to occur in our marriage, with our children as they grow, and certainly with external forces that are beyond our control. But we have a tool to remind us, as our compass, to guide our conversations and help us readjust the temperature whenever we get off track.

In my book **ReMember:** *renewing our memberships, relationships and focus in a distracting world,* you may recall my surfing analogy. Those learning to surf for the first time are often reminded, "Where you look is where you go!" Where you look your body will follow. Don't get distracted by the waves!

What gets your eyes, your focus, your attention, and your heart on a daily basis is where your body goes. Being able to articulate your core values or guiding principles is critical to being able to set the temperature you desire.

As the magnificent poet Mary Oliver, said, "This is the first, wildest, and wisest thing I know, that the soul exists, and it is built entirely out of attentiveness." What will get your eyes? What will get your heart? What will get your attentiveness as a leader, team or organization? Where you look is where you go!

The precision of the language is critical. What might mean one thing to one person means something else to another. Language isn't perfect, but it's all we've got. So, the precision of the words we choose and the definitions we design together are critical.

Revitalizing language that already exists is also a part of keeping values an active and growing tool. I've been involved in a number of companies in the last year who have values that have been around for decades, but the language is not driving the behavior they desire. It's time to revitalize the language.

One example is a national construction company that has been around for 70+ years. They have weathered changes in the economy, other companies folding, and a transitioning workforce. As we began to dive into revitalizing their values with fifty of their key leaders from across the country precision in language was essential.

The old tried and true language of "Safety First" was still a wonderful principle, but they were noticing that it just wasn't resonating as deeply with a new generation of workers. That language had once served them well and the idea was still a good one, but precision was needed.

Their passionate leaders chimed in and added perspectives from the field. We had many conversations that are the currency for change. We homed in on the language that really resonated with them. "Be Accident Free." It was even more specific and clear, and it was *their* language.

That seemingly small precise change to the language set the group off into wonderful conversations and ways of thinking about their safety program that hadn't been considered before. Now they were able to define what safety means at their company and what it looks like in action and behavior. It took them from a broad perspective to keep "safety first" into a proactive and participatory process to make sure preventive measures are taken to avoid accidents before they happen. They could finally articulate that "Safety First" was not enough; they actually desired to "Be Accident Free."

Accurate, Clear & Connected?

Have you ever driven down the road and seen a sign that makes you giggle because you know that the true message of the sign has been lost in translation? It is obvious that the sign does not really communicate its intended purpose. It's in those moments that I choose to believe the person making or placing the sign was probably in such a hurry to get the task done that they forgot to step back and make sure it communicated what they truly wanted. For example, here are two that I have seen:

Or even better:

I'm guessing these were not the messages they were trying to send. So often the messages we are sending to those around us are clear in our minds, but not always clear to the person on the other end. And when we assume that everyone on the team is on the same page or they "know" what temperature we are trying to set, it's easy for the communication to break down.

Is your message accurate? Does it communicate what really is going on? Is it clear? Can the person on the other end quickly and easily get it? And is it connected? Is it linked to human beings and to the bigger mission and culture you are trying to create? As you begin to think about leveraging your core values as a tool, you have to make sure the messages you're sending are accurate, clear, and connected.

The Hospital

The last few years have not been enjoyable as it relates to watching my parents struggle with their health. I lost my mother to cancer in 2015, and my father has been in and out of the hospital with everything known to man for the last five years. I do not wish those moments upon anyone, yet I realize that experiencing these types of pain and losing people we love are aspects of the human experience.

I remember standing in the hallway during one of my dad's extended stays in the hospital. I was pacing back and forth in an attempt to stretch my legs and keep my mind right for the grind of sitting and waiting. I noticed a team of doctors walk into his room, so I followed.

One of the physicians was clearly the lead doctor and the others were members of her team and/or residents. The six doctors in their white lab coats were huddled around my father's bed and whispering to each other and taking his vital signs. I

85

was very used to this routine by now so I stood back and let them do their poking and prodding.

As they came to the end of their examination, I stepped up and asked the question that I got in the habit of asking while different doctors came and went from his room. "Hello," I said. "I'm his son. Can you please tell me what you're observing with my dad and what the game plan is from here?" (*A real Point A to Point B kind of question*)

A moment of silence came upon the room as the team of six looked at each other to see who should speak first.

The lead doctor chimed in, "Yes, your dad seems to be doing a bit better, and I think what the next plan will be is for him to have a procedure to put in a pacemaker to help control his heart," she said confidently.

There was a silence. I let it silence linger for a few long seconds as I contemplated my response. Finally I spoke.

"Yes, thank you," I said. I paused again to make sure I had their attention. "My father already had that procedure this morning."

You could have heard a pin drop. It was as if the whole hospital froze in place. All six of the doctors were staring directly at me and clearly embarrassed.

"I am interested in talking to someone about what the game plan is now that he has had this procedure." I was calm and direct in my approach.

They said they needed to connect with the other specialists and then would be in touch with me. After some awkward stares and scattered eye contact, they quickly left the room.

I could write a whole book on the observations I've had in the last five years after spending way too much time in hospitals. Many amazing moments of care, service, and expertise, but unfortunately, also moments of disjointed communication and care. In this situation, their assessment of where we were on the map was off, and the way they articulated the message was off. Clearly not one of the doctors checked my father's chart or the previous notes. Their bedside poking and prodding did not include noticing he had been in surgery already.

It was clear the other doctors involved had not communicated with each other at all. Although the illusion was that proper communication had taken place, the message wasn't accurate. The message wasn't clear. The message certainly wasn't connected to a culture that the hospital is trying to create for its patients or families they serve.

Once you can clearly *articulate* your values as a team and all are looking in the same direction comes the compelling opportunity to tie them to *action*.

ARTICULATE

TEMPERATURE GAUGE

+ DO YOU HAVE CLEAR CORE VALUES OR GUIDING PRINCIPLE LANGUAGE FOR YOUR TEAM? YOUR ORGANIZATION? YOUR SIGNIFICANT RELATIONSHIPS?

+ CAN YOU AND EACH TEAM MEMBER ARTICULATE WHAT THE CORE VALUES LOOK LIKE IN ACTION AND BEHAVIOR? WHAT DOES IT LOOK LIKE WHEN THINGS ARE GOING WELL? WHAT DOES IT LOOK LIKE WHEN THE TEAM GETS OFF TRACK?

+ WHAT MESSAGES/STORIES ARE BEING SHARED ON THE TEAMS IN YOUR LIFE AND WORK?

+ HOW COULD YOU ARTICULATE YOUR VALUES MORE CLEARLY AND CONSISTENTLY, AND CONNECT WITH THOSE ON THE TEAM?

NOTES

"Vision without action is a daydream,
Action without vision is a nightmare."
— Japanese Proverb

Chapter 5

Act: **WHAT'S YOUR BIAS TOWARD ACTION?**

There are things we *know*.

Then there are things we *do*.

There is often a gap between the two.

The Dentist's Office

I hear the dreaded question:

"How have you been doing with your flossing?"

The deep swallow I take while the practitioner probes my open mouth and inspects my gums reveals the real answer to her question. I'm guessing many of you are with me on this one.

There are things we know we're supposed to do, but we don't always follow through. I know I'm supposed to floss, but I don't always do what I know.

Look at how long it took us as a society to shift the way we think and act about cigarettes. You think we didn't know they were bad for our health? You think we didn't have a sense that they might be a contributing player in our overall lung function, heart disease, and aging of our skin? You think we didn't have the sneaky suspicion that inhaling smoke all day might play a role in lung cancer?

There are things we know and then there are things we do.

Sociologists C. Kirk Hadaway and Penny Long Marler would refer to this as what they call "the halo effect,"which is the difference between what people tell interviewers or pollsters when surveyed compared to what people actually do. In all of their research, they observe a disconnect between what people say they do and what they actually do. People tend to inflate how often they engage in desirable or reputable behaviors such as voting or going to church and underestimate or under-report their less socially desirable behaviors such as drinking or drug use.

In the ecosystems of our teams, businesses, communities, and families, it is only human to acknowledge that a knowing and doing gap exists. We all have our shortcomings and disconnects between what we say we want and what we actually do. However, one of the most significant differentiating factors in all high-performing, connected, and thriving groups of people is their ability to bring the story of what they aspire to be into action.

Those who are able to shift their culture are intentionally putting actions into motion throughout their days. Those who are successful at setting the temperature they desire within their culture carry out the actions that align human beings around the compelling story they articulate about who they aspire to be.

They enter into a process to discover their highest priorities, commit to the most important things they know, and then do them with disciplined action. It is our actions that bring the core values posters off of the walls and put them on display within our people.

Keep Moving

When you walk into a *System of Strength* workout studio in Columbus, Ohio, words such as "Keep Moving" and "Find A Way" show up artistically all over their walls. The cinder block, exposed lighting, and mirror-covered walls create a hip industrial environment for those looking to sweat. Hip hop music often blares throughout the studio as those committed to the System compete against themselves in boot-camp-style classes. The room is packed and there is an energy steeped in positivity, passion, and perseverance.

But the room wasn't always packed. In fact, in the early days of its existence, founder Gretchen

Dusseau began with small groups of five or six in a smaller space that felt more like a garage than a studio. There were plenty of moments in those early days when it could have been easier (and surely justifiable) to listen to other voices, doubts, and give up. But, "Keep Moving" was at their core.

Now, only a handful of years later, Gretchen and her partner in the business, Keri Croft, have inspired a loyal following that has led to jam-packed sessions, three studio rooms (and positioned to grow), and a new virtual online workout platform for those traveling or in other parts of the country.

Their message, "Find A Way," resonates with their tribe at a time and in a culture when it is easy to give up and just jump to the next shiny object. Their message to "Keep Moving" is not about perpetuating busyness, but is deeply rooted in the spirit of taking the next step along your own personal journey. Be willing to challenge yourself. *Act.* Close the gap between what you know you want to do and what you actually will do.

I've been fortunate to experience their classes and see this spirit in action, as well as serve their leadership team with guidance and support related to their vision and culture. The successful temperature they are setting is a direct result of their ability to *articulate* their message and bring their story to life with intentional *action*. The proactive actions of their entire team are bringing people together, motivating them, and growing a loyal culture along the way.

They continue to keep moving daily with small, intentional actions and goals.

Three-Month Action Plan

Some of you have heard me say I'm not sure I believe in long-range plans anymore.

Let me explain. What I don't believe in is the arduous process that so many teams and companies have entered into, creating binders that chart every "i" they are going to dot and every "t" they are going to cross in the next ten years. So many places have entered into this process and then those binders sit on a shelf and collect dust. I do not believe in that.

What I do believe in is the exercise of creating long-term visions and short-term plans. To align your people, your leadership team, your spouse, your family, or the board of your organization around a vision (where you're heading) in the next one, three and five years, is powerful. It is big picture. It is the 30,000 foot view of the landscape where you hope to travel. And it is okay that not every "i" is dotted yet or "t" crossed because, the truth be told, you don't know what's going to happen. And it is perfectly okay to admit it.

The world is changing so quickly that it is impossible for you to know every element of what will emerge on the path ahead. There will be things that are out of sight now that will appear later. There will be obstacles. There will be detours. And yes, there will be surprises and successes, too. The exercise to visualize for the direction you're heading is critical. It is life-giving. If it is a compelling vision, it will align and energize people.

From the long-term vision comes the short-term plan. I do an exercise with many clients that I call the *Three-Month Action Plan*. It helps them boil their long-term vision into shorter, actionable moves. It helps them get clear on their own personal mission that will guide their performance for the next three months. It's their mantra, their focus for who they are striving to be.

We are living in the most distracted times in the history of our world. The *Three-Month Action Plan* exercise helps you concentrate on your top five priorities. I know we often want to jump from Point A to Point Z in one giant leap, but that never happens. We must identify what success with our top priorities will look like at the three-month mark.

Precisely what are the first actions necessary to stimulate progress this week, this month, next month, and month three? What's the objective? What's the message? Who owns it? When will the action be put into place?

One action at a time, we set the temperature and once cloudy visions are brought into existence. The culture begins to shift. The temperature in the room changes. Something is different, real. The once-distant light now is visible and shines brightly to everyone around us. It communicates that change is not only possible, it is happening. Now.

The Lost Boys

From the moment I first met Bol Aweng I knew something was shifting within me. He was one of those people who you meet and you know they are going to reveal a new perspective, story, or angle of the world to you. He did all three.

We sat at a table for an hour straight and he spoke and I listened. Bol was one of only two of the Lost Boys of Sudan to live within hundreds of miles of my hometown. The Lost Boys were more than 20,000 boys of the Nuer and Dinka ethnic groups who were chased out of their rural villages and orphaned during the Second Sudanese Civil War from 1983 - 2005. The boys traveled by foot thousands of miles and for weeks to years on end through villages in neighboring countries and refugee camps.

A grown man now, Bol's eyes still welled with tears as he recounted his journey as a young boy watching his friends be killed by soldiers, eaten by crocodiles as they attempted to cross a river, or fight off circling lions. He was one of the lucky few thousand rescued by the United States government and brought to our country. He quite literally has continued to keep moving in his life ever since. His story is captivating, but his spirit astonishing.

I was introduced to Bol by Steve Walker, a friend of mine who had befriended Bol after hearing his story and had put actions into motion to support Bol's dream of helping his people back in South Sudan. Steve had formed a steering committee and was leading the charge to bring basic medical supplies and care to Bol's old village in Piol. He had asked me to help them vision and assist with repositioning their organizational structure to bring the vision to life. I was humbled to be involved and am honored to still receive their updates.

I will never forget the day that an update appeared in my inbox; it shared their biggest celebration to date. After years of visioning and many small intentional actions to advance progress with their vision to open and operate a health clinic in the village, the moment had arrived. They shared the story of the day the solar panels that would provide the first electricity to bring light and energy to refrigerate the medicines were installed in the clinic.

In the pitch-black night of South Sudan, one small light began to shine. Out of the darkness, people from the village slowly appeared from their small dwellings and made their way toward the light. It was a sign to all in the village that something was changing. That progress was happening. It was a symbol that a different temperature was being set in their village. Movement was happening.

The action communicated hope. It was a reminder that light could appear in the darkness. It was a tangible action that reverberated to all. This one action represented all the tiny ones that came before it and led to the future delivery of food, supplies, and medications to a village that desperately needed them.

The actions we put into motion every day reverberate to those around us. They change the temperature.

You Are Responsible for Your Wake

It was a beautiful summer evening in Kiawah, South Carolina. The sun was setting over the tree line and reflections glistened off the surface of the inlet waterway. I paddled quietly in my kayak as my five year-old daughter leaned back in my lap. It was a postcard kind of moment and the exact *Step Back* that we were looking for and needing as a family.

A moment later, a fishing boat came ripping through the cove faster than was typical. The wake from the boat sent waves that sloshed our kayak back and forth and rocked us out of our peaceful moment. The unsteadiness of the waves caused a bit of panic for my daughter.

As the waves calmed, we paddled past a dock with a giant sign that read, "You Are Responsible For Your Wake."

The point of this is not about the flaws or mistakes of the people behind the wheel of the boat (we've all been there). I assume they were having their own beautiful moment and just didn't realize the impact their wake was making. Fortunately for this situation, no real damage was done, unlike other more serious examples when property has been damaged, people have been hurt, and the natural ecosystem disrupted.

Whether we fully realize it or not, our wake has a profound impact on those around us. The good and the bad of our actions send ripples, waves, and reverberations that affect those around us and the culture we try to create. Those ripples travel through our relationships, families, communities—and absolutely—throughout our teams and organizations every day.

The most effective teams and groups have clarity about *HOW* they aim to travel each day and are intentional about the wake they are trying to create together. They send ripples of leadership that create a positive, sustaining, and growing culture.

The clarity and commitment to the actions they put out into the world allow them to create waves for the culture they are leading on their section of the beach. As Denis Waitley gets credit for saying (and is similar to the Serenity Prayer that many know), "Change the changeable. Accept the unchangeable, and remove yourself from the unacceptable."

Alignment with the team around you, clarity about who you aspire to be, and a story that you can clearly articulate about the temperature you are trying to set together, allows you to focus on what you can control. It also helps you be better prepared for how to respond when big waves appear that are out of your control.

Jeni's Splendid Ice Creams

Leadership and culture are easy to talk about when things are going well, but reveal their true significance when tests and challenges arrive.

For any of you who appreciate creativity and the artful expression of culinary flavors, undoubtedly you know of Jeni's Splendid Ice Creams. Popular flavors such as Salty Caramel, Brambleberry Crisp, Goat Cheese with Red Cherries, Sweet Corn & Black Raspberries, and Ylang Ylang & Fennel, are just a few examples of the eclectic flavors that have captivated cult fans across the country. Their boldness and playful vibe has garnered the recognition of the *Food Network*, *New York Times*, *Huffington Post*, *People Magazine*, and the *Today* show, just to name a few.

From humble beginnings in Columbus, Ohio, owners Jeni Britton Bauer and Charly Bauer have experienced terrific success with fifteen stores across the United States, distribution in high-end grocery stores nationwide, and a large following with direct to consumer deliveries. They are a shining example to many for their entrepreneurial spirit and unique contributions to the world.

But all good things experience waves and obstacles. On April 23, 2015, Jeni's initiated a recall of inventory due to concerns of a possible listeria presence in their products. Listeria, a genus of bacteria that can cause serious infection when people eat it and is a special danger to pregnant women, is a constant battle that all food processing and packaging companies face. When the wake from this wave arrived, it was easy for all in the boat to feel very uneasy.

CEO John Lowe, in the midst of the fear and unknowns of the situation, remembers the first critical leadership meeting around their board table. The information in the center of the table for them to discuss was that they had received a "presumptive positive" test from one pint of their ice creams. All they knew was that there was one pint out there that was "possibly" contaminated. They didn't have all the information, but it was time to act.

One by one each member of the leadership team around the table spoke up. Unanimously, voice after voice advocated for pulling all inventory off of shelves. They spoke about the concern for their customers. If there was a possibility that listeria was in one of their pints of ice cream, how could they in good conscience assume that it was restricted to that one pint? They spoke passionately about the fact that nothing was worth risking any harm being done to someone eating their product.

Not one person around the table asked about the economic impact of pulling all inventory. Not one person asked about what this might do to the company. Not one person focused on the media storm of negativity that was going to come from pulling their product due to "possible" listeria concerns. Not one person let their personal concerns outweigh the greater good. Why?

When pressed on this question, Lowe responded, "Because at the core of everything Jeni and Charly have ever done, the business exists for good. It's at their core and has been at our core."

Their boat was being jostled by the wake of waves that they didn't see coming. But in that moment, their compass was the values that were at the center of their existence. When they needed to make a critical decision, they had clarity about the temperature they were committed to setting: the health and care for their customers came first. The only way to begin dealing with the waves was to put actions into motion that would send ripples of a different kind.

The next months were not easy. There were big questions. Big fears. Much work to be done to restore the company back to still waters and get everyone paddling in alignment. In the midst of the chaos, they had to keep their eyes on where they were going, not where they'd been. They had to stay focused on the loving customers who got their focus in the first place.

One day Lowe came out of his office and taped what he referred to as a "love note" onto the wall in their headquarters. It was an email that had come in from someone applauding their handling of the situation and sharing the love and appreciation from one of their customers. Over the next twenty-four hours, other employees printed "love notes" they received and taped them to the wall. Soon, the wall was covered with love.

We all experience the wake from waves that are out of initial sight (and often our control) in our personal lives and work. We all experience situations that challenge us, test us, and rock our boat. It is inevitable that every culture, every team, every family, every church, every organization, and every business will experience challenges at some point that upset their equilibrium.

In every culture there will be times when it gets too hot and too cold in the room. But the ones who are able to navigate through the waves and restore the temperature back to their desired culture, will be the ones who have clarity on the temperature they are trying to set, are rooted in their values, and are courageous enough to put actions into motion. They are the cultures that have thermostats (people) who will intentionally put actions into motion that restore the focus and reset the temperature.

The most compelling cultures are not the ones that are perfect (none are) but the ones that are able to adjust, shift, and adapt to internal and external factors, and in doing so, stimulate progress toward the culture they desire. Their actions are aligned with who they aspire to be.

Above & Below the Line

The most effective cultures are relentless in their pursuit of actions that set the temperature for the culture they desire. They are laser focused on what they are trying to create and identifying actions and behaviors that will support it. They work hard with their people to name, recognize, and plan actions that are the best of what they want. They know what is acceptable and gives life to their culture and they know what is unacceptable and suffocates their desired culture.

As far as I can discern, the phrase "Above the Line and Below the Line" was first coined at Procter & Gamble in 1954 when accountants and marketers tried to make sense of the return on investment (ROI) of all their different advertising efforts. They needed terminology to help them decipher what the purpose and targets of their efforts were. Since then, countless consultants and teams have utilized the phrase in a number of different ways to help people identify behaviors that either fit with what they are trying to accomplish or fall short of their desired culture.

Above-the-line actions are aligned with the culture companies and organizations are trying to build. They are actions where individuals take ownership for their role in having a positive impact on the outcome. They are actions that seek solutions and create change. They are actions that communicate that each person recognizes they are accountable to one another and the team as a whole. Above-the-line actions are the best of a group's core values being lived out. The core values posters on the wall are being displayed within the people.

Below-the-line actions are the behaviors and mindsets that suffocate others and are not aligned with the temperature the team is trying to set. They focus on blaming, complaining, and eluding any sense of accountability or ownership in the overall outcome. Below-the-line behaviors often show up as individual pursuits outweighing the mission of the team.

In any group of people aiming to design their new culture or shape their existing one, the needle on results truly begins to move when ideas and thoughts are moved into action. But the people within your ecosystem must be able to identify the actions that will contribute to building the culture they want as well as the actions that will get in the way. Every culture is dynamic and evolving moment by moment based on the actions that are put into motion. Culture change initiatives require buy-in, focus, and energy.

As Roger Connors and Tom Smith put it in their great book *Change the Culture Change the Game*, "Below the Line people spend time covering their tails, just in case the culture change effort gets derailed and they need to explain away their involvement and try to justify the lack of progress. Still, in our estimation, the greatest Below the Line threat to the progress of any culture change is a 'wait and see' attitude. In this state of mind, people simply wait and see if anything at all is going to happen, pretending they are enrolled in the change process, when all along they do nothing meaningful to move it forward."

Engaged and compelling cultures are filled with people who are enrolled in meaningful work to move things forward. They buy in to the future they are trying to create. They understand they must be a part of the future they wish to see. They understand that they too must put actions into motion. They must set the temperature for those around them.

You cannot control all the waves in the ocean that may come your way. You certainly can't clean up the entire coastline of the beach all by yourself and all at once, but you can take care of the small section of the beach that you occupy. There will be waves that will rock you from time to time, but you are responsible for your wake. With the people and projects within your section of the beach, your actions matter. They set the temperature.

So, what actions are needed in your life and work to begin moving toward the culture you desire?

TEMPERATURE GAUGE

+ **WHAT ACTIONS COULD YOU PUT INTO MOTION TODAY TO PUT YOUR CORE VALUES INTO MOTION IN YOUR LIFE AND WORK? THIS WEEK? THIS MONTH?**

+ **WHAT OBSTACLES ARE CURRENTLY IN YOUR PATH AND WILL REQUIRE YOU TO KEEP MOVING WITH PERSISTENCE AND RESILIENCE?**

+ **WHAT CHANGES CAN YOU CONTROL AND LEAD ON YOUR SECTION OF THE BEACH IN YOUR LIFE AND WORK?**

+ **WHAT'S YOUR THREE-MONTH ACTION PLAN?**
  (SEE THE BACK OF THE BOOK FOR MORE RESOURCES)

NOTES

ANCHOR

"We are what we repeatedly do. Excellence, therefore,
is not an act, but a habit."

— Aristotle

Chapter 6

Anchor: **DROP ANCHORS**

"Let's test them," I said with excitement in my voice. "After all, they say they are freaky fast."

The challenge was on.

I was standing at the creative business retreat center, sparkspace, and staring at their founder and good friend Mark Henson. Our mind-blowing creative meeting was about to begin, but first things first. We needed something to eat.

We looked up at the dry erase board in the office and saw the tally of the delivery times from the last seven orders from Jimmy John's. It was quite amazing to see delivery times of anywhere from six to ten minutes peppering the board. Jimmy John's mantra is "Freaky Fast."

Mark entered the credit card information on their website, gave me the look, and then hit "send" to submit the order. I started the stopwatch on my phone immediately. Now the game was really on.

The two of us stood up from our chairs and proceeded to walk down the hallway and into the room where we would be meeting. We entered the room and made our way over to the comfortable chairs positioned perfectly near the giant dry erase board. As soon as the fabric of my pants hit the seat cushion, a young man with one pant leg tucked into his sock and a bag in his hand came jogging into the room.

"Jimmy John's," he said as his panting voice made its way into the space.

Amazed, I quickly looked down at my stopwatch.

Three minutes and forty-seven seconds.

WHAT?

A new world record!

Mark and I looked at each other in disbelief as we laughed at the mere notion that Jimmy John's received the order, made the sandwiches, handed the package off to their delivery guy who tucked his pants into his sock and jumped on his bike, rode a block down the street, ran into the building and up the flight of stairs to the second floor, and handed us our bag of delicious food. In three minutes and forty-seven seconds.

It was Freaky Fast. And when the delivery guy learned that we had been timing him, he said, "Oh, I could have shaved at least twenty seconds off my time!"

It truly was Freaky Fast, and I needed to know more. So I called their store manager. I wanted to learn more about *how* they were accomplishing this. I figured there would be some leadership lessons to share. As a guy who speaks around the world about leadership, culture, service, mission, vision, and values, this was a worthy conversation. Once the manager got past the idea that I wasn't a wacko stalker (well, maybe), he confirmed what I suspected.

"Of course we have our ordering system and sandwich line organized efficiently, but the real key is that from Day 1 of anyone working here, we are crystal clear about *what* we expect and *how* we are going to accomplish it," he said. "Our culture attracts those looking for this kind of engaging environment. We live it every day."

Their guiding principle of "Freaky Fast" permeates all they do and has clarity of language, action, and behaviors that follow. The actions are anchored within their culture. They aren't one-time actions; they are repeatable actions that become habits.

Freaky Fast may not be the guiding principle that resonates with you or your team, but it is theirs. Authentically and uniquely theirs. They've named it, defined it, they act upon it, and they set up procedures and policies that help them anchor it within their culture. It becomes a habit.

Your journey along this path is to find the values that authentically guide you and your team. Whatever the values are that resonate most authentically with you, my invitation is for them to be *Thoughtfully Great*. We might not need to be *Freaky*

Fast, but we can strive to be *Thoughtfully Great* with the people, projects and mission that stand in front of us.

It's Not a Drive-Through Experience

I say to audiences and clients all the time that developing people and culture is not a drive-through experience. I know we often want everything in our lives to be freaky fast, but when it comes to leadership development with the people in your organization and shaping the culture you desire as a team, there are no quick-fix solutions.

That's why there are 6A's to this journey *(Assess, Align, Aspire, Articulate, Act, Anchor)* because you can't accomplish everything all in one leap. Each step along the way plays a monumental role in what the culture becomes. But, there certainly is no more important step in the process than the last A: Anchor.

I say that because this is often the step in the process where it is easy to lose momentum, focus, and is the spot where some leaders and teams stumble. Among the most common missteps leaders and teams make is that they go through the process to align their team around the values, articulate what they're hoping to create together, and even identify some first actions to begin bringing it to life, but then get distracted and default to old behaviors or routines.

Dropping anchors is about intentionally placing support messages, experiences, and learning opportunities at each stage of development along the continuum of someone's experience as part of your culture. From the first time they join your efforts to their last days as part of the group, what do you do to teach them and empower them to set the desired temperature?

Intentional or Scattered?

Have you ever seen an unkempt tree that has branches growing every which way? It looks scattered and not very visually appealing. For true landscaping gurus or lawn-maintenance czars, it makes them sick to their stomach.

The truth is that, as long as the tree continues to get sunlight and rain, it'll continue to grow. It'll grow in whichever direction it can and certainly won't groom itself. Trees are resilient organisms that find a way to just stay alive.

The truth is that many leaders, teams, and organizations are like these trees. Without any clarity about how they want to grow and which direction they want to head, or support from those around them, they just sprawl in all directions. They limp along. They maintain. They continue to exist. I'm sure you can think about groups or teams or companies in your life that seem to remain alive, but there isn't real clarity on how they want to grow. They know that with basic sunlight and water they can keep the lights on.

Last spring, I had the great honor to speak at another Global Leadership Conference for Entrepreneurs' Organization. This time the conference gathered in Bangkok, Thailand, and thousands of business owners from 51 countries came together to strengthen their own leadership and the future of their organizations. It is a fascinating group of people and many are doing amazing work to inspire and impact people's lives through business.

I spoke two of the days of the conference and then my wife, Amy, and I got to enjoy a little rest and relaxation on the breathtaking island of Phuket off the coast of Thailand. On one of the last mornings in Thailand, I was out walking around on my own and reflecting on the wonderful last couple of days.

I came around the corner of one of the buildings and I noticed again how beautiful the 360-degree views were of the ocean and trees that lined the property. The trees were magnificent and added beauty to the already gorgeous surroundings. (I am not an overly active landscaper, but my mom would be so proud of my observations.)

As I looked closer, I could see that each of the trees had little wooden support beams that had been nailed together around the trunk and lower branches of the trees to help them grow in a particular direction. In fact, as I looked to my left, I saw a two-person landscaping team nailing the support pieces in place for one of the younger trees on the property. Each support piece they placed with precision to help the tree grow in the direction they desired.

There couldn't have been a better image for this part of the book and much of the work I do with teams and organizations! Again, the trees are going to grow in whichever direction they can as long as they have water and sunlight. You can't force the trees to grow, but you do have the choice to either tend to them or ignore them. You can choose to leave them alone and allow them to scatter on their own or you can be intentional about the support beams you put in place. Without clarity and support they'll scatter. With support beams in place, they have a better opportunity to blossom and bloom in the direction you want them to.

The teams and organizations I've studied and worked with that do it best are the ones that anchor messages, experiences, and learning opportunities systematically throughout their culture. They intentionally insert support beams.

They recognize that anchoring the culture they desire begins with the way they interview prospective new teammates, how they onboard people into their organization culturally, how they coach and develop their people not only about what they do but also about how they do it, how their performance evaluations are linked to their desired culture, how they select and develop emerging leaders, and how their mid-upper leadership teams are committed to their ongoing development and alignment. It's intentional.

According to a recent national survey, the most common reason couples divorce is a "lack of commitment"(73%) and not far behind is "unrealistic expectations" (45%). The data support the idea that most relationships have a better chance for success when they have a shared vision for their future, aligned expectations for the temperature they're trying to set, and actions they anchor as habits. The most successful relationships and families put intentional support beams to help guide their way.

Talk to any successful major sports coach about the development of their team and you will see the intentionality that emerges in how they recruit, assimilate, train in the off-season, and develop their culture. The tree will grow. It can just maintain. But, if you want to maximize and guide the direction, intentional support anchors are needed.

Is your organization scattered and just maintaining? Or are you eager to intentionally put support anchors in place to grow the culture you desire?

The Rule of 7

You may know the old marketing adage about The Rule of 7. The concept is that someone has to hear a message seven times before they will take action and buy whatever you're selling. I'm guessing it actually is more than seven times in today's distracted world, but for now, let's just go with seven.

I invite you to think about this concept beyond just selling a product or service. I want you to think about it from the perspective of a parent, coach, department head, teacher, pastor, board chair, or anyone else trying to anchor important messages or teachings for a group of any kind.

Captain Obvious would tell us that you can't say something once and expect it to stick. You can't just put a poster on the wall and say "I told you so." You can't just send out one memo or email to the team and then cross it off your "to do" list. You can't just say it once at your annual meeting and expect it to live and breathe within your people every other day the rest of the year. You've got to practice the Rule of 7 to anchor the important messages in your culture. Over and over again.

For example, I often help organizations look at their onboarding experience and put more intentional anchors within their culture. If you only had five messages you could share with a new team member, what are the top five messages or stories you must share with them about the culture you're trying to create? What's your plan to anchor those messages seven different times in their first ninety days on the job?

The best cultures anchor their values and vision for the future within every element of their organizational story. They support the messages individually and collectively. They take individual one-time actions and develop them into habits that slowly become "the way we do it here." Many small, intentional actions over time.

Get Physical

So much of what we're talking about up to this point in the book is about aligning the thoughts, actions, and interactions of the people around us in order to create the culture we desire. If we don't bring the minds and hearts of people together than what I'm about to share doesn't really matter. But, in addition to the language we use to drive behavior and the actions we bring to life, the physical environment can either enhance or detract from the culture. The environment doesn't make the culture, but it sure can either enhance it or detract from it.

Mindfulness researcher Ellen Langer reminds us in her book *Counter Clockwise* that "Our physical environment primes our feelings and behavior, although we are typically oblivious to its influence. Primes often tell us what is expected of us, and too often we mindlessly comply."

"Primes" is a term that comes from psychologists Anthony Greenwald and Mazarin Banaji, who use that word to refer to the cues that activate particular associations and influence in our behavior. All day long we walk around and the environments give us cues about how we should act or behave. In some ways, it is a form of subtle manipulation, but in its most positive sense, the physical environment can help reinforce the values and spirit that we hope to encourage in our people. It's the reason a renovation of a home can give a completely different feeling to the exact same location and why more and more companies are being thoughtful about the physical space that they show up to each day.

Whether it's the music in the background and the messages they put on the cups at Starbucks, the smells that fill the streets at Disney World, or the way a stale doctor's office makes us feel cold, all have an impact on our experience. Airbnb, the growing online marketplace that allows people to list, find, or rent apartments or homes around the world, sets up their lobby in their headquarters in San Francisco to look exactly like a room in a property they list. This gives employees the physical reminder every day about the types of places they are representing. It puts them in a different mindset, one focused on those they are serving.

Have you ever noticed the way some airports have designed the walking path that leads you directly through the duty-free shops? That's because they realize that in the most highly distracted time in the history of the world, if you want someone to look at something or think about something, you need to put it right in front of them.

Writer Jennifer Hullinger explained "According to a study by the consulting company Internists, Duty-Free shops with 'Serpentine Walk-Through' designs have 60% more sales because 100% of customers are exposed."

Where we look is where we go! The physical environment we put into place will help enhance the culture you are trying to create—or it will detract from it. Wedding the language, values, and spirit of your people into the design of the physical environment has the ability to create synergy that anchors the culture even more significantly.

What's on Your Checklist?

Many times the habits we think we are anchoring are not truly being anchored.

The brilliant Atul Gawande in his book *The Checklist Manifesto* showed us all that we cannot assume that even the small "routine" actions are getting accomplished when we live in a quick, complex, and uncertain world. His passionate and persuasive message about the power of checklists cites case after case where simple reminders about the steps in a process allowed successful outcomes to be achieved.

In his work with a global steering committee associated with the World Health Organization (WHO), the group searched to come up with a checklist for surgeries that would improve global health. What was on the checklist? Simple things: did everyone coming into the surgery room wash their hands? Was the correct medicine given to the patient at the proper time in order for it to have the intended effect? Did they have all of necessary tools in the room for the surgery? And so on.

Seems like simple things to be a part of a checklist. Shouldn't we know those things? Yes, but remember there is a gap between what we know and what we do. Just because we know doesn't mean we will remember and certainly doesn't mean we'll do it.

So, what were some of the outcomes of this checklist? Where were the metrics that showed the checklist aid does anything more than take up time?

"Major complications for surgical patients in all eight hospitals fell by 36 percent after the introduction of the checklists. Deaths fell by 47 percent."

Nearly two hundred people in this test were spared from either harm or death just because of a checklist. An immediate thirty-six to forty-seven percent increase in positive outcomes. They studied and tracked each item on the checklist and saw positive results across the board.

As it related to appendicitis patients having surgery, "After three months, 89 percent of appendicitis patients got the right antibiotic at the right time. After ten months, 100 percent did. The checklist had become habitual—and it had also become clear that team members could hold up an operation until the necessary steps were completed."

The simple actions have been anchored within their culture over time so that they soon became habits. They had identified how they wanted to improve the culture and success of their hospitals, had identified actions and language that would help drive behavior, and then were disciplined enough to anchor them in their day-to-day processes.

On their checklists were the "non-negotiables" that they couldn't ever afford to forget. They were the items that could slip thru the cracks if people were moving too quickly, a complex situation arose, or they got distracted by a co-worker. They identified those things that have to happen repeatedly in order to improve the culture of their work. They had to ask themselves what habits they needed to form.

Some doctors were offended by the mere notion that they needed a checklist. After all, they were the experts. They had been doing these operations for thirty years in some cases.

"I've had years of training," they said. "I don't need a little checklist."

Just trust us and give it a shot, asked Gawande.

One of the last items on the checklist was for every person who was involved in the surgery to quickly introduce themselves by name and their role in the surgery. Some thought this was unnecessary too. Just do your job and I'll do mine was the mentality of some. It doesn't matter if I know the people I'm working with. "It's my patient," thought some. But Gawande reminded them, "Just ticking boxes is not the ultimate goal here. Embracing a culture of teamwork and discipline is."

The results followed.

So, what are the non-negotiables that would be on the checklist for your culture? In order to anchor the desired culture in your family, on your team, in your organization, in your faith community, in your business, what actions need to become habits? What anchors do you need to drop?

Opt Outside

Many of the important anchors you drop are internal, meant only for the development of the people in the trenches with you each day. But sometimes, it's important to drop anchors that reach externally in the world and set the temperature with those you serve.

Black Friday, the day that begins at midnight on Thanksgiving with millions of excited shoppers bum rushing retail locations for discounted items, has been growing rapidly. Last year Americans spent 1.7 billion dollars on Black Friday, up twenty percent from the year before. Despite studies that show that forty-nine percent of consumers disapprove of stores opening at midnight on Thanksgiving, the monetary success has been huge for many companies.

In 2015, REI, the mammoth specialty outdoor retailer and nation's largest consumer co-op, went against the grain. They decided to drop an anchor that would send a different message to their followers. They saw an opportunity to anchor many of their individual actions in a way that would align better with the temperature they are trying to set and the true spirit of their brand.

With their "OptOutside" (#OptOutside) campaign, they announced that they would be closing their doors on Black Friday. A huge gasp echoed throughout the retail world at the idea that they were turning away from the floods of people and dollars that Black Friday brings. Even better, REI announced to their 12,000 employees at all 143 of their retail locations, offices, and distribution centers, that they would be paid for the day and encouraged to go spend the day outside with their family and friends.

As CEO of REI, Jerry Stritzke, put it, "Black Friday is the perfect time to remind ourselves of the essential truth that life is richer, more connected and complete when you choose to spend it outside. We're closing our doors, paying our employees to get out there, and inviting America to OptOutside with us because we love great gear, but we are even more passionate about the experience it unlocks."

In a moment, REI had captivated the minds and hearts of its people far and wide and taken them back to the root of why they exist as a company. They anchored the message of their values in a concrete and visible action. It made their values even more clear and recognizable to all. Oh, and for those of you who still can't let go of the idea of all the business they were turning away by closing their doors, analytics after the weekend showed a twenty-six percent increase in online traffic.

It is important to point out that this same action would not have worked everywhere. Yes, it was a brilliant marketing idea, but it worked because it was authentic to REI. It was perfectly aligned with who they already had shown they were through the millions of tiny actions that went into building their brand. This is the perfect example of "shared-value" branding, a trend in marketing, that connects messages to the hearts and shared values of a group's followers.

The most successful teams, families, and entities of any kind continually find new ways to share stories and messages that anchor their values and the temperature they are trying to set. They find

135

new ways to make their actions into habits so that the "way we do it" is anchored in the very fiber of their being. It is intentional. It is thoughtful. It is authentic. Their strategic plan for the coming year has intentional spots where cultural actions are being anchored into their operations.

What's On Your LP?

In the 1930s, many major record companies were exploring ways to create longer-playing records that could fit more music onto them. Company after company failed attempts to jam more music onto their records and sound quality plummeted. Finally, one studio, Columbia, figured out how to create a new LP that had a stronger foundation, purposeful design, and actually increased the sound quality. The LP was born and revolutionized the music industry!

Well, many years later, entrepreneurs and time management teachers, Matt and Maria Granados, thought that the LP metaphor was one that needed to be applied to people's personal and career lives. They started the new LP and the Life Planner was born—a focused planning tool to help individuals establish their macro goals and boil them down into micro plans to achieve success.

Matt and I met following a speech I gave at a leadership conference in Asia and my description of the "Busy vs. Effective" leader in today's world was a beautiful connection to their work. Their Life Planner provides a disciplined tool to help people cut through the distractions and noise of everyday living and bring their focus to their daily and weekly goals to develop themselves personally/spiritually, in their careers, social/emotionally, and physically. The workbook guides your highest priorities and helps you set intentional actions to your daily and weekly plan.

The brilliance of the simple tool is in the actual time that the user makes to *step back* and write down their priorities and necessary actions. As they'll remind you, people who write things down are forty-two percent more likely to remember and achieve their goals. It is not scattered; it is intentional. It is not reactive; it is proactive. Those who use the tool experience their daily, weekly and monthly goals come to life through intentionality. The tool helps them anchor their actions into habits.

So the question is, what is on the LP of your life? What music do you want to play? It isn't about creating a "to do" list to heighten your scattered or busy feeling, but is about discovering the mindfulness necessary to live the life you want. It is about anchoring intentional actions that strengthen your habits and the work you do in your life and with those around you. It is about proactively setting an authentic and consistent temperature.

Where's the Magic?

Sorry to disappoint you, but this is the point in the book where I have to crush your dreams and remind you that there is no magic pill for any of this work. There is no easy button. There is no quick fix. Hopefully you're seeing that shaping the culture is a committed process. Moving the dial on your thermostats and setting the temperature within the teams in your work is a journey.

And guess what, the reward is in the journey. Going through the process itself with the most important thermostats in your life and work is what creates the desired outcomes. The magic is the journey, together.

Howard Behar, the former President of Starbucks Coffee and Starbucks International, he and his team grew the iconic chain from twenty-eight stores to fifteen thousand stores around the globe. He is a humble, caring, and courageous leader as well as a terrific friend and mentor. When you talk about the importance of culture with Howard, his eyes light up and he nearly jumps out of his chair. "Culture isn't an add-on to your business. It is everything!" he exclaims.

His latest book *The Magic Cup*, is a business parable about a leader, a team, and the power of putting people and values first. The story is about the discovery that many leaders go through in corporate life that leads some to realize that their significance is not in what they accomplish, but how they travel along the journey. The values of responsibility, curiosity, cooperation, trust, truth, hope, forgiveness, focus, stewardship, courage, and connection fill Howard's cup. The values are the magic that continues to be fuel for his journey.

He's not perfect. He's the first one to admit it and speak openly about mistakes he's made or things that didn't go the way he had hoped. The story isn't about perfection. It's about the commitment to the journey.

When you sit in his home office, the walls are littered with photos of people and quotes from his journey. The picture frames are not filled with articles about the milestones they achieved as a company or awards he won along the way. They are photos of people. With people. Photos and words that remind him that the sustaining success of the journey lies in the hearts and faces of the people he lives and works with.

It's about the people. It's about the temperature they worked hard to set for those around them and for those who would come after them. What filled their cup was being a part of something bigger than themselves and coming together with other people to create it. Their journey was focused on being the best thermostats they could be to reflect their values and to develop and inspire other thermostats. The magic was in the temperature they were setting together.

Set Your Dial

So we've walked this far together. It is time to remind you of some things you need to remember.

You're now standing in front of the thermostat dial for the teams in your life and work. You've reflected on the path ahead and the important people and intentional steps you want to take. Now it is time to set your dial to the temperature you want to create.

But there are a couple final things to remember as you begin the process. First, if you're an avid TV viewer or infomercial lover, the name Ron Popeil may ring a bell. If it doesn't, that is okay too. I didn't remember it either. Popeil is an American inventor and direct response marketing personality who became famous for his infomercial line that he would say over and over again with one of his products, "Set it, and forget it!" The catchy saying broke in to pop culture and it was not uncommon to hear someone urge another to "Set it, and forget it!"

Well, as popular as the saying became, it doesn't work here. In fact, the effectiveness of dropping anchors within your culture to set your

141

desired temperature will be directly linked to your ability to "Set it and *NOT* forget it!"

The 6 A's are not a one-time thing. They are continuous. The process never stops. Once you get through the anchoring process, then you go right back to the position to *Assess* and begin the next change process. The most compelling leaders and groups are committed to the process month after month, quarterly, and yearly. The temperature is always being adjusted.

Lastly, I need to remind you that the temperature won't drastically change overnight. *But the needle will move.* There will still be moments where it is too hot in the room or too cool. *But you'll recognize those moments with more clarity.* Some people will not like the temperature you're trying to set because they don't want to change. *But you will also find those who rise up to partner with you to move things forward.*

You need to set your own thermostat first so that you are able to help others. You might be the leader by title, but you are also a leader in the sense that someone is always watching what you're doing. They're taking their cues from you. The way you begin to shift your *Thinking, Acting* and *Interacting* will reverberate to others. Your vibrations will begin to spread a new temperature.

As Max De Pree once said, "We cannot become what we need to be by remaining what we are."

What do you want your culture to become?

Begin the process.

ANCHOR

TEMPERATURE GAUGE

+ DO YOU HAVE AN INTENTIONAL PLAN TO SET THE TEMPERATURE FOR YOUR TEAM, ORGANIZATION OR GROUP? OR, ARE YOU SCATTERED?

+ IN WHAT WAYS WILL YOU DROP ANCHORS TO DEVELOP YOUR PEOPLE AND CONTINUE TO INVEST IN THEIR DEVELOPMENT?

+ HOW WILL YOU PRACTICE THE RULE OF 7 TO COMMUNICATE THE IMPORTANT MESSAGES AND STORIES FOR YOUR CULTURE?

+ HOW WILL YOU ANCHOR YOUR VALUES IN YOUR HIRING, ONBOARDING, EVALUATIONS, AND ONGOING LEADERSHIP DEVELOPMENT?

NOTES

"What Is Honored
Will Be Cultivated."
- Plato

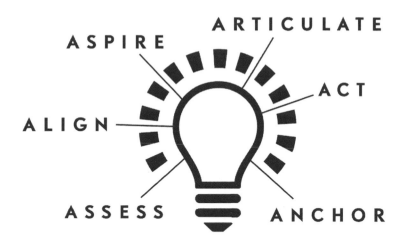

ASPIRE ARTICULATE ACT ANCHOR ASSESS ALIGN

Set Your Temperature

Share the 6 A Process With Your Team

Need a

Team Retreat?
Keynote Speech?
Guide for Your Culture Initiative?
Online Program or Distance Learning Tool?
Want to Put Your Team Through a Culture Program?

Visit **www.JasonVBarger.com**
to access more information, tools, and to inquire
about support for maximizing the 6A's with your
team! Contact us to involve Jason's team with setting
the temperature in your culture. Email
Info@JasonVBarger.com to request
discounted bulk copies of his books.

Resources

- Show Me The Money: The ROI on Employee Engagement, Decision-Wise. Haydon, Reese. https://www.decision-wise.com/show-me-the-money-the-roi-of-employee-engagement/
- Baldoni, John, Employee Engagement Does More Than Boost Productivity, Harvard Business Review...https://hbr.org/2013/07/employee-engagement-does-more, July 4, 2013.
- Why People Divorce in The United States. http://www.wf-lawyers.com/divorce-statistics-and-facts/
- Barger, Jason, Step Back from the Baggage Claim, One Love Publishers, 2008, 2010, 2011, 2012.
- Grant, Adam. Give and Take. New York, New York. Viking by Penguin Group, 2013.
- Manage Your Emotional Culture, Harvard Business Review, January-February 2016, P.3.
- Salesforce is One of Fortune's Top 10 Best Companies to Work For! Boutin, Sarah. March 5, 2015. https://www.salesforce.com/blog/2015/03/salesforce-fortunes-100-best-companies-work-for.html
- The Chipotle Effect. Washington Post. https://www.washingtonpost.com/news/wonk/wp/2015/02/02/the-chipotle-effect-why-america-is-obsessed-with-fast-casual-food/ Ferdman, Roberto. February 2, 2015.
- The $70 Billion Fantasy Football Market, Forbes. Goff, Brian. August 20, 2013. http://www.forbes.com/sites/briangoff/2013/08/20/the-70-billion-fantasy-football-market/#14e5368a41b7
- Sethi, Lokanksha, Social Media Addiction. Daze Info, January 12, 2015. http://dazeinfo.com/2015/01/12/social-media-addiction/

- Oliver, Mary. Quote. http://www.wisdomquotes.com/quote/mary-oliver-3.html
- Best Places To Work For LGBT Equality, https://www.paypal.com/stories/us/core-values-creating-a-best-place-to-work-for-lgbt-equality
- Collins, James and Porras, Jerry. Built to Last. New York, New York: HarperCollins Publishers, 1994, 1997, 2002.
- Gawande, Atul. Checklist Manifesto. New York, New York: Picador, 2009, 2010.
- Behar, Howard. It's Not About the Coffee. New York, New York. The Penguin Group, 2007, 2009.
- Krzyzewski Mike, http://en.wikipedia.org/wiki/Mike_Krzyzewski
- 7 Startling Facts: An Up Close Look at Church Attendance in America. Shattuck, Kelly. http://www.churchleaders.com/pastors/pastor-articles/139575-7-startling-facts-an-up-close-look-at-church-attendance-in-america.html
- Jeni's Splendid Ice Creams, www.Jenis.com
- System of Strength, www.systemofstrength.com
- Revenue Builder Blog, "ATL, BTL and TTL Marketing—Definitions and Examples. http://www.revenuebuilderblog.com/2013/10/atl-btl-ttl-marketing.html
- Connors, Roger and Smith, Tom. Change the Culture Change the Game. New York, New York: The Penguin Group, 1999, 2011.
- Langer, Ellen. Counter Clockwise. New York, New York. The Random House Publishing Group, 2009.
- A.G. Greenwald, M.R. Banaji, and L.A. Rudman, "A Unified Theory Of Implicit Attitudes, Stereotypes, Self-Esteem, and Self-Concept." Psychological Review 109, 1 (2002), pp.3-25.

- Hullinger, Jessica, Mental Floss. "12 Behind The Scenes Secrets of Airports," January 22, 2016.
- Why REI's Closure on Thanksgiving and Black Friday Pay Dividends? NBC News Business. Wong, Kristin. November 26, 2015.
- Brown, Molly, REI's move to close Black Friday pays off with 26 percent hike in online traffic. Geekwire, November 30, 2015.
- Life Planner, www.LifePlanner.guru, 2016 by Altimaxx Inc.
- Behar, Howard. The Magic Cup. New York, New York. Center Street, 2016.
- Popeil, Ron. https://en.wikipedia.org/wiki/Ron_Popeil

Jason Barger is a dad, husband, friend, chicken wing connoisseur, and curious human.

He's also the globally celebrated author of *Step Back from the Baggage Claim* and *ReMember*, as well as creator of the *Step Back from the Baggage Claim* movement — highlighted by the New York Times, ABC News, International Herald Tribune, and many other outlets worldwide.

As founder of Step Back Leadership Consulting LLC, Jason is a highly sought-after keynote speaker, retreat leader, coach and consultant, focused on leadership development, culture-shaping, service, and clarity of mission, vision, and values.

Prior to taking off to sleep in airports and observe human behavior, Jason led 1,700 people to construct 125 houses internationally for families living in poverty. He is a graduate of Denison University, where he served as Captain of the men's basketball team, and then received certification from Georgetown University in Nonprofit Executive Management. In 2004, he was one of five people in Columbus, Ohio, to receive a Jefferson Award, a national award given to "ordinary people doing extraordinary things." In 2014, he was a recipient of Business First's *Forty Under 40* award.

Today, Jason and his family live in Columbus, Ohio.

To learn more, visit JasonVBarger.com

The Invitation…

BE A THERMOSTAT

Jason Barger's books are not meant to sit on shelves. They are meant to be shared. They are meant to begin conversations. They are meant to spread positive messages around the world.

Be a thermostat by spreading the temperature to others and caring for others along your path.

Who in your life and work could benefit from the messages, questions, and lessons in this book?

Who are the individuals, teams, or organizations who could benefit from intentional time to set the temperature for their culture and leadership?

Dare to share.

Give it away to someone along your path!

JasonVBarger.com

(email Info@JasonVBarger.com to purchase discounted bulk copies for your team or organization or to inquire about keynotes, workshops & other programs)

SOMETHING NEW

P. G. WODEHOUSE

DOVER PUBLICATIONS, INC
Mineola, New York

Bibliographical Note

This Dover edition, first published in 2000, is an unabridged
republication of the work originally published by Daniel Appleton
& Company, Chicago, in 1915, and includes a later preface written
by the author.

Library of Congress Cataloging-in-Publication Data

Wodehouse, P. G. (Pelham Grenville), 1881–1975.
  [Something fresh]
  Something new / P.G. Wodehouse.
    p. cm.
  ISBN 0-486-41404-3 (pbk.)
    1. Blandings Castle (England : Imaginary place)—Fiction.
  2. Shropshire (England)—Fiction. I. Title.

PR6045.O53 S68 2000
823'.912—dc21

                                                              00-031776

Manufactured in the United States of America
Dover Publications, Inc., 31 East 2nd Street, Mineola, N.Y. 11501

PREFACE

When this book was first published—fifty-three years ago—writers in America, where I had been living since 1909, were divided into two sharply defined classes—the Swells who contributed regularly to the *Saturday Evening Post* and the Cannail or Dregs who thought themselves lucky if they landed an occasional story with *Munsey's*, the *Popular* or one of the other pulp magazines. I had been a chartered member of the latter section for five years when I typed the first words of *Something Fresh*.

Half-way through it I got married (and have been ever since) to an angel in human form who had seventy-five dollars. As I had managed to save fifty, we were fairly well fixed financially, but we felt we could do with a bit more, and by what I have always looked on as a major miracle we got it. My agent, who must have been an optimist to end all optimists, sent the story to the *Saturday Evening Post* and George Horace Lorimer, its world-famous editor, bought it as a serial and paid me the stupefying sum of $3,500 for it, at that time the equivalent of seven hundred gleaming golden sovereigns. I was stunned. I had always known in a vague sort of way that there was money like $3,500 in the world, but I had never expected to touch it. If I was a hundred bucks ahead of the game in those days, I thought I was doing well.

I have always had the idea that Lorimer must have been put in a receptive mood the moment he saw the title page. My pulp magazine stories had been by 'P. G. Wodehouse,' but *Something Fresh* was the work of: PELHAM GRENVILLE WODE-HOUSE, and I am convinced that that was what put it over.

A writer in America at that time who went about without three names was practically going around naked. Those were the days of Richard Harding Davis, of James Warner Bellah, of Margaret Culkin Banning, of Earl Derr Biggers, of Charles Francis Coe, Norman Reilly Raine, Mary Roberts Rinehart, Clarence Budington Kelland and Orison Swett—yes, really, I'm not kidding—Marden. Naturally a level-headed editor like Lorimer was not going to let a Pelham Grenville Wodehouse get away from him.

If you ask me to tell you frankly if I like the names Pelham Grenville, I must confess that I do not. I have my dark moods when they seem to me about as low as you can get. At the font I remember protesting vigorously when the clergyman uttered them, but he stuck to his point. 'Be that as it may,' he said firmly, having waited for a lull, 'I name thee Pelham Grenville'.

Apparently I was called that after a godfather, and not a thing to show for it except a small silver mug which I lost in 1897. I little knew how the frightful label was going to pay off thirty-four years later. (One could do a bit of moralizing about that if one wanted to, but better not for the moment. Some other time, perhaps.)

Something Fresh was the first of what I might call—in fact, I will call—the Blandings Castle Saga. Since then I have written nine novels and a number of short stories about that stately home of England. And I should like to give a warning to any young litterateur who is planning to go in for this Saga racket, and that is to be very careful in the early stages how he commits himself to dates and what is known as locale. When I wrote *Something Fresh* I rashly placed Blandings Castle in Shropshire because my happiest days as a boy were spent near Bridgnorth, over-looking the fact that to get to the heart of Shropshire by train takes four hours (or did in my time. No doubt British Railways by now have cut it down a lot). This meant that my characters were barred from popping up to London and popping back the same afternoon, which is so essential to characters in the sort of stories I write. Kent or Sussex would have served me better.

And as to dates. I wrote *Something Fresh* in 1914, and not realizing that this was not an end but a beginning and wanting to make Lord Emsworth fairly elderly I stated that he had been at Eton in the Sixties. This becomes awkward nowadays, for while the ninth earl is not supposed to be in his first youth, I certainly do not intend to portray him as a centenarian.

People are always asking me . . . well, someone did the other day . . . if I draw my characters from living originals. I don't. I never have, except in the case of Psmith. He was based more or less faithfully on Rupert D'Oyly Carte, the son of the Savoy Theatre man. He was at school with a cousin of mine, and my cousin happened to tell me about his monocle, his immaculate clothes and his habit, when asked by a master how he was, of replying, 'Sir, I grow thinnah and thinnah'. I instantly recognized that I had been handed a piece of cake and I bunged him down on paper (*circ.* 1908). But none of the Blandings circle owes his or her existence to anyone but me. I thought them all up, starting from scratch.

I have often felt that life at Blandings must have been a very pleasant affair, if not for Lord Emsworth and his pig, at any rate for visitors to the castle. Plenty of ridin', shootin' and fishin' for these sportively inclined, and the browsing and sluicing of course beyond criticism. I have always refrained from describing the meals there, not wishing to make my readers' mouths water excessively, but I can now divulge that they were of the best and rendered all the more toothsome by being presided over by butler Beach, who also never failed to bring the tray of beverages into the drawing-room at 9.30.

The one thing that might be considered to militate against the peace of life at Blandings was the constant incursion of impostors. Blandings had impostors the way other houses have mice. I have recorded so far the activities of six of them, and no doubt more to come.

I am not certain who is the Empress's pig man now that La Simmons has left. I may be wrong, but I have a sort of idea that he will turn out to be the latest of that long line of impostors. It is about time that another was coming along. Without at least one impostor on the premises, Blandings Castle is never itself.

P. G. WODEHOUSE

CHAPTER ONE

I

The sunshine of a fair Spring morning fell graciously upon London town. Out in Piccadilly its heartening warmth seemed to infuse into traffic and pedestrians alike a novel jauntiness, so that bus-drivers jested and even the lips of chauffeurs uncurled into not unkindly smiles. Policemen whistled at their posts, clerks on their way to work, beggars approached the task of trying to persuade perfect strangers to bear the burden of their maintenance with that optimistic vim which makes all the difference. It was one of those happy mornings.

At nine o'clock precisely the door of No. 7A, Arundell Street, Leicester Square, opened, and a young man stepped out.

Of all the spots in London which may fairly be described as back-waters, there is none that answers so completely to the description as Arundell Street, Leicester Square. Passing along the north pavement of the Square, just where it joins Piccadilly, you hardly notice the bottle-neck opening of the tiny *cul-de-sac*.

Day and night the human flood roars past, ignoring it. Arundell Street is less than forty yards in length, and, though there are two hotels in it, they are not fashionable hotels. It is just a back-water.

In shape Arundell Street is exactly like one of those flat stone jars in which Italian wine of the cheaper sort is stored. The narrow neck which leads off Leicester Square opens abruptly into a small court. Two sides of this hotels occupy; the third is at present given up to furnished lodgings for the impecunious. These are always just going to be pulled down in the name of Progress, to make room for another hotel, but they never do meet with that fate, and as they stand now so will they, in all probability stand for generations to come.

They provide single rooms of moderate size, the bed modestly hidden during the day behind a battered screen. They contain a table, an easy-chair, a hard chair, a bureau, and a round tin bath, which, like the bed, goes into hiding after its

9

useful work is performed. And you may rent one of these rooms, with breakfast thrown in, for five dollars a week.

Ashe Marson had done so. He had rented the second-floor front of No. 7A.

Twenty-six years before this story opens there had been born to the Reverend Joseph Marson, minister, and Sarah his wife, of Much Middlefold, Salop, a son. This son, christened Ashe after a wealthy uncle who subsequently double-crossed them by leaving his money to charities, in due course proceeded to Oxford to read for the Church. So far as can be ascertained from contemporary records, he did not read a great deal for the Church, but he did succeed in running the mile in four and a half minutes and the half-mile at a correspondingly rapid speed, and his researches in the art of long-jumping won him the respect of all.

He secured his Blue for Athletics, and gladdened thousands by winning the mile and the half-mile two years in succession against Cambridge at Queen's Club. But, owing to the pressure of other engagements, he unfortunately omitted to do any work, and, when the hour of parting arrived, he was peculiarly unfitted for any of the learned professions. Having, however, managed to obtain a sort of degree, enough to enable him to call himself a Bachelor of Arts, and realizing that you can fool some of the people some of the time, he applied for and secured a series of private tutorships. Having saved a little money at this dreadful trade, Ashe came to London and tried newspaper work. After two years of moderate success, he got in touch with the Mammoth Publishing Company.

The Mammoth Publishing Company, which controls several important newspapers, a few weekly journals, and a number of other things, does not disdain the pennies of the office-boy and the junior clerk. One of its many profitable ventures is a series of paper-covered tales of crime and adventure. It was here that Ashe found his niche. Those 'Adventures of Gridley Quayle, Investigator', which are so popular with a certain section of the reading public, were his work. Until the advent of Ashe and Mr. Quayle, the 'British Pluck Library' had been written by many hands and had included the adventures of many heroes; but in Gridley Quayle the proprietors held that the ideal had been reached, and Ashe received a commission to conduct the entire 'British Pluck Library' (monthly) himself. On the meagre salary paid him for these labours he had been supporting himself ever since.

10

That was how Ashe came to be in Arundell Street, Leicester Square, on this May morning.

He was a tall, well-built, fit-looking young man, with a clear eye and a strong chin; and he was dressed, as he closed the front door behind him, in a sweater, flannel trousers, and rubber-soled gymnasium shoes. In one hand he bore a pair of Indian clubs, in the other a skipping-rope.

Having drawn in and expelled the morning air in a measured and solemn fashion which the initiated observer would have recognized as that 'scientific deep breathing' which is so popular nowadays, he laid down his clubs, adjusted his rope, and began to skip.

When one considers how keenly London, like all large cities, resents physical exercise, unless taken with some practical and immediately utilitarian object in view, this young man's calm, as he did this peculiar thing, was amazing. The rules governing exercise in London are clearly defined. You may run, if you are running after a hat, or an omnibus; you may jump, if you do so with the idea of avoiding a taxi-cab or because you have stepped on a banana-skin. But, if you run because you wish to develop your lungs or jump because jumping is good for the liver, London punishes you with its mockery. It rallies round and points the finger of scorn.

Yet this morning, Arundell Street bore the spectacle absolutely unmoved. Due West, the proprietor of the Hotel Previtali leaned against his hostelry, his mind an obvious blank; due North, the proprietor of the Hotel Mathis propped up his caravanserai, manifestly thinking of nothing. In various windows of the two hotels the upper portions of employees appeared, and not a single employee ceased his task for a moment to fling a jibe. Even the little children who infested the court forbore to scoff, and the customary cat rubbing itself against the railings rubbed on without a glance.

The whole thing affords a remarkable object-lesson of what a young man can achieve with patience and perseverance.

When he had taken the second-floor front of No. 7A three months before, Ashe Marson had realized that he must forget those morning exercises which had become a second nature to him, or else defy London's unwritten law and brave London's mockery. He had not hesitated long. Physical fitness was his gospel. On the subject of exercise he was confessedly a crank. He decided to defy London.

The first time he appeared in Arundell Street in his sweater

11

and flannels, he had barely whirled his Indian clubs once round his head before he had attracted the following audience:

(a) two cabmen (one intoxicated);
(b) four waiters from the Hotel Mathis;
(c) six waiters from the Hotel Previtali;
(d) six chambermaids from the Hotel Mathis;
(e) five chambermaids from the Hotel Previtali;
(f) the proprietor of the Hotel Mathis;
(g) the proprietor of the Hotel Previtali;
(h) a street-cleaner;
(i) eleven nondescript loafers;
(j) twenty-seven children;
(k) a cat.

They all laughed, even the cat, and kept on laughing. The intoxicated cabman called Ashe 'Bill Bailey!' And Ashe kept on swinging his clubs.

A month later, such is the magic of perseverance, his audience had narrowed down to the twenty-seven children. They still laughed, but without that ringing conviction which the sympathetic support of their elders had lent them.

And now, after three months, the neighbourhood having accepted Ashe and his morning exercises as a natural phenomenon, paid him no further attention.

On this particular morning, Ashe Marson skipped with even more than his usual vigour. This was because he wished to expel by means of physical fatigue a small devil of discontent of whose presence within him he had been aware ever since getting out of bed. It is in the Spring that the ache for the Larger Life comes upon us, and this was a particularly mellow Spring morning. It was the sort of morning when the air gives us a feeling of anticipation, a feeling that, on a day like this, things surely cannot go joggling along in the same dull old groove, a premonition that something romantic and exciting is about to happen to us. On such a morning you will see stout old gentlemen make sudden rollicking swings with their umbrellas; and a note of shrill optimism thrills in the errand-boy's whistle, as he sees life opening before him, large and splendid.

But the south-west wind of Spring brings also remorse. We catch the vague spirit of unrest in the air, and we regret our misspent youth.

Ashe was doing this. Even as he skipped, he was conscious

12

of a wish that he had worked harder at Oxford, and was now in a position to be doing something better than hack-work for a soulless publishing company. Never before had he been so completely certain that he was sick to death of the rut into which he had fallen. The thought that after breakfast he must sit down and hammer out another Gridley Quayle adventure numbed him like a blow from what the papers always call 'some blunt instrument'. The mere thought of Gridley Quayle was loathsome on a morning like this, with all creation shouting at him that Summer was on its way and that there were brave doings afoot just round the corner.

Skipping brought no balm. He threw down his rope, and took up the Indian clubs.

Indian clubs left him still unsatisfied. The thought came to him that it was a long time since he had done his Larsen Exercises. Perhaps they would heal him.

A gentleman named Lieutenant Larsen, of the Danish Army, as the result of much study of the human anatomy, some time ago evolved a series of Exercises. All over the world at the present moment his apostles are twisting themselves into knots in accordance with the dotted lines in the illustrative plates of his admirable book. From Peebles to Baffin's Bay arms and legs are being swung in daily thousands from point A to point B, and flaccid muscles are gaining the consistency of india-rubber. Larsen's Exercises are the last word in exercises. They bring into play every sinew of the body. They promote a brisk circulation. They enable you, if you persevere, to fell oxen, if desired, with a single blow.

But they are not dignified. Indeed, to one seeing them suddenly and without warning for the first time, they are markedly humorous. The only reason why King Henry of England, whose son sank with the White Ship, never smiled again, was because Lieutenant Larsen had not then invented his admirable Exercises.

So complacent, so insolently unselfconscious had Ashe become in the course of three months, owing to his success in inducing the populace to look on anything he did with the indulgent eye of understanding, that it simply did not occur to him, when he abruptly twisted his body into the shape of a cork-screw in accordance with the directions in the Lieutenant's book for the consummation of Exercise One, that he was doing anything funny. And the behaviour of those present seemed to justify his confidence. The proprietor of the Hotel

Mathis regarded him without a smile. The proprietor of the Hotel Previtali might have been in a trance for all the interest he displayed. The hotel employees continued their tasks impassively. The children were blind and dumb. The cat across the way stropped its backbone against the railings unheeding.

But, even as he unscrambled himself and resumed a normal posture, from his immediate rear there rent the quiet morning air a clear and musical laugh. It floated out upon the breeze, and hit him like a bullet.

Three months ago Ashe would have accepted the laugh as inevitable, and would have refused to allow it to embarrass him. But long immunity from ridicule had sapped his resolution. He spun round with a jump, flushed and self-conscious.

From the window of the first floor front of No. 7A a girl was leaning. The Spring sunshine played on her golden hair and lit up her bright blue eyes, fixed on his flannelled and sweatered person with a fascinated amusement. Even as he turned, the laugh smote him afresh.

For the space of perhaps two seconds they stared at each other, eye to eye. Then she vanished into the room.

Ashe was beaten. Three months ago a million girls could have laughed at his morning exercises without turning him from his purpose. Today this one scoffer, alone and unaided, was sufficient for his undoing. The depression which exercise had begun to dispel surged back upon him. He had no heart to continue. Sadly gathering up his belongings, he returned to his room, and found a cold bath tame and uninspiring.

The breakfasts (included in rent) provided by Mrs. Bell, the landlady of No. 7A, were not exhilarating feasts. By the time Ashe had done his best with the dishevelled fried egg, the chicory, blasphemously called coffee, and the charred bacon, Misery had him firmly in its grip. And when he forced himself to the table, and began to try to concoct the latest of the adventures of Gridley Quayle, Investigator, his spirit groaned within him.

With that musical laugh ringing in his ears, he found himself wishing that he had never thought of Gridley Quayle, that the baser elements of the British reading public had never taken him for their hero, and that he personally was dead.

The unholy alliance had been in progress now for more than two years, and it seemed to Ashe that Gridley grew less human each month. He was so complacent and so maddeningly blind to the fact that only the most amazing luck enabled him to

14

detect anything. To depend on Gridley Quayle for one's income was like being chained to some horrible monster.

This morning, as he sat and chewed his pen, his loathing for Gridley seemed to have reached its climax. It was his habit, in writing these stories, to think of a good title first, and then fit an adventure to it.

And overnight, in a moment of inspiration, he had jotted down on an envelope the words:

THE ADVENTURE OF THE WAND OF DEATH

It was with the sullen repulsion of a vegetarian who finds a caterpillar in his salad that he now sat glaring at them.

The title had seemed so promising overnight, so full of strenuous possibilities. It was still speciously attractive, but, now that the moment had arrived for writing the story, its flaws became manifest.

What was a Wand of Death? It sounded good, but, coming down to hard facts, what *was* it? You cannot write a story about a wand of death without knowing what a wand of death is; and, conversely, if you have thought of such a splendid title, you cannot jettison it offhand.

Ashe rumpled his hair, and gnawed his pen.

There came a knock at the door.

Ashe spun round in his chair. This was the last straw. If he had told Mrs. Bell once that he was never to be disturbed in the morning on any pretext whatsoever, he had told her twenty times. It was simply too infernal to be endured if his work-time was to be cut into like this. He ran over in his mind a few opening remarks.

'Come in,' he shouted, and braced himself for battle.

A girl walked in, the girl of the first-floor front, the girl with the blue eyes who had laughed at his Larsen Exercises.

II

Various circumstances contributed to the poorness of the figure which Ashe cut in the opening moments of this interview. In the first place, he was expecting to see his landlady, whose height was about four feet six, and the sudden entry of someone who was about five feet seven threw the universe temporarily out of focus. In the second place, in anticipation of Mrs. Bell's entry, he had twisted his face into a forbidding

15

scowl and it was no slight matter to change this on the spur of the moment into a pleasant smile. Finally a man who has been sitting for half an hour in front of a sheet of paper bearing the words:

THE ADVENTURE OF THE WAND OF DEATH

and trying to decide what a wand of death may be, has not his mind under proper control.

The net result of these things was that, for perhaps half a minute, Ashe behaved absurdly. He goggled and he yammered. A lunacy commissioner, had one been present, would have made up his mind about him without further investigation. It was not for an appreciable time that he thought of rising from his seat. When he did, the combined leap and twist which he executed practically amounted to a Larsen Exercise.

Nor was the girl unembarrassed. If Ashe had been calmer, he would have observed upon her cheek the flush that told that she too was finding the situation trying. But, women being ever better equipped with poise than man, it was she who spoke first.

'I'm afraid I'm disturbing you.'

'No, no,' said Ashe. 'Oh no, not at all, not at all, no, oh no, not at all, no,' and would have continued to play upon the theme indefinitely, had not the girl spoken again.

'I wanted to apologize,' she said, 'for my abominable rudeness in laughing at you just now. It was idiotic of me, and I don't know why I did it. I'm sorry.'

Science, with a thousand triumphs to her credit, has not yet succeeded in discovering the correct reply for a young man to make who finds himself in the appalling position of being apologized to by a pretty girl. If he says nothing, he seems sullen and unforgiving. If he says anything, he makes a fool of himself. Ashe, hesitating between these two courses, suddenly caught sight of the sheet of paper over which he had been poring so long.

'What is a wand of death?' he asked.

'I beg your pardon?'

'A wand of death.'

'I don't understand.'

The delirium of the conversation was too much for Ashe. He burst out laughing. A moment later the girl did the same. And simultaneously embarrassment ceased to be.

16

'I suppose you think I'm mad?' said Ashe.

'Certainly,' said the girl.

'Well, I should have been if you hadn't come in.'

'Why was that?'

'I was trying to write a detective story.'

'I was wondering if you were a writer.'

'Do *you* write?'

'Yes. Do you ever read "Home Gossip"?'

'Never.'

'I congratulate you. It's a horrid little paper, all brown-paper patterns and advice to the love-lorn. I do a short story for it every week, under various names. A duke or an earl goes with each story. I loathe it intensely.'

'I am sorry for your troubles,' said Ashe firmly, 'but we are wandering from the point. What is a wand of death?'

'A wand of death?'

'A wand of death.'

The girl frowned reflectively.

'Why, of course it's the sacred ebony stick stolen from the Indian temple which is supposed to bring death to whoever possesses it. The hero gets hold of it, and the priests dog him and send him threatening messages. What else could it be?'

Ashe could not restrain his admiration.

'This is genius!'

'Oh no.'

'Absolute genius. I see it all. The hero calls in Gridley Quayle, and that patronizing ass, by the aid of a series of wicked coincidences, solves the mystery, and there am I with another month's work done.'

She looked at him with interest.

'Are you the author of "Gridley Quayle"?'

'Don't tell me you read him!'

'I do *not* read him. But he is published by the same firm that publishes "Home Gossip," and I can't help seeing his cover sometimes while I am waiting in the waiting-room to see the editress.'

Ashe felt like one who meets a boyhood's chum on a desert island. Here was a real bond between them.

'Do the Mammoth publish you too? Why, we are comrades in misfortune—fellow-serfs. We should be friends. Shall we be friends?'

'I should be delighted.'

'Shall we shake hands, sit down, and talk about ourselves a

17

little?'

'But I am keeping you from your work.'

'An errand of mercy.'

She sat down. It is a simple act, this of sitting down, but like everything else it may be an index to character. There was something wholly satisfactory to Ashe in the manner in which this girl did it. She neither seated herself on the extreme edge of the easy-chair, as one braced for instant flight; nor did she wallow in the easy-chair, as one come to stay for the week-end. She carried herself in an unconventional situation with an unstudied self-confidence which he could not sufficiently admire. Etiquette is not rigid in Arundell Street, but, nevertheless, a girl in a first-floor front may be excused for showing surprise and hesitation when invited to a confidential chat with a second-floor front young man whom she has only known five minutes. But there is a Free Masonry among those who live in large cities on small earnings.

'Shall we introduce ourselves?' said Ashe. 'Or did Mrs. Bell tell you my name. By the way, you have not been here long, have you?'

'I took my room the day before yesterday. But your name, if you are the author of Gridley Quayle, is Felix Clovelly, isn't it?'

'Good Heavens, no! Surely you don't think anyone's name could really be Felix Clovelly? That is only the cloak under which I hide my shame. My real name is Marson. Ashe Marson. And yours?'

'Valentine. Joan Valentine.'

'Will you tell me the story of your life, or shall I tell mine first?'

'I don't know that I have any particular story.'

'Come, come!'

'Well, I haven't.'

'Think again. Let us thrash this thing out. You were born!'

'I was.'

'Where?'

'In London.'

'Now we seem to be started. I was born in Much Middleford.'

'I'm afraid I never heard of it.'

'Strange! I know your birth-place quite well. But I have not yet made Much Middleford famous. In fact, I doubt if I ever shall. I am beginning to realize that I am one of the failures.'

18

'How old are you?'

'Twenty-six.'

'You are twenty-six, and you call yourself a failure? I think that is a shameful thing to say.'

'What would you call a man of twenty-six whose only means of making a living was the writing of Gridley Quayle stories? An empire builder?'

'How do you know it's your only means of making a living? Why don't you try something new?'

'Such as——?'

'How should I know? Anything that comes along. Good gracious, Mr. Marson, here you are in the biggest city in the world, with chances of adventure simply shrieking to you on every side——'

'I must be deaf. The only thing I have heard shrieking to me on every side has been Mrs. Bell—for the week's rent.'

'Read the papers. Read the advertisement columns. I'm sure you will find something sooner or later. Don't get into a groove. Be an adventurer. Snatch at the next chance, whatever it is.'

Ashe nodded.

'Continue,' he said. 'Proceed. You are stimulating me.'

'But why should you want a girl like me to stimulate you? Surely London is enough to do it without my help? You can always find *something* new, surely? Listen, Mr. Marson. I was thrown on my own resources about five years ago. Never mind how. Since then I have worked in a shop, done typewriting, been on the stage, had a position as governess, been a lady's maid——'

'A *what*? A lady's maid?'

'Why not? It was all experience, and I can assure you I would much rather be a lady's maid than a governess.'

'I think I know what you mean. I was a private tutor once. I suppose a governess is the female equivalent. I have often wondered what General Sherman would have said about private tutoring, if he expressed himself so breezily about mere War. Was it fun being a lady's maid?'

'It was pretty good fun, and it gave me an opportunity of studying the aristocracy in its native haunts, which has made me "Home Gossip's" established authority on dukes and earls.'

Ashe drew a deep breath—not a scientific deep breath, but one of admiration.

'You are perfectly splendid?'

19

'Splendid?'

'I mean, you have such pluck!'

'Oh well, I keep on trying. I'm twenty-three, and I haven't achieved anything much yet, but I certainly don't feel like sitting back and calling myself a failure.'

Ashe made a grimace.

'All right,' he said. 'I got it!'

'I meant you to,' said Joan placidly. 'I hope I haven't bored you with my autobiography, Mr. Marson? I'm not setting myself up as a shining example, but I do like action and hate stagnation.'

'You are absolutely wonderful,' said Ashe. 'You are a human correspondence course in Efficiency—one of the ones you see in the back pages of the magazines, beginning, "Young man are you earning enough?" with a picture showing the dead-beat gazing wistfully at the boss's chair. You would galvanize a jellyfish.'

'If I have really stimulated you——'

'I think,' said Ashe pensively, 'that that was another insult. Well, I deserve it. Yes, you *have* stimulated me. I feel a new man. It's queer that you should have come to me right on top of everything else. I don't remember when I have felt so restless and discontented as this morning.'

'It's the Spring.'

'I suppose it is. I feel like doing something big and adventurous.'

'Well, do it then. You have a *Morning Post* on the table. Have you read it yet?'

'I glanced at it.'

'But you haven't read the advertisement pages? Read them. They may contain just the opening you want.'

'Well, I'll do it, but my experience of advertisement pages is that they are monopolized by philanthropists who want to lend you any sum from ten to a hundred thousand pounds on your note of hand only. However, I will scan them.'

Joan rose, and held out her hand.

'Good-bye, Mr. Marson. You've got your detective story to write, and I have to think out something with a duke in it by tonight, so I must be going.' She smiled. 'We have travelled a good way from the point we started at, but I may as well go back to it before I leave you. I'm sorry I laughed at you this morning.'

Ashe clasped her hand in a fervent grip.

20

'I'm not. Come and laugh at me whenever you feel like it. I like being laughed at. Why, when I started my morning exercises, half London used to come and roll about the pavements in convulsions. I'm not an attraction any longer, and it makes me feel lonely. There are twenty-nine of those Larsen Exercises, and you only saw part of the first. You have done so much for me that, if I can be of any use to you in helping you to greet the day with a smile, I shall be only too proud. Exercise Six is funny without being vulgar. I'll start with it tomorrow morning. I can also recommend Exercise Eleven. Don't miss it.'

'Very well. Well, good-bye for the present.'

'Good-bye.'

She was gone; and Ashe, thrilling with new emotions, stared at the door which had been closed behind her. He felt as if he had been awakened from sleep by a powerful electric shock.

A wonderful girl ... An astounding girl ... An amazing girl....

Close beside the sheet of paper on which he had inscribed the now luminous and suggestive title of his new Gridley Quayle story lay the *Morning Post*, whose advertisement columns he had promised her to explore. The least he could do was to begin at once.

His spirits sank as he did so. It was the same old game. A Mr. Brian MacNeill, though doing no business with minors, was willing, even anxious, to part with his vast fortune to anyone over the age of twenty-one whose means happened to be a trifle straitened. This good man required no security whatever. Nor did his rivals in generosity, the Messrs. Angus Bruce, Duncan Macfarlane, Wallace Mackintosh, and Donald MacNab. They, too, showed a curious distaste for dealing with minors, but anyone of maturer years could simply come round to the office and help himself.

Beneath these was the heart-cry of Young Man (Christian) who wanted a thousand pounds at once to enable him to complete his education with the Grand Tour.

Ashe threw the paper down wearily. He had known all along that it was no good. Romance was dead, and the Unexpected no longer happened.

He picked up his pen, and began to write the Adventure of the Wand of Death.

CHAPTER TWO

I

In a bedroom on the fourth floor of the Hotel Guelph in Piccadilly, the Hon. Frederick Threepwood sat in bed with his knees drawn up to his chin and glared at the day with a glare of mental anguish. He had very little mind, but what he had was suffering.

He had just remembered.

It is like that in this life. You wake up, feeling as fit as a fiddle; you look at the window and see the sun and thank Heaven for a fine day; You begin to plan a perfectly corking luncheon-party with some of the chappies you met last night at the National Sporting Club, and then—you remember.

'Oh, dash it!' said the Hon. Freddie. And after a moment's pause, 'And I was feeling so dashed happy!'

For the space of some minutes he remained plunged in sad meditation. Then, picking up the telephone on the table at his side, he asked for a number.

'Hello?'

'Hello?' responded a rich voice at the other end of the wire.

'Oh, I say, is that you, Dickie?'

'Who is that?'

'This is Freddie Threepwood, I say, Dickie, old top, I want to see you about something devilish important. Will you be in at twelve?'

'Certainly. What's the trouble?'

'I can't explain over the wire, but it's deuced serious.'

'Very well. By the way, Freddie, congratulations on the engagement.'

'Thanks, old man. Thanks very much, and so forth, but you won't forget to be in at twelve, will you? Good-bye.'

He replaced the receiver quickly, and sprang out of bed, for he had heard the door-handle turn. When the door opened he was giving a correct representation of a young man wasting no time in beginning his toilet for the day.

An elderly, thin-faced, bald-headed, amiably vacant man entered. He regarded the Hon. Freddie with a certain disfavour.

'Are you only just getting up, Frederick?'

'Hullo, guv'nor. Good morning. I shan't be two ticks now,'

'You should have been out and about two hours ago. The day is glorious.'

'Shan't be more than a minute, guv'nor, now. Just got to have a tub and chuck on a few clothes.'

He disappeared into the bathroom. His father, taking a chair, placed the tips of his fingers together and in this attitude remained motionless, a figure of disapproval and suppressed annoyance.

Like many fathers in his rank of life, the Earl of Emsworth had suffered much through that problem which—with the exception of Mr. Lloyd George—is practically the only fly in the British aristocratic amber—the problem of What To Do With The Younger Sons. It is useless to try to gloss over the fact, the Younger Son is not required. You might reason with a British peer by the hour—you might point out to him how, on the one hand, he is far better off than the male codfish, who may at any moment find itself in the distressing position of being called on to provide for a family of over a million; and remind him, on the other, that every additional child he acquires means a corresponding rise for him in the estimation of ex-President Roosevelt; but you would not cheer him up in the least. He does not want the Younger Son.

Apart, however, from the fact that he was a younger son, and, as such a nuisance in any case, the Honourable Freddie had always annoyed his father in a variety of ways. The Earl of Emsworth was so constituted that no man or thing really had the power to trouble him deeply, but Freddy had come nearer to doing it than anybody else in the world. There had been a consistency, a perseverance, about his irritating performances which had acted on the placid peer as dripping water on a stone. Isolated acts of annoyance would have been powerless to ruffle his calm; but Freddie had been exploding bombs under his nose since he went to Eton.

He had been expelled from Eton for breaking out at night and roaming the streets of Windsor in a false moustache. He had been sent down from Oxford for pouring ink from a second-storey window on to the Junior Dean of his college. He had spent two years at an expensive London crammer's and failed to pass into the Army. He had also accumulated an almost record series of racing debts, besides as shady a gang of friends, for the most part vaguely connected with the turf, as any young man of his age ever contrived to collect.

These things try the most placid of parents, and finally Lord

23

Emsworth had put his foot down. It was the only occasion in his life when he had acted with decision, and he did it with the accumulated energy of years. He stopped his son's allowance, haled him home to Blandings Castle, and kept him there so relentlessly that, until the previous night, when they had come up together by an afternoon train, Freddie had not seen London for nearly a year.

It was possibly the reflection that, whatever his secret troubles, he was at any rate once more in his beloved metropolis that caused Freddie at this point to burst into discordant song. He splashed and warbled simultaneously.

Lord Emsworth's frown deepened, and he began to tap his fingers together irritably. Then his brow cleared, and a pleased smile flickered over his face. He, too, had remembered.

What Lord Emsworth had remembered was this. Late in the previous autumn, the next estate to Blandings had been rented by an American, a Mr. Peters, a man with many millions, chronic dyspepsia, and one fair daughter, Aline. The two families had met. Freddie and Aline had been thrown together. And, only a few days before, the engagement had been announced, and for Lord Emsworth the only flaw in this best of all possible worlds had been removed.

The singing in the bathroom was increasing in volume, but Lord Emsworth heard it now without wincing. It was amazing what a difference it made to a man's comfort, this fair prospect of getting his younger son off his hands. For nearly a year Freddie, a prisoner at Blandings, had afflicted his father's nerves with a never-failing discomfort. Blandings was a large house, but not so large that father and son did not occasionally meet; and on these occasions it had maddened Lord Emsworth to perceive the martyred aspect of the young man. To Lord Emsworth the park and gardens of Blandings were the nearest earthly approach to Paradise. Freddie, chafing at captivity, had mooned about them with an air of crushed gloom which would have caused comment in Siberia.

Yes, he was glad Freddie was engaged to be married to Aline Peters. He liked Aline. He liked Mr. Peters. Such was the relief he experienced that he found himself feeling almost affectionate towards Freddie, who emerged from the bathroom at this moment clad in a pink bath-robe, to find the paternal wrath evaporated and all, so to speak, right with the world.

Nevertheless, he wasted no time about his dressing. He was always ill at ease in his father's presence, and he wished to be

24

elsewhere with all possible speed. He sprang into his trousers with such energy that he nearly tripped himself up.

As he disentangled himself, he recollected something which had slipped his memory.

'By the way, guv'nor, I met an old pal of mine last night, and asked him down to Blandings this week. That's all right, isn't it, what?'

For a moment Lord Emsworth's geniality faltered. He had had experience of Freddie's old pals.

'Who is he? Kindly remember that Mr. Peters and Aline and nearly all your relations will be at Blandings this week. If he is one of——'

'Oh no, that's all right. Honour bright. He isn't one of the old crowd. He's a man named Emerson. Most respectable chap. Policeman or something in Hong-Kong. He knows Aline quite well, he says. Met her on the boat coming over.'

'I do not remember any friend of yours named Emerson.'

'Well, as a matter of fact I met him last night for the first time. But it's all right. He's a good chap, don't you know, and all that sort of rot.'

Lord Emsworth was feeling too benevolent to raise the objections which he would certainly have raised, had his mood been less sunny.

'Certainly, let him come, if he wishes.'

'Thanks, guv'nor.'

Freddie completed his toilet.

'Doing anything special this morning, guv'nor? I rather thought of getting a bit of breakfast and then strolling round a bit. Have you had breakfast?'

'Two hours ago. I trust that, in the course of your strolling, you will find time to call at Mr. Peter's and see Aline. I shall be going there directly after lunch. Mr. Peters wishes to show me his collection of—I think scarabs was the word he used.'

'Oh, I'll look in all right. Don't you worry. Or, if I don't, I'll call the old boy up on the phone and pass the time of day. Well, I rather think I'll be popping off now and getting that bit of breakfast, what?'

Several comments on this speech suggested themselves to Lord Emsworth. In the first place, he did not approve of Freddie's allusion to one of America's merchant-princes as 'the old boy'. Secondly, his son's attitude did not strike him as the ideal attitude of a young man towards his betrothed. There seemed a lack of warmth. But, he reflected, possibly this was simply another manifestation of the Modern Spirit, and in any case it was not worth bothering about, so he offered no criticism; and presently, Freddie having given his shoes a flick with a silk handkerchief and thrust the latter carefully up his sleeve, they passed out and down into the main lobby of the hotel, where they parted, Freddie to his bit of breakfast, his father to potter about the streets and kill time till lunch. London was always a trial to the Earl of Emsworth. His heart was in the country, and the city held no fascinations for him.

II

On one of the floors in one of the buildings in one of the streets which slope precipitously from the Strand to the Thames Embankment, there is a door, which would be all the better for a lick of paint, which bears what is perhaps the most modest and unostentatious announcement of its kind in London.

The grimly ground-glass displays the words:

- R. JONES,

simply that, and nothing more.

Situated between a door profusely illustrated with the legend, 'Sarawak and New Guinea Rubber Estates Exploitation Company. General Manager, Jno. Bradbury-Eggleston' and a door belonging to the Bhangaloo Ruby Mines Incorporated, it has a touch of the woodland violet nestling among orchids.

R. JONES.

It is rugged in its simplicity. You wonder, as you look at it, if you have time to look at and wonder about these things, who this Jones may be and what is the business which he conducts with such a coy reticence.

As a matter of fact, these speculations had passed through suspicious minds at Scotland Yard, which had for some time taken not a little interest in R. Jones. But, beyond ascertaining that he bought and sold curios, did a certain amount of book-making during the flat-racing season, and had been known to lend money. Scotland Yard did not find out much about Mr. Jones, and presently dismissed him from its thoughts. Not that Scotland Yard was satisfied. To a certain extent, baffled would

26

be a better description of its attitude. The suspicion that R. Jones was, among other things, a receiver of stolen goods still lingered, but proof was not forthcoming.

R. Jones saw to that. He did a great many things, for he was one of the busiest men in London; but what he did best was seeing to it that proof was not forthcoming.

On the theory, given to the world by my brother-author, William Shakespeare, that it is the lean and hungry-looking men who are dangerous and that the fat, the sleek-headed men and such as sleep o' nights, are harmless, R. Jones should have been above suspicion. He was infinitely the fattest man in the west-central postal district of London. He was a round ball of a man, who wheezed when he walked upstairs, which was seldom, and shook like a jelly if some tactless friend, wishing to attract his attention, tapped him unexpectedly on the shoulder. But this occurred still less frequently than his walking upstairs, for in R. Jones' circle it was recognized that nothing is a greater breach of etiquette and worse form than to tap people unexpectedly on the shoulder. That, it was felt, should be left to those who are paid by the Government to do it.

R. Jones was about fifty years old, grey-haired, of a mauve complexion, jovial among his friends, and perhaps even more jovial with chance acquaintances. It was estimated by envious intimates that his joviality with chance acquaintances, especially with young men of the upper classes with large purses and small foreheads, was worth hundreds of pounds a year to him. There was something about his comfortable appearance and his jolly manner which irresistibly attracted a certain type of young man. It was his good fortune that this type of young man should be the type, financially, most worth attracting.

Freddie Threepwood had fallen under his spell during his short but crowded life in London. They had met for the first time at the Derby, and ever since R. Jones had held, in Freddie's estimation, that position of guide, philosopher, and friend, which he held in the estimation of so many young men of Freddie's type.

That was why, at twelve o'clock punctually on this Spring morning, he tapped with his cane on R. Jones' ground-glass, and showed such satisfaction and relief when the door was opened by the proprietor in person.

'Well, well, well!' said R. Jones, rollickingly. 'Whom have we here? The dashing bridegroom-to-be, and no other!'

R. Jones, like Lord Emsworth, was delighted that Freddie

27

was about to marry a nice girl with plenty of money. The sudden turning-off of the tap from which Freddie's allowance had flowed had hit him hard. He had other sources of income, of course, but few so easy and unfailing as Freddie had been in the days of his prosperity.

'The prodigal son, by George! Creeping back into the fold after all this weary time! It seems years since I saw you, Freddie. The old guv'nor put his foot down, didn't he, and stopped the funds? Damned shame! I take it that things have loosened up a bit since the engagement was announced, eh?'

Freddie sat down, and chewed the knob of his cane unhappily.

'Well, as a matter of fact, Dickie, old top,' he said, 'not so that you could notice it, don't you know. Things are still pretty much the same. I managed to get away from Blandings for a night, because the governor had to come to London, but I've got to go back with him on the three o'clock train. And, as for money, I can't get a quid out of him. As a matter of fact, I'm in the deuce of a hole, and that's why I've come to you.'

Even fat, jovial men have their moments of depression. R. Jones' face clouded, and jerky remarks about the hardness of times and losses on the Stock Exchange began to proceed from him. As Scotland Yard had discovered, he lent money on occasion, but he did not lend it to youths in Freddie's unfortunate position.

'Oh, I don't want to make a touch, you know,' Freddie hastened to explain. 'It isn't that. As a matter of fact, I managed to raise five hundred of the best this morning. That ought to be enough.'

'Depends what you want it for,' said R. Jones, magically genial once more. The thought entered his mind, as it had so often done, that the world was full of easy marks. He wished he could meet the money-lender who had been rash enough to advance the Honourable Freddie five hundred pounds. These philanthropists cross our path too seldom.

Freddie felt in his pocket, produced a cigarette-case, and from it extracted a newspaper-clipping.

'Did you read about poor old Percy in the papers? The case, you know?'

'Percy?'

'Lord Stockheath, you know.'

'Oh, the Stockheath breach-of-promise case? I did more than that. I was in court all three days.' R. Jones emitted a cosy chuckle. 'Is he a pal of yours? A cousin, eh? I wish you had seen him in the witness-box, with Jellicoe-Smith cross-examining him! The funniest thing I ever heard. And his letters to the girl! They read them out in court, and of all the——'

'Don't, old man! Dickie, old top, please! I know all about it. I read the reports. They made poor old Percy look an absolute ass.'

'Well, Nature had done that already, but I'm bound to say they improved on Nature's work. I should think your cousin Percy must have felt like a plucked chicken.'

A spasm of pain passed over the Honourable Freddie's vacant face. He wriggled in his chair.

'Dickie, old man, I wish you wouldn't talk like that. It makes me feel ill.'

'Why, is he such a pal of yours as all that?'

'It's not that. It's—the fact is, Dickie, old top, I'm in exactly the same bally hole as poor old Percy was, myself.'

'What! You have been sued for breach of promise?'

'Not absolutely that—yet. Look here, I'll tell you the whole thing. Do you remember a show at the Piccadilly about a year ago, called, 'The Girl from Dublin?' There was a girl in the chorus.'

'Several. I remember noticing.'

'No. I mean one particular girl—a girl called Joan Valentine. The rotten part is that I never met her.'

'Pull yourself together, Freddie. What exactly is the trouble?'

'Well, don't you see, I used to go to the show every other night, and I fell frightfully in love with this girl——'

'Without having met her?'

'Yes. You see, I was rather an ass in those days.'

'No, no,' said R. Jones, handsomely.

'I must have been, or I wouldn't have been such an ass, don't you know. Well, as I was saying, I used to write this girl letters, saying how much I was in love with her, and—and——'

'Specifically proposing marriage?'

'Eh?'

'I say, specifically proposing marriage?'

'I can't remember. I expect I did. I was awfully in love.'

'How was it that you never met her?'

'She wouldn't meet me. She wouldn't even come out to lunch. She didn't even answer my letters—just sent word down by the Johnnie at the stage-door. And then——'

29

Freddie's voice died away. He thrust the knob of his cane into his mouth in a sort of frenzy.

'What then?' inquired R. Jones.

A scarlet blush manifested itself on Freddie's young face. His eyes wandered sideways. After a long pause a single word escaped him, almost inaudible.

'Poetry!'

R. Jones trembled as if an electric current had been passed through his plump frame. His little eyes sparkled with merriment.

'You wrote her poetry!'

'Yards of it, old boy, yards of it!' groaned Freddie.

Panic filled him with speech.

'You see the frightful hole I'm in? This girl is bound to have kept the letters. I don't remember if I actually proposed to her or not, but anyway she's got enough material to make it worthwhile to have a dash at an action, especially after poor old Percy has just got soaked for such a pile of money, and made breach-of-promise cases the fashion, so to speak. And now that the announcement of my engagement is out, she's certain to get busy. Probably she has been waiting for something of the sort. Don't you see that all the cards are in her hands? We couldn't afford to let the thing come into court. That poetry would dish my marriage for a certainty. I'd have to emigrate or something! Goodness knows what would happen at home. My old governor would murder me. So you see what a frightful hole I'm in, don't you, Dickie, old man?'

'And what do you want me to do?'

'Why, to get hold of this girl and get back the letters, don't you see? I can't do it myself, cooped up miles away in the country. And besides I shouldn't know how to handle a thing like that. It wants a chappie with a lot of sense and a persuasive sort of way with him.'

'Thanks for the compliment, Freddie, but I should imagine that something a little more solid than a persuasive way would be required in a case like this. You said something a while ago about five hundred pounds?'

'Here it is, old man, in notes. I brought it on purpose. Will you really take the thing on? Do you think you can work it for five hundred?'

'I can have a try.'

Freddie rose with an expression approximating to happiness on his face. Some men have the power of inspiring confidence

30

in some of their fellows, while filling others with distrust. Scotland Yard might look askance at R. Jones, but to Freddie he was all that was helpful and reliable. He shook R. Jones' hand several times in his emotion.

'That's absolutely topping of you, old man,' he said. 'Then I'll leave the whole thing to you. Write me the moment you have done anything, won't you. Good-bye, old top, and thanks ever so much.'

The door closed. R. Jones remained where he sat, his fingers straying luxuriously among the crackling paper. A feeling of complete happiness warmed R. Jones' bosom. He was not certain whether or not his mission would be successful, and, to be truthful, he was not letting this worry him much. What he was certain of, was the fact that the Heavens had opened unexpectedly and dropped five hundred pounds into his lap.

CHAPTER THREE

I

The Earl of Emsworth stood in the doorway of the Senior Conservative Club's vast dining-room, and beamed with a vague sweetness upon the two hundred or so Senior Conservatives, who, with much clattering of knife and fork, were keeping body and soul together by means of the coffee-room luncheon. He might have been posing for a Statue of Amiability. His pale blue eyes shone with a friendly light through their protecting glasses; the smile of a man at peace with all men curved his weak mouth; his bald head, reflecting the sunlight, seemed almost to wear a halo.

Nobody appeared to notice him. He so seldom came to London these days that he was practically a stranger in the club; and in any case your Senior Conservative, when at lunch, has little leisure for observing anything not immediately on the table in front of him. To attract attention in the dining-room of the Senior Conservative Club between the hours of one and two-thirty, you have to be a mutton-chop, not an earl.

It is possible that, lacking the initiative to make his way down the long aisle and find a table for himself, he might have stood there indefinitely, but for the restless activity of Adams,

31

the head steward. It was Adams' mission in life to flit to and fro, hauling would-be lunchers to their destinations, as a St. Bernard dog hauls travellers out of Alpine snow-drifts.

He sighted Lord Emsworth, and secured him with a genteel pounce.

'A table, your lordship? This way, your lordship.'

Adams remembered him, of course. Adams remembered everybody.

Lord Emsworth followed him beamingly, and presently came to anchor at a table at the farther end of the room. Adams handed him the bill of fare, and stood brooding over him like a Providence.

'Don't often see your lordship in the club,' he opened chattily. It was his business to know the tastes and dispositions of all the five thousand or so members of the Senior Conservative Club and to suit his demeanour to them. To some he would hand the bill of fare swiftly, silently, almost brusquely, as one who realizes that there are moments in life too serious for talk. Others, he knew, liked conversation, and to these he introduced the subject of food almost as a sub-motive.

Lord Emsworth, having examined the bill of fare with a mild curiosity, laid it down and became conversational.

'No, Adams, I seldom visit London nowadays. London does not attract me. The country ... the fields ... the woods ... the birds ...'

Something across the room seemed to attract his attention, and his voice trailed off. He inspected this for some time with bland interest, then turned to Adams once more.

'What was I saying, Adams?'

'The birds, your lordship.'

'Birds? What birds? What about birds?'

'You were speaking of the attractions of life in the country, your lordship. You included the birds in your remarks.'

'Oh yes, yes, yes. Oh yes, yes. Oh yes, to be sure. Do you ever go the country, Adams?'

'Generally to the seashore, your lordship, when I take my annual vacation.'

Whatever was the attraction across the room once more exercised its spell. His lordship concentrated himself upon it to the exclusion of all other mundane affairs. Presently he came out of his trance again.

'What were you saying, Adams?'

'I said that I generally went to the seashore, your lordship.'

32

'Eh? When?'

'For my annual vacation, your lordship.'

'Your what?'

'My annual vacation, your lordship.'

'What about it?'

Adams never smiled during business hours, unless professionally, as it were, when a member made a joke, but he was storing up in the recesses of his highly respectable body, a large laugh, to be shared with his wife when he reached home that night. Mrs. Adams never wearied of hearing of the eccentricities of the members of the club. It occurred to Adams that he was in luck today. He was expecting a little party of friends to supper that night, and he was a man who loved an audience. You would never have thought it, to look at him when engaged on his professional duties, but Adams had built up a substantial reputation as a humorist in his circle by his imitations of certain members of the club, and it was a matter of regret to him that he got so few opportunities nowadays of studying the absent-minded Lord Emsworth. It was rare luck, his lordship coming in today evidently in his best form.

'Adams, who is the gentleman over by the window? The gentleman in the brown suit?'

'That is a Mr. Simmonds, your lordship. He joined us last year.'

'I never saw a man take such large mouthfuls. Did *you* ever see a man take such large mouthfuls, Adams?'

Adams refrained from expressing an opinion, but inwardly he was thrilling with artistic fervour. Mr. Simmonds, eating, was one of his best imitations, though Mrs. Adams was inclined to object to it on the score that it was a bad example for the children. To be privileged to witness Lord Emsworth watching and criticizing Mr. Simmonds was to collect material for a double-barrelled character-study which would assuredly make the hit of the evening.

'That man,' went on Lord Emsworth, 'is digging his grave with his teeth. Digging his grave with his teeth, Adams. Do *you* take large mouthfuls, Adams?'

'No, your lordship.'

'Quite right. Very sensible of you, Adams. Very sensible of you. Very sen ... What was I saying, Adams?'

'About my not taking large mouthfuls, your lordship.'

'Quite right. Quite right. Never take large mouthfuls, Adams. Never gobble. Have you any children, Adams?'

'Two, your lordship.'

'I hope you teach them not to gobble. They pay for it in later life. Americans gobble when young, and ruin their digestions. My American friend, Mr. Peters, suffers terribly from his digestion.'

Adams lowered his voice to a confidential murmur.

'If you will pardon the liberty, your lordship—I saw it in the paper——'

'About Mr. Peters' digestion?'

'About Miss Peters, your lordship, and the Honourable Frederick. May I be permitted to offer my congratulations?'

'Eh? Oh yes, the engagement. Yes, yes, yes. Yes, to be sure. Yes, very satisfactory in every respect. High time he settled down and got a little sense. I put it to him straight. I cut off his allowance, and made him stay at home. That made him think, lazy young devil. I——'

Lord Emsworth had his lucid moments, and in the one that occurred now it came home to him that he was not talking to himself, as he had imagined, but confiding intimate family secrets to the head steward of his club's dining-room. He checked himself abruptly, and with a slight decrease of amiability fixed his gaze on the bill of fare, and ordered clear soup. For an instant he felt resentful against Adams for luring him on to soliloquize, but the next moment his whole mind was gripped by the fascinating spectacle of Mr. Simmonds dealing with a wedge of Stilton cheese, and Adams was forgotten.

The clear soup had the effect of restoring his lordship to complete amiability, and, when Adams in the course of his wanderings again found himself at the table, he was once more disposed for light conversation.

'So you saw the news of the engagement in the paper, did you, Adams?'

'Yes, your lordship, in the "Mail". It had quite a long piece about it. And the Honourable Frederick's photograph and the young lady's were in the "Mirror". Mrs. Adams clipped them out and put them in an album knowing that your lordship was a member of ours. If I may say so, your lordship, a beautiful young lady.'

'Devilish attractive, Adams, and devilish rich. Mr. Peters is a millionaire, Adams.'

'So I read in the paper, your lordship.'

'Damme, they all seem millionaires in America. Wish I knew how they managed it. Honestly, I hope. Mr. Peters is an honest man, but his digestion is bad. He used to bolt his food. *You* don't bolt your food, I hope, Adams?'

'No, your lordship, I am most careful.'

'The late Mr. Gladstone used to chew each mouthful thirty-three times. Deuced good notion, if you aren't in a hurry. What cheese would you recommend, Adams?'

'The gentlemen are speaking well of the gorgonzola.'

'All right, bring me some. You know, Adams, what I admire about Americans is their resource. Mr. Peters tells me that, as a boy of eleven, he earned twenty dollars a week selling mint to saloon-keepers, as they call publicans over there. Why they wanted mint I cannot recollect. Mr. Peters explained the reason to me, and it seemed highly plausible at the time, but I have forgotten it. Possibly for mint-sauce. It impressed me, Adams. Twenty dollars is four pounds. *I* never earned four pounds a week when I was a boy of eleven. In fact, I don't think I ever earned four pounds a week. His story impressed me, Adams. Every man ought to have an earning capacity.... Tell me Adams, have I eaten my cheese?'

'Not yet, your lordship. I was about to send the waiter for it.'

'Never mind. Tell him to bring the bill instead. I remember that I have an appointment. I must not be late.'

'Shall I take the fork, your lordship?'

'The fork?'

'Your lordship has inadvertently put a fork in your coat-pocket.'

Lord Emsworth felt in the pocket indicated, and, with the air of an inexpert conjuror whose trick has succeeded contrary to his expectations, produced a silver-plated fork. He regarded it with surprise, then he looked wonderingly at Adams.

'Adams, I'm getting absent-minded. Have you ever noticed any traces of absent-mindedness in me before?'

'Oh no, your lordship.'

'Well, it's deuced peculiar. I have no recollection whatsoever of placing that fork in my pocket.... Adams, I want a taxi-cab.'

He glanced round the room, as if expecting to locate one by the fireplace.

'The hall-porter will whistle one for you, your lordship.'

'So he will, by George, so he will. Good day Adams.'

'Good day, your lordship.'

The Earl of Emsworth ambled benevolently to the door,

35

leaving Adams with the feeling that his day had not been ill-spent. He gazed almost with reverence after the slow-moving figure.

'What a nut!' said Adams to his immortal soul.

Wafted through the sun-lit streets in his taxi-cab, the Earl of Emsworth smiled benevolently upon London's teeming millions. He was as completely happy as only a fluffy-minded old man with excellent health and a large income can be. Other people worried about all sorts of things—strikes, wars, suffragettes, diminishing birth-rates, the growing materialism of the age, and a score of similar subjects. Worrying, indeed, seemed to be the twentieth century's speciality. Lord Emsworth never worried. Nature had equipped him with a mind so admirably constructed for withstanding the disagreeableness of life that, if an unpleasant thought entered it, it passed out again a moment later. Except for a few of Life's fundamental facts, such as that his cheque-book was in the right-hand top drawer of his desk, that the Honourable Freddie Threepwood was a young idiot who required perpetual restraint, and that, when in doubt about anything, he had merely to apply to his secretary, Rupert Baxter—except for these basic things, he never remembered anything for more than a few minutes.

At Eton, in the sixties, they had called him Fathead.

His was a life which lacked, perhaps, the sublimer emotions which raised Man to the level of the gods, but it was undeniably an extremely happy one. He never experienced the thrill of ambition fulfilled, but, on the other hand, he never knew the agony of ambition frustrated. His name, when he died, would not live for ever in England's annals; he was spared the pain of worrying about this by the fact that he had no desire to live for ever in England's annals. He was possibly as nearly contented as a human being can be in this century of alarms and excursions. Indeed, as he bowled along in his cab, and reflected that a really charming girl, not in the chorus of any West-end theatre, a girl with plenty of money and excellent breeding had—in a moment, doubtless, of mental aberration—become engaged to be married to the Honourable Freddie, he told himself that life was at last absolutely without a crumpled rose-leaf.

The cab drew up before a house gay with flowered window-boxes. Lord Emsworth paid the driver, and stood on the side-

36

walk looking up at this cheerful house, trying to remember why on earth he had told the man to drive there.

A few moments' steady thought gave him the answer to the riddle. This was Mr. Peter's town house, and he had come to it by invitation to look at Mr. Peters' collection of scarabs.

To be sure. He remembered now. His collection of scarabs.

Or was it Arabs?

He smiled. Scarabs, of course. You couldn't collect Arabs. He wondered idly, as he rang the bell, what scarabs might be. But he was interested in a fluffy kind of way in all forms of collecting, and he was very pleased to have the opportunity of examining these objects, whatever they were.

He rather thought they were a kind of fish.

II

There are men in this world who cannot rest, who are so constituted that they can only take their leisure in the shape of a change of work. To this fairly numerous class belonged Mr. J. Preston Peters, father of Freddie's Aline. And to this merit—or defect—is to be attributed his almost maniacal devotion to that rather unattractive species of curio—the Egyptian scarab.

Five years before, a nervous breakdown had sent Mr. Peters to a New York specialist.

The specialist had grown rich on similar cases, and his advice was always the same. He insisted on Mr. Peters taking up a hobby.

'What sort of a hobby?' inquired Mr. Peters irritably. His digestion had just begun to trouble him at the time, and his temper was not of the best.

The very word hobby seemed futile and ridiculous to him. His hobby was avoiding hobbies and attending to business. Which, the specialist pointed out, was precisely the reason why he had just written a hundred-dollar cheque for his advice. This impressed Mr. Peters. He disliked writing unnecessary cheques, and, if the only way to avoid doing so was to have a hobby, a hobby he must have.

'Any sort of hobby,' said the specialist. 'There must be something outside of business in which you are interested?'

Mr. Peters could not think of anything. Even his meals were beginning to interest him less.

'Now my hobby,' said the specialist, 'is the collecting of

37

scarabs. Why should you not collect scarabs?'

'Because,' said Mr. Peters, 'I shouldn't know one if you brought it to me on a plate. What *are* scarabs?'

'Scarabs,' said the specialist, warming to his subject, 'are Egyptian hieroglyphs.'

'And what,' inquired Mr. Peters, 'are Egyptian hieroglyphs?'

The specialist began to wonder whether it would not have been better to advise Mr. Peters to collect postage-stamps.

'A scarab,' he said, 'derived from the Latin *scarabeus,* is literally a beetle.'

'I will *not* collect beetles,' said Mr. Peters definitely. 'I despise beetles. Beetles give me that pain.'

'Scarabs are Egyptian symbols in the form of beetles,' the specialist hurried on. 'The most common form of scarab is in the shape of a ring. Scarabs were used for seals. They were also employed as beads or ornaments. Some scarabei bear inscriptions having reference to places, as, for instance, "Memphis is mighty for ever".'

Mr. Peters' scorn changed suddenly to active interest.

'Have you got one like that?'

'Like——?'

'A scarab boosting Memphis. It's my home town.'

'I think it possible that some other Memphis was alluded to.'

'There isn't any other except the one in Tennessee,' said Mr. Peters patriotically.

The specialist owed the fact that he was a nerve doctor instead of a nerve patient to his habit of never arguing with his visitors.

'Perhaps,' he said, 'you would care to glance at my collection? It is in the next room.'

That was the beginning of Mr. Peters' devotion to scarabs. At first he did his collecting without any love of it, partly because he had to collect something or suffer, but principally because of a remark the specialist made as he was leaving the room.

'How long would it take me to get together that number of the things?' he inquired, when, having looked his fill upon the dullest assortment of objects which he remembered ever to have seen, he was preparing to take his leave.

The specialist was proud of his collection.

'How long? To make a collection as large as mine? Many years, Mr. Peters. Oh, many, many years.'

'I'll bet you a hundred dollars I do it in six months.'

And from that moment Mr. Peters had brought to the collecting of scarabs the same furious energy which had given him so many dollars and so much indigestion. He went after scarabs like a dog after rats. He scooped in scarabs from all the four corners of the earth, until, at the end of a year, he found himself possessed of what, purely as regarded quantity, was a record collection.

This marked the end of the first phase of, so to speak, the scarabean side of his life. Collecting had become a habit with him, but he was not yet a real enthusiast. It occurred to him that the time had arrived for a certain amount of pruning and elimination. He called in an expert, and bade him go through the collection and weed out what he felicitously termed the 'dead ones'. The expert did his job thoroughly. When he had finished, the collection was reduced to a mere dozen specimens.

'The rest,' he explained, 'are practically valueless. If you are thinking of making a collection that will have any value in the eyes of archaeologists, I should advise you to throw them away. The remaining twelve are good.'

'How do you mean "Good"? Why is one of these things valuable and another so much junk? They all look alike to me.'

And then the expert had talked to Mr. Peters for nearly two hours about the New Kingdom, the Middle Kingdom, Osiris, Ammon, Mut, Bubastis, Dynasties, Cheops, the Hyksos kings, cylinders, bezels, Amenophis III, Queen Taia, the Princess Gilukhipa of Mitanni, the Lake of Zarukhe, Naucratis, and the Book of the Dead. He did it with a relish. He liked doing it.

When he had finished, Mr. Peters thanked him and went to the bathroom, where he bathed his temples with eau de Cologne.

That talk changed J. Preston Peters from a supercilious scooper-up of random scarabs to a genuine scarab-maniac. It does not matter what a man collects; if Nature has given him the collector's mind, he will become a fanatic on the subject of whatever collection he sets out to make. Mr. Peters had collected dollars, he began to collect scarabs with precisely the same enthusiasm. He would have become just as enthusiastic about butterflies, or old china, if he had turned his thoughts to them, but it chanced that what he had taken up was the collecting of the scarab, and it gripped him more and more as the years went on. Gradually he came to love his scarabs with that love passing the love of women which only collectors know. He became an expert on these curious relics of a dead civilization. For a time they ran neck and neck in his thoughts with business. When he retired from business, he was free to make them the master passion of his life. He treasured each individual scarab in his collection as a miser treasures gold.

Collecting, as Mr. Peters did it, resembles the drink habit. It begins as an amusement, and ends as an obsession.

He was gloating over his treasures when the maid announced Lord Emsworth.

A curious species of mutual toleration—it could hardly be dignified by the title of friendship—had sprung up between these two men, so opposite in practically every respect. Each regarded the other with that feeling of perpetual amazement with which we encounter those whose whole view-point and mode of life is foreign to our own. The American's force and nervous energy fascinated Lord Emsworth. In a purely detached way Lord Emsworth liked force and nervous energy. They interested him. He was glad he did not possess them himself, but he enjoyed them as a spectacle, just as a man who would not like to be a purple cow may have no objection to seeing one. As for Mr. Peters, nothing like the earl had ever happened to him before in a long and varied life. He had seen men and cities, but Lord Emsworth was something new. Each, in fact, was to the other a perpetual freak-show with no charge for admission. And, if anything had been needed to cement the alliance, it would have been supplied by the fact that they were both collectors.

They differed in collecting as they did in everything else. Mr. Peters' collecting, as has been shown, was keen, furious, concentrated; Lord Emsworth's had the amiable dodderingness which marked every branch of his life. In the museum at Blandings Castle you might find every manner of valuable and valueless curio. There was no central motive, the place was simply an amateur junk-shop. Side by side with a Gutenberg Bible for which rival collectors would have bidden without a limit, you would come upon a bullet from the field of Waterloo, one of a consignment of ten thousand shipped there for the use of tourists by a Birmingham firm. Each was equally attractive to its owner.

'My dear Mr. Peters,' said Lord Emsworth sunnily, advanc-

40

ing into the room, 'I trust I am not unpunctual. I have been lunching at my club.'

'I'd have asked you to lunch here,' said Mr. Peters, 'but you know how it is with me. I've promised the doctor I'll give those nuts and grasses of his a fair trial, and I can do it pretty well when I'm alone or with Aline. But to have to sit by and see someone else eating real food would be trying me too high.'

Lord Emsworth murmured sympathetically. The other's digestive tribulations touched a ready chord. An excellent trencherman himself, he understood what Mr. Peters must suffer.

'Too bad,' he said.

Mr. Peters turned the conversation into other channels.

'These are my scarabs,' he said.

Lord Emsworth adjusted his glasses, and the mild smile disappeared from his face, to be succeeded by a set look. A stage director of a moving-picture firm would have recognized the look; Lord Emsworth was 'registering' interest—interest which, he perceived from the first instant, would have to be completely simulated; for instinct told him as Mr. Peters began to talk, that he was about to be bored as he had seldom been bored in his life.

We may say what we will against the aristocracy of England; we may wear red ties and attend Socialist meetings; but we cannot deny that in certain crises blood will tell. An English peer of the right sort can be bored nearer to the point where mortification sets in, without showing it, than anyone else in the world. From early youth he has been accustomed to staying at English country-houses, where, though horses bored him intensely, he has had to accompany his host round the stables every morning and pretend to enjoy it, and this Spartan upbringing stands him in good stead in after years.

It was pleasant, then, to see the resolute, if painful, politeness with which Lord Emsworth accepted the trying role of the man who listens to a monomaniac discoursing on his pet subject. His mind was elsewhere, but early in the proceedings he began to make use of a musical 'Ah!' which, emitted at regular intervals, seemed to be all that Mr. Peters demanded of him.

Mr. Peters, in his character of showman, threw himself into his work with even more than his customary energy. He was both exhaustive and exhausting. His flow of speech never faltered. He spoke of the New Kingdom, the Middle Kingdom, Osiris, and Ammon; waxed eloquent concerning Mut, Bubastis, Cheops, the Hyksos kings, cylinders, bezels, and Amenophis III; and became at times almost lyrical when touching on Queen Taia, the Princess Gilukhipa of Mitanni, the Lake of Zarukhe, and the Book of the Dead.

Time slid by . . .

'Take a look at this, Lord Emsworth.'

As one who, brooding on love or running over business projects in his mind, walks briskly into a lamp-post and comes back to the realities of life with a sense of jarring shock, Lord Emsworth started, blinked, and returned to consciousness. Far away his mind had been, seventy miles away, in the pleasant hothouses and shady garden-walks of Blandings Castle. He came back to London to find that his host, with a mingled air of pride and reverence, was extending towards him a small, dingy-looking something.

He took it and looked at it. That, apparently, was what he was meant to do. So far, all was well.

'Ah!' he said.

That blessed word, covering everything. He repeated it, pleased at his ready resource.

'A Cheops of the Fourth Dynasty,' said Mr. Peters fervently.

'I beg your pardon?'

'A Cheops! Of the Fourth Dynasty!'

Lord Emsworth began to feel like a hunted stag. He could not go on saying 'Ah!' indefinitely, yet what else was there to say to this curious little beastly sort of a beetle kind of thing?

'Dear me! A Cheops!'

'Of the Fourth Dynasty!'

'Bless my soul! The Fourth Dynasty!'

'What do you think of that, eh?'

Strictly speaking, Lord Emsworth, thought nothing of it, and he was wondering how to veil this opinion in diplomatic words, when the providence which looks after all good men saved him by causing a knock at the door to occur.

In response to Mr. Peters' irritated cry, a maid entered.

'If you please, sir. Mr. Threepwood wishes to speak to you on the telephone.'

Mr. Peters turned to his guest.

'Excuse me for one moment.'

'Certainly,' said Lord Emsworth gratefully. 'Certainly, certainly, certainly. By all means.'

The door closed behind Mr. Peters. Lord Emsworth was

42

alone.

For some moments he stood where he had been left, a figure with small signs of alertness about it. But Mr. Peters did not return immediately. The booming of his voice came faintly from some distant region. Lord Emsworth strolled to the window and looked out.

The sun still shone brightly on the quiet street. Across the road were trees. Lord Emsworth was fond of trees; he looked at these approvingly. Then round the corner came a vagrant man, wheeling flowers in a barrow.

Flowers! Lord Emsworth's mind shot back to Blandings like a homing pigeon. Flowers! Had he or had he not given head-gardener Thorne adequate instructions as to what to do with those hydrangeas? Assuming that he had not, was Thorne to be depended on to do the right thing by them by the light of his own intelligence?

Lord Emsworth began to brood upon head-gardener Thorne.

He was aware of some curious little object in his hand; he accorded it a momentary inspection. It had no message for him. It was probably something, but he couldn't remember what.

He put it in his pocket, and returned to his meditations.

III

At about the hour when the Earl of Emsworth was driving to keep his appointment with Mr. Peters, a party of two sat at a corner table at Simpson's Restaurant in the Strand. One of the two was a small, pretty, good-natured looking girl of about twenty, the other a sturdy young man with a small moustache, a wiry crop of red-brown hair, and an expression of mingled devotion and determination. The girl was Aline Peters, the young man's name was George Emerson. He was, as Freddie had said, a policeman or something in Hong-Kong. That is to say, he was second-in-command of the police force in that distant spot. At present, he was home on leave. He had a strong, square face, with a dogged and persevering chin.

There is every kind of restaurant in London, from the restaurant which makes you fancy you are in Paris to the restaurant which makes you wish you were. There are palaces in Piccadilly, quaint lethal chambers in Soho, and strange food factories in Oxford Street and the Tottenham Court Road.

43

There are restaurants which specialize in ptomaine, and restaurants which specialize in sinister vegetable-messes. But there is only one Simpson's.

Simpson's in the Strand is unique. Here if he wishes, the Briton may, for the small sum of half a dollar, stupefy himself with food. The God of Fatted Plenty has the place under his protection. Its keynote is solid comfort. County clergymen, visiting London for the annual Clerical Congress, come here to get the one square meal which will last them till next year's Clerical Congress. Fathers and uncles with sons or nephews on their hands rally to Simpson's with silent blessings on the head of the genius who founded the place, for here only can the young boa-constrictor really fill himself at moderate expense. Militant suffragettes come to it to make up leeway after their last hunger-strike.

A pleasant, soothing hearty place. A restful Temple of Food. No strident orchestra forces the diner to bolt beef in rag-time. No long, central aisle distracts his attention with its stream of new arrivals. There he sits, alone with his food, while white-robed priests, wheeling their smoking trucks, move to and fro, ever ready with fresh supplies.

All round the room, some at small tables, some at large tables, the worshippers sit, in their eyes that resolute, concentrated look which is the peculiar property of the British luncher, ex-President Roosevelt's man-eating fish, and the American army-worm.

Conversation does not flourish at Simpson's. Only two of all those present on this occasion showed any disposition towards chattiness. They were Aline Peters and her escort.

'The girl you ought to marry,' Aline was saying, 'is Joan Valentine.'

'The girl I am going to marry,' said George Emerson, 'is Aline Peters.'

For answer Aline picked up from the floor beside her an illustrated paper, and, having opened it at a page towards the end, handed it across the table.

George Emerson glanced at it disdainfully. There were two photographs on the page. One was of Aline, the other of a heavy, loutish-looking youth, who wore that peculiar expression of pained glassiness which Young England always adopts in the face of a camera.

Under one photograph were printed the words, 'Miss Aline Peters, who is to marry the Hon. Frederick Threepwood in

44

June.' Under the other, 'The Hon. Frederick Threepwood, who is to marry Miss Aline Peters in June.' Above the photographs was the legend, 'Forthcoming International Wedding. Son of the Earl of Emsworth to marry American heiress.' In one corner of the picture a Cupid draped in the Stars and Stripes aimed his bow at the gentleman; in the other another Cupid, clad in a natty Union Jack, was drawing a bead on the lady.

The sub-editor had done his work well. He had not been ambiguous. What he intended to convey to the reader was that Miss Aline Peters of America was going to marry the Hon. Frederick Threepwood, son of the Earl of Emsworth; and that was exactly the impression the average reader got.

George Emerson, however, was not an average reader. The sub-editor's work did not impress him.

'You mustn't believe everything you see in the papers,' he said. 'What are the stout children in the bathing-suits supposed to be doing?'

'Those are Cupids, George, aiming at us with their little bows—a pretty and original idea.'

'Why Cupids?'

'Cupid is the God of Love. I can see that *you* never went to night-school.'

'What has the God of Love got to do with it?'

Aline placidly devoured a fried potato.

'You're simply trying to make me angry,' she said, 'and I call it very mean of you. You know perfectly well how fatal it is to get angry at meals. It was eating while he was in a bad temper that ruined father's digestion. George, that nice, fat carver is wheeling his truck this way. Flag him, and make him give me some more of that mutton.'

George looked round him morosely.

'Why is it,' he said, 'that every one in London looks exactly the same as every one else? They used to tell me that I should find that all Chinamen looked alike. There isn't a Chinaman in Hong-Kong that I would have the least difficulty in recognizing. But these blighters——' His eyes roamed about the room. It returned to a stout young man at a neighbouring table, who had been the original cause of this homily, owing to the fact that he had reminded him of the Hon. Freddy Threepwood. He scowled at this harmless youth, who was browsing contentedly on fish-pie. 'Do you see the fellow in the grey suit?' he said. 'Look at the stodgy face. Mark the glassy eye. If that

45

man sandbagged your Freddie and tied him up somewhere and turned up at the church instead of him, can you honestly tell me that you would know the difference? Come now, wouldn't you simply say, "Why, Freddie, how natural you look," and go through the ceremony without a suspicion?'

'He isn't a bit like Freddie. And you oughtn't to speak of him as Freddie. You don't know him.'

'Yes, I do. And what is more he expressly asked me to call him Freddie. "Oh, dash it, old top, don't keep on calling me Threepwood. Freddie to pals." Those were his very words.'

'George, you're making this up.'

'Not at all. We met last night at the National Sporting Club. Porky Jones was going twenty rounds with Eddie Flynn. I offered to give three to one on Eddie. Freddie, who was sitting next to me, took me in fivers. And if you want any further proof of your young man's fat-headedness, mark that. A child could have seen that Eddie had him going. Afterwards Threepwood chummed up with me, and told me that to real pals like me he was Freddie. I was a real pal, as I understood it, because I would have to wait for my money. The fact was, he explained, that his old governor had cut off his bally allowance.'

'You're simply trying to poison my mind against him, and I don't think it's very nice of you, George.'

'What do you mean, poison your mind? I'm not poisoning your mind, I'm simply telling you a few things about him. You know perfectly well that you don't love him, and that you aren't going to marry him, and that you are going to marry me.'

'How do you know I don't love my Freddie?'

'If you can look me straight in the eyes and tell me that you do, I will drop the whole thing and put on a little page's dress and carry your train up the aisle! Now then?'

'And all the while you're talking you're letting my carver get away,' said Aline.

George signalled to the willing priest, who steered his truck towards them. Aline directed his dissection of the shoulder of mutton with word and gesture.

'Enjoy yourself,' said Emerson coldly.

'So I do, George, so I do. What excellent meat they have in England.'

'I wish you would be a bit more spiritual. I don't want to sit here discussing food-products.'

'If you were in my position, George, you wouldn't want to

talk about anything else. It's doing him a world of good, poor dear, but there are times when I'm sorry father ever started this food-reform thing. You don't know what it means for a healthy young girl to try and support life on nuts and grasses.'

'And why should you?' broke out Emerson. 'I'll tell you what it is Aline, you are perfectly absurd about your father. I don't want to say anything against him to you, naturally, but——'

'Go ahead, George. Why this diffidence? Say what you like.'

'Very well, then, I will. I'll give it to you straight. You know quite well that you let your father bully you. I don't say it is your fault or his fault or anybody's fault. I just state it as a fact. It's temperament, I suppose. You are yielding, and he is aggressive, and he has taken advantage of it. Take this food business, for a start. Your father's digestion has gone wrong, and as a result he has to live on nuts and bananas and things. Why should you let him make you do the same?'

'It isn't a question of making. He doesn't make me, I do it to encourage him, to show him that it can be done. If I weakened he would lose all his resolution in a moment, and rush out and start a regular debauch of *pâté de fois gras* and lobster. And then he would suffer agonies. What a terrible thing it is, George, that father should combine a schoolboy appetite with a Rockefeller digestion. Either by itself wouldn't be so bad, but the combination is awful.'

George, baffled, but determined, resumed the attack.

'All right, then, if you really are starving yourself of your own free will, there is no more to say.'

'But you are going to say it, aren't you, George?'

'We now come to this idiot Freddie marriage business. Your father has forced you into that. It's all very well to say that you are a free agent, and that fathers don't coerce their daughters nowadays. The trouble is that your father does. You let him do what he likes with you. And you won't break away from this Freddie foolishness because you can't find the pluck. I'm going to help you find it. I'm coming down to Blandings Castle when you go there on Friday.'

'Coming to Blandings?'

'Freddie invited me last night. I think it was done by way of interest on the money he owed me, but he did it, and I accepted.'

'But, George, my dear, dear boy, do you *never* read the Etiquette Books and the hints in the papers on how to be the

47

Perfect Gentleman? Don't you know that you can't be a man's guest and take advantage of his hospitality to try to steal his fiancée away from him?'

'Watch me!'

A dreamy look came into Aline's eyes.

'I wonder what it feels like being a countess,' she said.

'You will never know,' George looked at her pityingly. 'My poor girl,' he said, 'have you been lured into this engagement in the belief that Freddie, the Idiot Child, is going to be an earl some day? They were ragging you. Freddie is not the heir. His elder brother, Lord Bosham, is as fit as a prize-fighter and has three healthy sons. Freddie has about as much chance of getting the title as I have.'

'George, your education has been sadly neglected. Don't you know that the heir to the title always goes for a yachting cruise with his whole family and gets drowned, and the children too? It happens in every English novel you read.'

'Listen, Aline, let us get this thing straight. I have been in love with you ever since we met on the *Olympic*. I proposed to you twice on the voyage and once in the train on the way to London. That was eight months ago, and I have been proposing to you at intervals ever since. I go to Scotland for a few weeks to see my people, and when I come back, what do I find? I find you engaged to be married to this Freddie excrescence.'

'I like your chivalrous attitude towards Freddie. So many men in your position might say horrid things about him.'

'Oh, I've nothing against Freddie. He is practically an imbecile and I don't like his face, but apart from that he's all right. But you will be glad later that you did not marry him. You are much too real a person. What a wife you will make for a hard-working man!'

'What does Freddie work hard at?'

'I am alluding at the moment not to Freddie but to myself. I shall come home tired out. Things will have gone wrong at my office. I shall be fagged, disheartened. And then you will come with cool, white hands, and placing them gently on my forehead——'

Aline shook her head.

'It's no good, George. Really, you had better realize it. I'm very fond of you, but we are not suited.'

'Why not?'

'You are too overwhelming, too much like a bomb. I think

48

you must be one of these Supermen one reads about. You would want your own way and nothing but your own way. I expect it's through having to be constantly moving people on out in Hong-Kong, and all that sort of thing. Now Freddie will roll through hoops and sham dead, and we shall be the happiest pair in the world. I am much too placid and mild to make you happy. You want someone who would stand up to you. Somebody like Joan Valentine.'

'That's the second time you have mentioned this Joan Valentine. Who *is* she?'

'She is a girl who was at school with me. I was at school in England, you know—Mother wanted me to get the tone, or something. We were the greatest chums. At least, I worshipped her and would have done anything for her, and I think she liked me. Then I went back to America and we lost touch with one another. I met her on the street yesterday, and she is just the same. She has been through the most awful times. Her father was quite rich, and he died suddenly, and she found that he hadn't left a penny. He had been living right up to his income all the time. His life wasn't even insured. She came to London, and, as far as I could make out from the short talk we had, she had done pretty nearly everything since we last met. She worked in a shop and went on the stage, and all sorts of things. Isn't it awful, George?'

'Frightful,' said Emerson. He was but faintly interested in Miss Valentine.

'She is so plucky and full of life. She would stand up to you.'

'Thanks! My idea of marriage is not a perpetual fight. My notion of a wife is something cosy and sympathetic and soothing. That is why I love you. We shall be the happiest——'

Aline laughed.

'Dear old George! And now pay the bill; and get me a taxi. I've endless things to do at home. If Freddie is in town, I suppose he will be calling to see me. Who is Freddie, do you ask? Freddie is my fiancé, George. My betrothed. The young man I'm going to marry.'

Emerson shook his head resignedly.

'Curious how you cling to that Freddie idea. Never mind. I'll come down to Blandings on Friday, and we will see what happens. Bear in mind the broad fact that you and I are going to get married and that nothing on earth is going to stop us.'

The reason why all we novelists with bulging foreheads and expensive educations are abandoning novels and taking to writing motion-picture scenarii is because the latter are so infinitely the more simple and pleasant.

If this narrative, for instance, were a film-drama, the operator at this point would flash on the screen the words:

MR. PETERS DISCOVERS THE LOSS OF THE SCARAB,

and for a brief moment the audience would see an interior set, in which a little angry man with a sharp face and starting eyes would register first, Discovery; next Dismay. The whole thing would be over in an instant.

The printed word demands a greater elaboration.

It was Aline who had to bear the brunt of her father's mental agony when he discovered, shortly after his guest had left him, that the gem of his collection of scarabs had done the same. It is always the innocent bystander who suffers.

'The darned old sneak-thief!' said Mr. Peters.

'Father!'

'Don't just sit there saying "Father!" What's the use of saying, "Father"? Do you think it is going to help, your saying "Father!"? I'd rather the old pirate had taken the house and lot than that scarab. He knows what's what! Trust him to walk off with the pick of the whole bunch. I did think I could trust the father of the man who's going to marry my daughter for a second alone with the things. There's no morality among collectors, none. I'd trust a syndicate of Jesse James, Captain Kidd, and Dick Turpin sooner than I would a collector. My Cheops of the Fourth Dynasty! I wouldn't have lost it for five thousand dollars.'

'But, Father, couldn't you write him a letter, asking for it back? He's such a nice old man; I'm sure he didn't mean to steal the scarab.'

Mr. Peters' overwrought soul blew off steam in the shape of a passionate snort.

'Didn't mean to steal it! What do you think he meant to do—take it away and keep it safe for me in case I should lose it? Didn't mean to steal it! I bet you he's well known in Society as a kleptomaniac. I bet you that, when his name is announced, his friends lock up their spoons and send in a hurry-call to police headquarters for a squad to come and see that he doesn't sneak the front door. Of course, he meant to steal it. He has a museum of his own down in the country. My Cheops is going to lend tone to that. I'd give five thousand dollars to get it back. If there's a burglar in this country with the spirit to break into the Castle and steal that scarab and hand it back to me, there's five thousand waiting for him right here, and, if he wants to, he can knock that old pirate on the head with a jemmy into the bargain.'

'But, father, why can't you simply go to him and say it's yours and that you must have it back?'

'And have him come back at me by calling off this engagement of yours! Not if I know it. You can't go about the place charging a man with theft and expect him to go on being willing to have his son marry your daughter, can you? The slightest suggestion that I thought he had stolen this scarab, and he would do the Proud Old English Aristocrat and end everything. He's in the strongest position a thief has ever been in. You can't get at him.'

'I didn't think of that.'

'You don't think at all. That's the trouble with you,' said Mr. Peters.

You see now why we prefer writing motion-picture scenarii. It is painful to a refined and sensitive young novelist to have to set down such a scene between father and child. But what is one to do? Years of indigestion had made Mr. Peters' temper, even when in a normal mood, perfectly impossible; in a crisis like this it ran amuck. He vented it on Aline because he had always vented his irritabilities on Aline, because the fact of her sweet, gentle disposition, combined with the fact of their relationship, made her the ideal person to receive the overflow of his black moods. While his wife had lived, he had bullied her. On her death, Aline had stepped into the vacant position.

Aline did not cry, because she was not a girl who was given to tears, but for all her placid good-temper, she was wounded. She was a girl who liked everything in the world to run smoothly and easily, and these scenes with her father always depressed her. She took advantage of a lull in Mr. Peters' flow of words and slipped from the room.

Her cheerfulness had received a shock. She wanted sympathy. She wanted comforting. For a moment she considered George Emerson in the rôle of comforter. But there were

51

objections to George in this character. Aline was accustomed to tease and chaff George, but at heart she was a little afraid of him, and instinct told her that, as comforter, he would be too volcanic and super-manly for a girl who was engaged to marry another man in June. George as comforter would be far too prone to trust to action rather than to the soothing power of the spoken word. George's idea of healing the wound, she felt, would be to push her into a cab and drive to the nearest registrar's.

No, she would not go to George; to whom, then?

The vision of Joan Valentine came to her—of Joan as she had seen her yesterday, strong, cheerful, self-reliant, bearing herself in spite of adversity with a valiant jauntiness. Yes, she would go and see Joan.

She put on her hat and stole from the house.

Curiously enough, only a quarter of an hour before, R. Jones had set out with exactly the same object in view.

v

How pleasant it is, after assisting at a scene of violence and recrimination, to be transferred to one of peace and goodwill. It is with a sense of relief that I find that the snipe-like flight of this story takes us next, far from Mr. Peters and his angry outpourings, to the cosy smoking-room of Blandings Castle.

At almost exactly the hour when Aline Peters set off to visit her friend Miss Valentine, three men sat in the cosy smoking-room of Blandings Castle.

They were variously occupied. In the long chair nearest the door, the Hon. Frederick Threepwood—Freddie to pals—was reading. Next to him sat a young man whose eyes, glittering through rimless spectacles, were concentrated on the upturned faces of several neat rows of playing-cards. (Rupert Baxter, Lord Emsworth's invaluable secretary, had no vices, but he sometimes relaxed his busy brain with a game of solitaire.) Beyond Baxter, a cigar in his mouth and a weak high-ball at his side, the Earl of Emsworth took his ease. After the scene we have just been through it does one good merely to contemplate such a picture.

The book which the Hon. Freddie was reading was a small, paper-covered book. Its cover was decorated with a colour-scheme in red, black, and yellow, depicting a tense moment in the lives of a man with a black beard, a man with a yellow

52

beard, a man without any beard at all, and a young woman, who, at first sight, appeared to be all eyes and hair. The man with the black beard, to gain some private end, had tied this young woman with ropes to a complicated system of machinery, mostly wheels and pulleys. The man with the yellow beard was in the act of pushing or pulling a lever. The beardless man, protruding through a trap-door in the floor, was pointing a large revolver at the parties of the second part.

Beneath this picture were the words, 'Hands up, you scoundrels!' Above it, in a meandering scroll across the page, 'Gridley Quayle, Investigator. The Adventure of the Secret Six. By Felix Clovelly.'

The Hon. Freddie did not so much read as gulp the adventure of the Secret Six. His face was crimson with excitement; his hair was rumpled; his eyes bulged. He was absorbed.

This is peculiarly an age in which each one of us may, if he do but search diligently, find the literature suited to his mental powers. Grave and earnest men, at Eton and elsewhere had tried Freddie Threepwood with Greek, with Latin, and with English, and the sheeplike stolidity with which he declined to be interested in the masterpieces of all three tongues had left them with the conviction that he would never read anything.

And then, years afterwards, he had suddenly blossomed out as a student. Only, it is true, a student of the Adventures of Gridley Quayle, but still a student. His was a dull life, and Gridley Quayle was the only person who brought romance into it. Existence for the Hon. Freddie was simply a sort of desert punctuated with monthly oases in the shape of new Quayle adventures.

It was his ambition to meet the man who wrote them.

Lord Emsworth sat and smoked and sipped and smoked again, at peace with all the world. His mind was as nearly a blank as it is possible for the human mind to be.

The hand which had not the task of holding the cigar was at rest in his trouser-pocket. The fingers of it fumbled idly with a small, hard object.

Gradually it filtered into his lordship's mind that this small hard object was not familiar. It was something new—something that was neither his keys, his pencil, nor his small change.

He yielded to a growing curiosity, and drew it out.

He examined it.

It was a little something, rather like a fossilized beetle. It touched no chord in him. He looked at it with an amiable distaste.

'Now, how in the world did that get there?' he said.

The Hon. Freddie paid no attention to the remark. He was now at the very crest of his story, when every line intensified the thrill. Incident was succeeding incident. The Secret Six were here, there, and everywhere, like so many malignant June bugs. Annabel, the heroine, was having a perfectly rotten time, kidnapped and imprisoned every few minutes. Gridley Quayle, hot on the scent, was covering someone or other with his revolver almost continuously. The Hon. Freddie had no time for chatting with his father.

Not so Rupert Baxter. Chatting with Lord Emsworth was one of the things for which he received his salary. He looked up from his cards.

'Lord Emsworth?'

'I have found a curious object in my pocket, Baxter. I was wondering how it got there.'

He handed the thing to his secretary. Rupert Baxter's eyes lit up with a sudden enthusiasm. He gasped.

'Magnificent!' he cried. 'Superb!'

Lord Emsworth looked at him inquiringly.

'It is a scarab, Lord Emsworth, and, unless I am mistaken— and I think I may claim to be something of an expert—a Cheops of the Fourth Dynasty. A wonderful addition to your museum.'

'Is it, by gad! You don't say so, Baxter!'

'It is indeed. If it is not a rude question, how much did you give for it, Lord Emsworth? It must have been the gem of someone's collection. Was there a sale at Christy's this afternoon?'

Lord Emsworth shook his head.

'I did not get it at Christy's for I recollect that I had an important engagement which prevented my going to Christy's. I had—to be sure, yes. I had promised to call on Mr. Peters and examine his collection of—now I wonder what it was that Mr. Peters said he collected?'

'Mr. Peters is one of the best-known living collectors of scarabs.'

'Scarabs! You are quite right, Baxter. And now that I recall the episode, this is a scarab, and Mr. Peters gave it to me.'

'*Gave* it to you, Lord Emsworth!'

54

'Yes. The whole scene comes back to me. Mr. Peters, after telling me a great many exceedingly interesting things about scarabs, which I regret to say I cannot remember, gave me this. And you say it is really valuable, Baxter?'

'It is, from a collector's point of view, of extraordinary value.'

'Bless my soul!' Lord Emsworth beamed. 'This is extremely interesting, Baxter. One has heard so much of the princely hospitality of Americans. How exceedingly kind of Mr. Peters. I shall certainly treasure it, though I must confess that, from a purely spectacular standpoint, it leaves me a little cold. However, I must not look a gift horse in the mouth, eh, Baxter?'

From afar came the silver booming of a gong. Lord Emsworth rose.

'Time to dress for dinner? I had no idea it was so late. Baxter, you will be going past the museum door. Will you be a good fellow and place this among the exhibits? You will know what to do with it better than I. I always think of you as the curator of my little collection, Baxter; ha, ha! Mind how you step when you are in the museum. I was painting a chair there yesterday, and I think I left the paint-pot on the floor.'

He cast a less amiable glance at his studious son.

'Get *up*, Frederick, and go and dress for dinner. What is that trash you are reading?'

The Hon. Freddie came out of his book much as a sleep-walker awakes, with a sense of having been violently assaulted. He looked up with a kind of stunned plaintiveness.

'Eh? governor?'

'Make haste. Beach rang the gong five minutes ago. What is that you are reading?'

'Oh, nothing, governor. Just a book.'

'I wonder how you can waste your time on such trash. Make haste.'

He turned to the door, and the benevolent expression once more wandered athwart his face.

'*Extremely* kind of Mr. Peters!' he said. 'Really, there is something almost oriental in the lavish generosity of our American cousins.'

VI

It had taken R. Jones just six hours to discover Joan Valentine's address. That it had not taken him longer is a proof of

55

his energy and of the excellence of his system of obtaining information. But R. Jones, when he considered it worth his while, could be extremely energetic, and he was a past master at the art of finding out things.

He poured himself out of his cab, and rang the bell of No. 7A. A dishevelled maid answered the ring.

'Miss Valentine in?'

'Yes, sir.'

R. Jones produced his card.

'On important business, tell her. Half a minute, I'll write it.'

He wrote the words on the card, and devoted the brief period of waiting to a careful scrutiny of his surroundings. He looked out into the court and he looked as far as he could down the dingy passage, and the conclusions he drew from what he saw were complimentary to Miss Valentine.

'If this girl is the sort of girl who would hold up Freddie's letters,' he mused, 'she wouldn't be living in a place like this. If she were on the make, she would have more money than she evidently possesses. Therefore, she is not on the make, and I should be prepared to bet that she destroyed the letters as fast as she got them.'

Those were, roughly, the thoughts of R. Jones, as he stood in the doorway of No. 7A, and they were important thoughts, inasmuch as they determined his attitude towards Joan in the approaching interview. He perceived that this matter must be handled delicately, that he must be very much the gentleman. It would be a strain, but he must do it.

The maid returned and directed him to Joan's room with a brief word and a sweeping gesture.

'Eh?' said R. Jones. 'First floor?'

'Front,' said the maid.

R. Jones trudged laboriously up the short flight of stairs. It was very dark on the stairs, and he stumbled. Eventually, however, light came to him through an open door. Looking in, he saw a girl standing at the table. She had an air of expectation, so he deduced that he had reached his journey's end.

'Miss Valentine?'

'Please come in.'

R. Jones waddled in.

'Not much light on your stairs.'

'No. Will you take a seat?'

'Thanks.'

56

One glance at the girl convinced R. Jones that he had been right. Circumstances had made him a rapid judge of character, for in the profession of living by one's wits in a large city, the first principle of offence and defence is to sum people up at first sight. This girl was not on the make.

Joan Valentine was a tall girl, with wheat-gold hair and eyes as brightly-blue as a November sky when the sun is shining on a frosty world. There was in them a little of November's cold glitter, too, for Joan had been through much in the last few years, and experience, even if it does not harden, erects a defensive barrier between its children and the world. Her eyes were eyes that looked straight and challenged. They could thaw to the satin blue of the Mediterranean Sea where it purrs about the little villages of Southern France, but they did not thaw for everyone. She looked what she was—a girl of action, a girl whom Life had made both reckless and wary, wary of friendly advances, reckless when there was a venture afoot.

Her eyes, as they met R. Jones' now, were cold and challenging. She, too, had learned the trick of swift diagnosis of character, and what she saw of R. Jones' in that first glance did not impress her very favourably.

'You wished to see me on business?'

'Yes,' said R. Jones. 'Yes ... Miss Valentine, may I begin by begging you to realize that I have no intention of insulting you?'

Joan's eyebrows rose. For an instant she did her visitor the injustice of suspecting that he had been dining too well.

'I don't quite understand.'

'Let me explain. I have come here,' R. Jones went on, getting more gentlemanly every moment, 'on a very distasteful errand, to oblige a friend. Will you bear in mind that, whatever I say, is said entirely on his behalf?'

By this time Joan had abandoned the idea that this stout person was a life-insurance tout, and was inclining to the view that he was collecting funds for a charity.

'I came here at the request of the Hon. Frederick Threepwood.'

'I don't quite understand.'

'You never met him, Miss Valentine, but, when you were in the chorus at the Piccadilly Theatre, I believe he wrote you some very foolish letters. Possibly you have forgotten them?'

'I certainly have.'

'You have probably destroyed them, eh?'

'Certainly. I don't often keep letters. Why do you ask?'

'Well, you see, Miss Valentine, the Hon. Frederick Threepwood is about to be married, and he thought that possibly, on the whole, it would be better that the letters—and poetry—which he wrote you were non-existent.'

Not all R. Jones' gentlemanliness—and during this speech he diffused it like a powerful scent in waves about him—could hide the unpleasant meaning of the words.

'He was afraid I might try and blackmail him?' said Joan with formidable calm.

R. Jones raised and waved a fat hand deprecatingly.

'My dear Miss Valentine!'

Joan rose and R. Jones followed her example. The interview was plainly at an end.

'Please tell Mr. Threepwood to make his mind quite easy. He is in no danger.'

'Exactly, exactly, precisely. I assured Threepwood that my visit here would be a mere formality. I was quite sure you had no intention whatever of worrying him. I will tell him definitely then, that you have destroyed the letters?'

'Yes. Good evening.'

'Good evening, Miss Valentine.'

The closing of the door behind him left him in total darkness, but he hardly liked to return and ask Joan to reopen it in order to light him on his way. He was glad to be out of her presence. He was used to being looked at in an unfriendly way by his fellows, but there had been something in Joan's eyes which had curiously discomfited him. He groped his way down, relieved that all was over and had ended well. He believed what she had told him, and he could conscientiously assure Freddie that the prospect of his sharing the fate of poor old Percy was non-existent. It is true that he proposed to add in his report that the destruction of the letters had been purchased with difficulty, at a cost of just five hundred pounds, but that was a mere business formality.

He had almost reached the last step when there was a ring at the front door. With what he was afterwards wont to call an inspiration, he retreated with unusual nimbleness till he had almost reached Joan's door again. Then he leaned over the banisters and listened.

The dishevelled maid opened the door. A girl's voice spoke.

'Is Miss Valentine in?'

'She's in, but she's engaged.'

'I wish you would go up and tell her that I want to see her. Say it's Miss Peters. Miss Aline Peters.'

The banisters shook beneath R. Jones' sudden clutch. For a moment he had felt almost faint. Then he began to think swiftly. A great light had dawned upon him, and the thought outstanding in his mind was that never again would he trust a man or woman on the evidence of his senses. He could have sworn that this Valentine girl was on the level. He had been perfectly satisfied with her statement that she had destroyed the letters. And all the while she had been playing as deep a game as he had ever come across in the whole course of his professional career. He almost admired her. How she had taken him in! It was obvious now what her game was. Previous to his visit she had arranged a meeting with Freddie's fiancée, with the view of opening negotiations for the sale of the letters. She had held him, Jones, at arms' length, because she was going to sell the letters to whoever would pay the best price. But for the accident of his happening to be here when Miss Peters arrived, Freddie and his fiancée would have been bidding against each other, and raising each other's price. He had worked the same game himself a dozen times, and he resented the entry of female competition into what he regarded as essentially a male field of enterprise.

As the maid stumped up the stairs, he continued his retreat. He heard Joan's door open, and the stream of light showed him the dishevelled maid standing in the doorway.

'Ow, I thought there was a gentleman with you, miss.'

'He left a moment ago. Why?'

'There's a lady wants to see you. Miss Peters her name is.'

'Will you ask her to come up?'

The dishevelled maid was no polished mistress of ceremonies. She leaned down into the void, and hailed Aline.

'She says, will you come up.'

Aline's feet became audible on the staircase. There were greetings.

'Whatever brings you here, Aline?'

'Am I interrupting you, Joan, dear?'

'No. Do come in. I was only surprised to see you so late. I didn't know you paid calls at this hour. Is anything wrong? Come in.'

The door closed, the maid retired to the depths, and R. Jones stole cautiously down again. He was feeling absolutely bewildered. Apparently his deductions, his second thoughts had been all wrong, and Joan was, after all, the honest person he had imagined at first sight. These two girls had talked to each other as if they were old friends, as if they had known each other all their lives. That was the thing that perplexed R. Jones.

With the tread of a Red Indian he approached the door, and put his ear to it. He found that he could hear quite comfortably.

Aline meanwhile, inside the room, had begun to draw comfort from Joan's very appearance. She looked so capable.

Joan's eyes had changed the expression they had contained during the recent interview. They were soft now, with a softness that was half compassionate, half contemptuous. It is the compensation which Life gives to those whom it has handled roughly that they shall be able to regard with a certain contempt the small troubles of the sheltered. Joan remembered Aline of old, and knew her for a perennial victim of small troubles. Even in their school days she had always needed to be looked after and comforted. Her sweet temper had seemed to invite the minor slings and arrows of fortune. Aline was a girl who inspired protectiveness in a certain type of her fellow human beings. It was this quality in her which kept George Emerson awake at nights; and it appealed to Joan now. Joan, for whom life was a constant struggle to keep the wolf within a reasonable distance from the door, and who counted that day happy on which she saw her way clear to paying her weekly rent and possibly having a trifle over for some coveted hat or pair of shoes, could not help feeling, as she looked at Aline, that her own troubles were as nothing, and that the immediate need of the moment was to pet and comfort her friend. Her knowledge of Aline told her that the probable tragedy was that she had lost a brooch or had been spoken to crossly by somebody, but it also told her that such tragedies bulked very large on Aline's horizon. Trouble, after all, like beauty, is in the eye of the beholder, and Aline was far less able to endure with fortitude the loss of a brooch than she herself the loss of a position whose emoluments meant the difference between having just enough to eat and starving.

'You're worried about something,' she said. 'Sit down and tell me about it.'

Aline sat down, and looked about her at the shabby room. By that curious process of the human mind which makes the spectacle of another's misfortune a palliative for one's own, she was feeling oddly comforted already. Her thoughts were not definite, and she could not analyse them, but what they amounted to was that, while it was an unpleasant thing to be bullied by a dyspeptic father, the world manifestly held worse tribulations which her father's other outstanding quality besides dyspepsia—wealth, to wit—enabled her to avoid. It was at this point that the dim beginnings of a philosophy began to invade her mind. The thing resolved itself almost into an equation. If father had not had indigestion, he would not have bullied her. But, if father had not made a fortune, he would not have had indigestion. Therefore, if father had not made a fortune, he would not have bullied her. Practically, in fact, if father did not bully her, he would not be rich. And, if he were not rich.... She took in the faded carpet, the stained wallpaper, and the soiled curtains, in a comprehensive glance.... It certainly cut both ways. She began to be a little ashamed of her misery.

'It's nothing at all, really,' she said. 'I think I've been making rather a fuss about very little.'

Joan was relieved. The struggling life breeds moods of depression, and such a mood had come to her just before Aline's arrival. Life, at that moment, had seemed to stretch before her like a dusty, weary road, without hope. She was sick of fighting. She wanted money and ease and a surcease from this perpetual race with weekly bills. The mood had been the outcome partly of R. Jones' gentlemanly-veiled insinuations, but still more, though she did not realize it, of her yesterday's meeting with Aline. Mr. Peters might be unguarded in his speech, when conversing with his daughter, he might play the tyrant towards her in many ways, but he did not stint her in the matter of dress allowance, and on the occasion when she met Joan, Aline had been wearing so Parisian a hat and a tailor-made suit of such obviously expensive simplicity that green-eyed envy had almost spoiled Joan's pleasure at meeting this friend of her opulent days. She had suppressed the envy, and it had revenged itself by assaulting her afresh in the form of the worst fit of blues which she had had in two years. She had been loyally ready to sink her depression in order to alleviate Aline's, but it was a distinct relief to find that the feat would not be necessary.

'Never mind,' she said, 'tell me what the very little thing was.'

'It was only father,' said Aline simply.

'Was he angry with you about something?'

'Not exactly angry with me. But—well, I was there.'

Joan's depression lifted slightly. She had forgotten, in the stunning anguish of the sudden spectacle of that hat and that tailor-made suit, that Paris hats and twenty-five pound suits not infrequently had their accompanying disadvantages. After all, she was independent. She might have to murder her beauty with hats and frocks which had never been nearer Paris than the Tottenham Court Road, but at least no one bullied her because she happened to_be at hand when tempers were short.

'What a shame!' she said. 'Tell me all about it.'

With a prefatory remark that it was all so ridiculous really, Aline embarked upon the narrative of the afternoon's events.

Joan heard her out, checking a strong disposition to giggle. Her view-point was that of the Average Person, and the Average Person cannot see the importance of the scarab in the scheme of things. The opinion she formed of Mr. Peters was of an eccentric old gentleman making a great to-do about nothing at all. Losses had to have a concrete value before they could impress Joan. It was beyond her to grasp that Mr. Peters would sooner have lost a diamond necklace, if he had happened to possess one, than his Cheops of the Fourth Dynasty.

It was not until Aline, having concluded her tale, added one more strand to it that she found herself treating the matter seriously.

'Father says he would give a thousand pounds to anyone who would get it back for him.'

'What!'

The whole story took on a different complexion for Joan. Money talks. Mr. Peters' words might have been merely the rhetorical outburst of a heated moment, but, even discounting them, there seemed to remain a certain exciting substratum. A man who shouts that he will give a thousand pounds for a thing may very well mean that he will give a hundred, and Joan's finances were perpetually in a condition which makes a hundred pounds a sum to be gasped at.

'He wasn't serious, surely?'

'I think he was,' said Aline.

'But a thousand pounds!'

'It isn't really very much to father, you know. He gives away a hundred thousand dollars a year to a University.'

'But for a grubby little scarab!'

'You don't understand how father loves his scarabs. Since he retired from business, he has been simply wrapped up in them. You know, collectors are like that. You read in the papers about men giving all sorts of money for funny things.'

Outside the door, R. Jones, his ear close to the panel, drank in all these things greedily. He would have been willing to remain in that attitude indefinitely in return for this kind of special information, but, just as Aline said these words, a door opened on the floor above and somebody came out, whistling, and began to descend the stairs.

R. Jones stood not upon the order of his going. He was down in the hall and fumbling with the handle of the front door with an agility of which few casual observers of his dimensions would have deemed him capable.

The next moment he was out in the street, walking calmly towards Leicester Square, pondering over what he had heard.

Much of R. Jones' substantial annual income was derived from pondering over what he had heard.

In the room, Joan was looking at Aline with the distended eyes of one who sees visions or has inspirations. She got up. There are occasions when one must speak standing.

'Then you mean to say that your father would really give a thousand pounds to anyone who got this thing back for him?'

'I am sure he would. But who could do it?'

'I could,' said Joan. 'And what is more, I'm going to.'

Aline stared at her helplessly. In their schooldays, Joan had always swept her off her feet. Then, she had always had the feeling that with Joan nothing was impossible. Heroine-worship, like hero-worship, dies hard. She looked at Joan now with the stricken sensation of one who has inadvertently set powerful machinery in motion.

'But, Joan!'

It was all she could say.

'My dear child, it's perfectly simple. This earl of yours has taken the thing off to his castle, like a brigand. You say you are going down there on Friday for a visit. All you have to do is to take me along with you.'

'But, Joan!'

'Where's the difficulty?'

'I don't see how I could take you down very well.'

'Why not?'

'Oh, I don't know.'

'But, what is your objection?'

'Well, don't you see.... If you come down there as a friend of mine, and were caught stealing the scarab, there would be ... just the trouble father wants to avoid. About my engagement, you see, and so on.'

It was an aspect of the matter which had escaped Joan. She frowned thoughtfully.

'I see. Yes, there is that. But there must be a way.'

'You mustn't, Joan, really. Don't think any more about it.'

'Not think any more about it! My child, do you even faintly realize what a thousand pounds, or a quarter of a thousand pounds means to me? I would do anything for it, *anything*. And there's the fun of it. I don't suppose you can realize that either. I want a change. I want something new. I've been grubbing away here on nothing a week for years, and it's time I had a vacation. There must be a way by which you could get me down.... Why, of course! Why didn't I think of it before! You shall take me on Friday as your lady's maid!'

'But, Joan, I couldn't.'

'Why not?'

'I—I couldn't.'

'Why not?'

'Oh well!'

Joan advanced upon her where she sat, and grasped her firmly by the shoulders. Her face was inflexible.

'Aline, my pet, it's no good arguing. You might just as well argue with a wolf on the trail of a fat Russian peasant. I need that money. I need it in my business. I need it worse than anybody has ever needed anything. And I'm going to have it. From now on till further notice, I am your lady's maid. You can give your present one a holiday.'

Aline met her eyes waveringly. The spirit of the old school-days, when nothing was impossible where Joan was concerned, had her in its grip. Moreover, the excitement of the scheme began to attract her.

'But, Joan,' she said, 'you know it's simply ridiculous. You could never pass as a lady's maid. The other servants would find you out. I expect there are all sorts of things a lady's maid has got to do and not do.'

'My dear Aline, I know them all. You can't stump me on below-stairs etiquette. I have *been* a lady's maid!'

'Joan!'

'It's quite true. Three years ago, when I was more than usually impecunious. The wolf was glued to the door like a postage stamp, so I answered an advertisement and became a lady's maid.'

'You seem to have done everything.'

'I have—pretty nearly. It's all right for you Idle Rich, Aline, you can sit still and contemplate Life, but we of the submerged tenth have got to work.'

Aline laughed.

'You know, you always could make me do anything you wanted, in the old days, Joan. I suppose I have got to look on this as quite settled now?'

'Absolutely settled. Oh, Aline, there's one thing you must remember. Don't call me Joan when I'm down at the Castle. You must call me Valentine.' She paused. The recollection of the Hon. Freddie had come to her. No, Valentine would not do. 'No, not Valentine,' she went on. 'It's too jaunty. I used it three years ago, but it never sounded just right. I want something more respectable, more suited to my position. Can't you suggest something?'

Aline pondered.

'Simpson?'

'Simpson! It's exactly right. You must practise it. Simpson! Say it kindly and yet distantly, as if I were a worm, but a worm for whom you felt a mild liking. Roll it round your tongue.'

'Simpson.'

'Splendid! Now, once again—a little more haughtily.'

'Simpson ... Simpson ... Simpson....'

Joan regarded her with affectionate approval.

'It's wonderful,' she said. 'You might have been doing it all your life.'

'What are you laughing at?' asked Aline.

'Nothing,' said Joan. 'I was just thinking of something. There's a young man who lives on the floor above this, and I was lecturing him yesterday on Enterprise. I told him to go and find something exciting to do. I wonder what he would say if he knew how thoroughly I am going to practise what I preach.'

65

CHAPTER FOUR

I

On the morning following Aline's visit to Joan Valentine, Ashe sat in his room, the *Morning Post* on the table before him. The heady influence of Joan had not yet ceased to work within him, and he proposed, in pursuance of his promise to her, to go carefully through the column of advertisements however pessimistic he might feel concerning the utility of that action.

His first glance assured him that the vast fortunes of the philanthropists whose acquaintance he had already made in print were not yet exhausted. Brian MacNeill still dangled his gold before the public. So did Angus Bruce. So did Duncan Macfarlane. So, likewise, Wallace Mackintosh and Donald MacNab. They still had the money and they still wanted to give it away.

The young Christian still wanted that thousand....

He was reading listlessly down the column, when, from the mass of advertisements, one of an unusual sort detached itself:

WANTED—Young Man of Good Appearance, who is poor and reckless, to undertake delicate and dangerous enterprise. Good pay for the right man. Apply between the hours of ten and twelve at offices of Mainprice, Mainprice & Boole, 3 Denvers Street, Strand.

And, as he read it, half past ten struck on the little clock on his mantelpiece.

It was probably this fact that decided Ashe. If he had been compelled to postpone his visit to the offices of Messrs. Mainprice, Mainprice & Boole until the afternoon, it is possible that barriers of laziness might have reared themselves in the path of adventure, for Ashe, an Adventurer at heart, was also uncommonly lazy. But as it was, he could make an immediate start.

Pausing but to put on his shoes, and having satisfied himself by a glance at the mirror that his appearance was reasonably good, he seized his hat, shot out of the narrow mouth of Arundell Street like a shell, and scrambled into a taxi-cab with the feeling that, short of murder, they couldn't make it too delicate and dangerous for him.

He was conscious of strange thrills. This, he told himself, was the only possible mode of life with Spring in the air. He had always been partial to those historical novels in which the characters are perpetually vaulting on to chargers and riding across country on perilous errands. This leaping into taxi-cabs to answer stimulating advertisements in the *Morning Post* was very much the same sort of thing. It was with a fine fervour animating him that he entered the gloomy offices of Mainprice, Mainprice & Boole. His brain was afire, and he felt ready for anything.

'I have come in answ——' he began to the diminutive office-boy, who seemed to be the nearest thing visible to a Mainprice or a Boole.

'Siddown. Gottatakeyerturn,' said the office-boy, and for the first time Ashe perceived that the ante-room in which he stood was crowded to overflowing.

This, in the circumstances, was something of a damper. He had pictured himself, during the ride in the cab, striding into the office and saying, 'The delicate and dangerous enterprise. Lead me to it.' He had not realized till now that he was not the only man in London who read the advertisement columns of the *Morning Post,* and for an instant his heart sank at the sight of all this competition.

A second and more comprehensive glance at his rivals gave him confidence.

The 'Wanted' column of the morning paper is a sort of dredger which churns up strange creatures from the mud of London's underworld. Only in response to the dredger's operations do they come to the surface in such numbers as to be noticeable, for as a rule they are of a solitary habit and shun company: but when they do come they bring with them something of the horror of the depths. It is the saddest spectacle in the world, that of the crowd collected by a 'Wanted' advertisement. They are so palpably not wanted by anyone for any purpose whatsoever: yet every time they gather together with a sort of hopeful hopelessness. What they were originally, the units of these collections, Heaven knows. Fate has battered out of them every trace of individuality. Each now is exactly like his neighbour, no worse, no better.

Ashe, as he sat and watched them, was filled with conflicting emotions. One half of him, thrilled with the glamour of adven-

67

ture, was chafing at the delay and resentful of these poor creatures as of so many obstacles to the beginning of all the brisk and exciting things which lay behind the mysterious brevity of the advertisement. The other, pitifully alive to the tragedy of the occasion, was grateful for the delay. On the whole he was glad to feel that if one of these derelicts did not secure the 'good pay for the right man', it would not be his fault. He had been the last to arrive, and he would be the last to pass through that door which was the gateway of adventure, the door with 'Mr. Boole' inscribed on its ground-glass, beyond which sat the author of the mysterious request for assistance, interviewing applicants. It would be through their own short-comings, not because of his superior attractions, if they failed to please that unseen arbiter.

That they were so failing was plain. Scarcely had one scarred victim of London's unkindness passed through, than the bell would ring, the office-boy who, in the intervals of frowning sternly on the throng as much as to say that he would stand no nonsense, would cry 'Next!' and another dull-eyed wreck would drift through, to be followed a moment later by yet another. The one fact at present ascertainable concerning the unknown searcher for reckless young men of good appearance was that he appeared to be possessed of consider-able decision of character, a man who did not take long to make up his mind. He was rejecting applicants now at the rate of two a minute.

Expeditious as he was, however, he kept Ashe waiting for a considerable time. It was not till the hands of the fat clock over the door pointed to twenty minutes past eleven that the office-boy's 'Next!' found him the only survivor. He gave his clothes a hasty smack with the palm of his hand and his hair a fleeting dab, to accentuate his good appearance, and turned the handle of the door of fate.

The room assigned by the firm to their Mr. Boole for his personal use was a small and dingy compartment, redolent of that atmosphere of desolation which lawyers alone know how to achieve. It gave the impression of not having been swept since the foundation of the firm in the year 1786. There was one small window, covered with grime. It was one of those windows which you see only in lawyer's offices. Possibly, some reckless Mainprice or hairbrained Boole had opened it, in a fit of mad excitement induced by the news of the Battle of Waterloo, in 1815, and had been instantly expelled from the

68

firm. Since then no one had dared to tamper with it.

Looking out of this window, or rather, looking at it, for X-rays could hardly have succeeded in actually penetrating the alluvial deposits upon the glass, was a little man. As Ashe entered, he turned, and looked at him as if he hurt him rather badly in some tender spot.

Ashe was obliged to own to himself that he felt a little nervous. It is not every day that a young man of good appearance, who has led a quiet life, meets face to face one who is prepared to pay him well for doing something delicate and dangerous. To Ashe the sensation was entirely novel. The most delicate and dangerous act he had performed to date had been the daily mastication of Mrs. Bell's breakfasts (included in rent). Yes, he had to admit it, he was nervous: and the fact that he was nervous made him hot and uncomfortable.

To judge him by his appearance, the man at the window was also hot and uncomfortable. He was a little, truculent-looking man, and his face at present was red with a flush which sat unnaturally on a normally leaden-coloured face. His eyes looked out from under thick grey eyebrows with an almost tortured expression. This was partly owing to the strain of interviewing Ashe's preposterous predecessors, but principally to the fact that the little man had suddenly become seized with acute indigestion, a malady to which he was peculiarly subject.

He removed from his mouth the black cigar which he was smoking, inserted a digestive tabloid, and replaced the cigar. Then he concentrated his attention upon Ashe. As he did so, the hostile expression of his face became modified. He looked surprised and—grudgingly—pleased.

'Well, what do *you* want?' he said.

'I came in answer to——'

'In answer to my advertisement? I had given up hope of seeing anything part-human. I thought you must be one of the clerks. You're certainly more like what I advertised for. Of all the seedy bunches of dead-beats I ever struck, the aggregation I've just been interviewing was the seediest. When I spend good money advertising for a young man of good appearance, then I want a young man of good appearance, not a tramp of fifty-five.'

Ashe was sorry for his predecessors, but he was bound to admit that they certainly had corresponded somewhat faithfully to the description just given. The comparative cordiality of his own reception removed the slight nervousness which had been troubling him. He began to feel confident, almost jaunty.

'I'm through,' said the little man wearily. 'I've had enough of interviewing applicants. You're the last one I'll see. Are there any more hoodoos outside?'

'Not when I came in.'

'Then we'll get down to business. I'll tell you what I want done, and, if you are willing, you can do it: if you are not willing, you can leave it and go to the devil. Sit down.'

Ashe sat down. He resented the little man's tone, but this was not the moment for saying so.

His companion scrutinized him narrowly.

'As far as appearance goes,' he said, 'you are what I want.' Ashe felt inclined to bow.

'Whoever takes on this job has got to act as my valet, and you look like a valet.' Ashe felt less inclined to bow. 'You're tall and thin and ordinary-looking. Yes, as far as appearance goes, you fill the bill.'

It seemed to Ashe that it was time to correct an impression which the little man appeared to have formed.

'I am afraid,' he said, 'that, if all you want is a valet, you will have to look elsewhere. I got the idea from your advertisement that something rather more exciting than that was in the air. I can recommend you to several good employment agencies, if you wish.'

He rose. 'Good morning,' he said. He would have liked to fling the massive pewter ink-pot at this little creature who had so keenly disappointed him.

'Sit down!' snapped the other.

Ashe resumed his seat. The hope of adventure dies hard on a Spring morning, when one is twenty-six, and he had the feeling that there was more to come.

'Don't be a damned fool,' said the little man. 'Of course I'm not asking you to be a valet and nothing else.'

'You would want me to do some cooking and plain sewing on the side, perhaps?'

Their eyes met in a hostile glare. The flush on the little man's face deepened.

'Are you trying to get gay with me?' he demanded dangerously.

'Yes,' said Ashe.

The answer seemed to disconcert his adversary. He was silent for a moment.

'Well,' he said at last, 'maybe it's all for the best. If you weren't full of gall, probably you wouldn't have come here at all, and whoever takes on this job of mine has got to have gall, if he has nothing else. I think we shall suit each other.'

'What is the job?'

The little man's face showed doubt and perplexity.

'It's awkward. If I'm to make the thing clear to you, I've got to trust you. And I don't know a thing about you. I wish I had thought of that before I inserted the advertisement.'

Ashe appreciated the difficulty.

'Wouldn't you make an A B case out of it?'

'Maybe I could, if I knew what an A B case was.'

'Call the people mixed up in it A and B.'

'And forget half-way through who was which! No, I guess I'll have to trust you.'

'I'll play square.'

The little man fastened his eyes on Ashe's in a piercing stare. Ashe met them smilingly. His spirits, always fairly cheerful, had risen high by now. There was something about the little man, in spite of his brusqueness and ill-temper, which made him feel flippant.

'Pure white,' he said.

'Eh?'

'My soul. And this'—he thumped the left section of his waistcoat—'solid gold. Proceed.'

'I don't know where to begin.'

'Without presuming to dictate, why not at the beginning?'

'It's all so darned complicated that I don't rightly know which *is* the beginning. Well, see here. I collect scarabs. I'm crazy about scarabs. Ever since I quit business, you might say that I have practically lived for scarabs.'

'Though it sounds an unkind thing to say of anyone,' said Ashe, 'incidentally, what *are* scarabs?' He held up his hand. 'Wait! It all comes back to me. Expensive Classical education now bearing belated fruit. Scarabaeus—Latin-noun, nominative —a beetle. Scarabeum, accusative, the beetle. Scarabei, of the beetle. Scarabeo, to or for the beetle. I remember now. Egypt— Rameses—Pyramids—sacred scarabs. Right!'

'Well, I guess I've gotten together the best collection of scarabs outside the British Museum, and some of them are worth what you like to me. I don't reckon money when it comes to a question of my scarabs Do you understand?'

'I take you, laddie.'

71

Displeasure clouded the little man's face.

'Don't call me "laddie"!'

'I used the word figuratively, as it were.'

'Well, don't do it again. My name is J. Preston Peters, and "Mr. Peters" will do as well as anything else when you want to attract my attention.'

'Mine is Marson. You were saying, Mr. Peters?'

'Well, it's this way,' said the little man.

Shakespeare and Pope have both emphasized the tediousness of a twice-told tale, so the episode of the stolen scarab need not be repeated at this point, though it must be admitted that Mr. Peters' version of it differed considerably from the calm, dispassionate description which the author, in his capacity of official historian, has given earlier in the story. In Mr. Peters' version, the Earl of Emsworth appeared as a smooth and purposeful robber, a sort of elderly Raffles, worming his way into the homes of the innocent and only sparing that portion of their property which was too heavy for him to carry away. Mr. Peters, indeed, specifically described the Earl of Emsworth as an oily old plug-ugly.

It took Ashe some little time to get a thorough grasp of the tangled situation, but he did it at last. Only one point perplexed him.

'You want to employ somebody to go to the castle and get this scarab back for you. I follow that. But why must he go as your valet?'

'That's simple enough. You don't think I'm asking him to buy a black mask and break in, do you? I'm making it as easy for him as possible. I can't take a secretary down to the Castle, for everybody knows that, now I've retired, I haven't got a secretary; and, if I engaged a new one and he was caught trying to steal my scarab from the Earl's collection, it would look suspicious. But a valet is different. Anyone can get fooled by a crook valet with bogus references.'

'I see. There's just one other point. Suppose your accomplice does get caught. What then?'

'That,' said Mr. Peters, 'is the catch, and it's just because of that that I am offering good pay to my man. We'll suppose for the sake of argument that you accept the contract, and get caught. Well, if that happens, you've got to look after yourself. I couldn't say a word. If I did, it would all come out, and, as far as the breaking-off of my daughter's engagement to young Threepwood was concerned, it would be just as bad as if I had

72

tried to get the thing back myself. You've got to bear that in mind. You've got to remember it if you forget everything else. I don't appear in this business in any way whatsoever. If you get caught, you take what's coming to you without a word. You don't turn round and say, "I am innocent. Mr. Peters will explain all," because Mr. Peters certainly won't. Mr. Peters won't utter a syllable of protest if they want to hang you. No, if you go into this, young man, you go into it with your eyes open. You go into it with a full understanding of the risks, because you think the reward, if you are successful, makes the taking of those risks worth while. You and I know that what you are doing isn't really stealing; it's simply a tactful way of getting back my own property. But the judge and jury will have different views.'

'I am beginning to understand,' said Ashe thoughtfully, 'why you called the job "delicate and dangerous".'

Certainly it had been no over-statement. As a writer of detective-stories for the British office-boy, he had imagined in his time many undertakings which might be so described, but few to which the description was more admirably suited.

'It is,' said Mr. Peters, 'and this is why I'm offering good pay. Whoever carries this job through gets five thousand dollars cash.'

Ashe started.

'Five thousand dollars! A thousand pounds?'

'Yes.'

'When do I begin?'

'You'll do it?'

'For a thousand pounds I certainly will.'

'With your eyes open?'

'Wide open.'

A look of positive geniality illuminated Mr. Peters' pinched features. He even went so far as to pat Ashe on the shoulder.

'Good boy!' he said. 'Meet me at Paddington Station at four o'clock on Friday. And if there's anything more you want to know, come round to this address.'

II

There remained the telling of Joan Valentine. For it was obviously impossible not to tell her. When you have revolutionized your life at the bidding of another, you cannot well conceal the fact, as if nothing had happened.

73

Ashe had not the slightest desire to conceal the fact. On the contrary, he was glad to have such a capital excuse for renewing the acquaintance.

He could not tell her, of course, the secret details of the thing. Naturally, those must remain hidden. No, he would just go airily in and say, 'You know what you told me about doing something new? Well, I've just got a job as a valet.'

So he went airily in and said it.

'To whom?' said Joan.

'To a man named Peters. An American.'

Women are trained from infancy up to conceal their feelings. Joan did not start or otherwise express emotion.

'Not Mr. Preston Peters?'

'Yes. Do you know him? What a remarkable thing.'

'His daughter,' said Joan, 'has just engaged me as a lady's maid.'

'What!'

'It will not be quite the same thing as three years ago,' Joan explained. 'It is just a cheap way of getting a holiday. I used to know Miss Peters very well, you see. It will be more like travelling as her guest.'

Ashe had not yet overcome his amazement.

'But—but——'

'Yes?'

'But what an extraordinary coincidence.'

'Yes. By the way, how did you get the situation? And what put it into your head to be a valet at all? It seems such a curious thing for you to think of doing.'

Ashe was embarrassed.

'I—I—well, you see, the experience will be useful to me, of course, in my writing.'

'Oh! Are you now thinking of taking up my line of work, Dukes?'

'No, no. Not exactly that.'

'It seems so odd. How did you happen to get in touch with Mr. Peters?'

'Oh, I answered an advertisement.'

'I see.'

Ashe was becoming conscious of an undercurrent of something not altogether agreeable in the conversation. It lacked the gay ease of their first interview. He was not apprehensive lest she might have guessed his secret. There was, he felt, no possible means by which she could have done that. Yet the fact

74

remained that those keen blue eyes of hers were looking at him in a peculiar and penetrating manner. He felt dampened.

'It will be nice being together,' he said feebly.

'Very,' said Joan.

There was a pause.

'I thought I would come and tell you.'

'Quite so.'

There was another pause.

'It seems so funny that you should be going out as a lady's maid.'

'Yes?'

'But of course you have done it before.'

'Yes.'

'The really extraordinary thing is that we should be going to the same people.'

'Yes.'

'It—it's remarkable, isn't it?'

'Yes.'

Ashe reflected. No, he did not appear to have any further remarks to make.

'Good-bye for the present,' he said.

'Good-bye.'

Ashe drifted out. He was consious of a wish that he understood girls. Girls, in his opinion, were odd.

When he had gone, Joan Valentine hurried to the door, and having opened it an inch, stood listening. When the sound of his door closing came to her, she ran down the stairs and out into Arundell Street.

She went to the Hotel Mathis.

'I wonder,' she said to the sad-eyed waiter, 'if you have a copy of the *Morning Post*?'

The waiter, a child of romantic Italy, was only too anxious to oblige Youth and Beauty. He disappeared, and presently returned with a crumpled copy. Joan thanked him with a bright smile.

Back in her room she turned to the advertisement page. She knew that life was full of what the unthinking call coincidences, but the miracle of Ashe having selected by chance the father of Aline Peters as an employer was too much of a coincidence for her. Suspicion furrowed her brow.

It did not take her long to discover the advertisement which had sent Ashe hurrying in a taxi-cab to the offices of Messrs.

Mainprice, Mainprice & Boole. She had been looking for something of the kind.

She read it through twice and smiled. Everything was very clear to her. She looked at the ceiling above her, and shook her head.

'You are quite a nice young man, Mr. Marson,' she said softly, 'but you mustn't try and jump my claim. I dare say you need that money too, but I'm afraid you must go without. I am going to have it, and nobody else.'

CHAPTER FIVE

I

The four-fifteen express slid softly out of Paddington Station, and Ashe settled himself in the corner seat of his second-class compartment. Opposite him, Joan Valentine had begun to read a magazine. Along the corridor, in a first-class smoking compartment, Mr. Peters was lighting a big black cigar. Still farther along the corridor, in a first-class, non-smoking compartment, Aline Peters looked out of the window and thought of many things.

Ashe was feeling remarkably light-hearted. He wished that he had not bought Joan that magazine and thus deprived himself temporarily of the pleasure of her conversation: but that was the only flaw in his happiness. With the starting of the train, which might be considered the formal and official beginning of the delicate and dangerous enterprise on which he had embarked, he had definitely come to the conclusion that the life adventurous was the life for him. He had frequently suspected this to be the case, but it had required the actual experiment to bring certainty.

Almost more than physical courage the ideal adventurer needs a certain lively inquisitiveness, the quality of not being content to mind his own affairs: and in Ashe this quality was highly developed. From boyhood up he had always been interested in things which were none of his business. And it is just that attribute which the modern young man, as a rule, so sadly lacks.

The modern young man may do adventurous things if they

76

are thrust upon him, but, left to himself, he will edge away uncomfortably and look in the other direction when the Goddess of Adventure smiles at him. Training and tradition alike pluck at his sleeve and urge him not to risk making himself ridiculous. And from sheer horror of laying himself open to the charge of not minding his own business he falls into a stolid disregard of all that is out of the ordinary and exciting. He tells himself that the shriek from the lonely house he passed just now was only the high note of some amateur songstress, and that the maiden in distress whom he saw pursued by the ruffian with a knife was merely earning the salary paid her by some motion-picture firm. And he proceeds on his way, looking neither to left nor right.

Ashe had none of this degenerate coyness towards adventure. It is true that it had needed the eloquence of Joan Valentine to stir him from his groove, but that was because he was also lazy. He loved new sights and new experiences.

Yes, he was happy. The rattle of the train shaped itself into a lively march. He told himself that he had found the right occupation for a young man in the Spring.

Joan, meanwhile, entrenched behind her magazine, was also busy with her thoughts. She was not reading the magazine: she held it before her as a protection, knowing that, if she laid it down, Ashe would begin to talk. And just at present she had no desire for conversation. She, like Ashe, was contemplating the immediate future, but unlike him was not doing so with much pleasure. She was regretting heartily that she had not resisted the temptation to uplift this young man, and wishing that she had left him to wallow in the slothful peace in which she had found him. It is curious how frequently in this world our attempts to stimulate and uplift swoop back on us and smite us like boomerangs. Ashe's presence was the direct outcome of her lecture on Enterprise, and it added a complication to an already complicated venture.

She did her best to be fair to Ashe. It was not his fault that he was about to try to deprive her of five thousand dollars which she looked upon as her personal property. But, illogically, she found herself feeling a little hostile.

She glanced furtively at him over the magazine, choosing by ill chance a moment when he had just directed his gaze at her. Their eyes met, and there was nothing for it but to talk. So she tucked away her hostility in a corner of her mind where she could find it again when she wanted it, and prepared for the

77

time being to be friendly. After all, except for the fact that he was her rival, this was a pleasant and amusing young man, and one for whom, till he made the announcement which had changed her whole attitude towards him, she had entertained a distinct feeling of friendship.

Nothing warmer. There was something about him which made her feel that she would have liked to stroke his hair in a motherly way and straighten his tie and have cosy chats with him in darkened rooms by the light of open fires, and make him tell her his inmost thoughts and stimulate him to do something really worthwhile with his life: but this, she held, was merely the instinct of a generous nature to be kind and helpful even to a comparative stranger.

'Well, Mr. Marson,' she said. 'Here we are!'

'Exactly what I was thinking,' said Ashe.

He was conscious of a marked increase in the exhilaration which the starting of the expedition had brought to him. At the back of his mind, he realized, there had been all along a kind of wistful resentment at the change in this girl's manner towards him. During the brief conversation when he had told her of his having secured his present situation, and later, only a few minutes back, on the platform of Paddington Station, he had sensed a coldness, a certain hostility, so different from her pleasant friendliness at their first meeting.

She had returned now to her earlier manner, and he was surprised at the difference it made. He felt somehow younger, more alive. The lilt of the train's rattle changed to a gay ragtime.

This was curious, because Joan was nothing more than a friend. He was not in love with her. One does not fall in love with a girl whom one has met only three times. One is attracted, yes; but one does not fall in love.

A moment's reflection enabled him to diagnose his sensations correctly. This odd impulse to leap across the compartment and kiss Joan was not love. It was merely the natural desire of a good-hearted young man to be decently chummy with his species.

'Well, what do you think of it all, Mr. Marson?' said Joan. 'Are you sorry or glad that you let me persuade you to do this perfectly mad thing? I feel responsible for you, you know. If it had not been for me, you would have been comfortably at Arundell Street, writing your "Wand of Death".'

'I'm glad.'

'You don't feel any misgivings now that you are actually committed to domestic service?'

'Not one.'

Joan, against her will, smiled approval on this uncompromising attitude. This young man might be her rival, but his demeanour on the eve of perilous times appealed to her. That was the spirit she liked and admired, that reckless acceptance of whatever might come. It was the spirit in which she herself had gone into the affair, and she was pleased to find that it animated Ashe also. Though, to be sure, it had its drawbacks. It made his rivalry the more dangerous.

This reflection injected a touch of the old hostility into her manner.

'I wonder if you will continue to feel so brave.'

'What do you mean?'

Joan perceived that she was in danger of going too far. She had no wish to unmask Ashe at the expense of revealing her own secret. She must resist the temptation to hint that she had discovered his.

'I meant,' she said quickly, 'that from what I have seen of him, Mr. Peters seems likely to be a rather trying man to work for.'

Ashe's face cleared. For a moment he had almost suspected that she had guessed his errand.

'Yes. I imagine he will be. He is what you might call quick-tempered. He has dyspepsia, you know.'

'I know.'

'What he wants is plenty of fresh air and no cigars, and a regular course of those Larsen exercises which amused you so much.'

Joan laughed.

'Are you going to try and persuade Mr. Peters to twist himself about like that? Do let me see it if you do.'

'I wish I could.'

'Do suggest it to him.'

'Don't you think he would resent it from a valet?'

'I keep forgetting that you are a valet. You look so unlike one.'

'Old Peters didn't think so. He rather complimented me on my appearance. He said I was ordinary looking.'

'I shouldn't have called you that. You look so very strong and fit.'

'Surely there are muscular valets?'

'Well yes, I suppose there are.'

Ashe looked at her. He was thinking that never in his life had he seen a girl so amazingly pretty. What it was that she had done to herself was beyond him, but something, some trick of dress, had given her a touch of the demure which made her irresistible. She was dressed in sober black, the ideal background for her fairness.

'While on the subject,' he said. 'I suppose you know you don't look in the least like a lady's maid. You look like a disguised princess.'

She laughed.

'That's very nice of you, Mr. Marson, but you're quite wrong. Anyone could tell I was a lady's maid a mile away. You aren't criticizing the dress, surely?'

'The dress is all right. It's the general effect. I don't think your expression is right. It's—it's—there's too much *attack* in it. You aren't meek enough.'

Joan's eyes opened wide.

'*Meek!* Have you ever seen a lady's maid, Mr. Marson?'

'Why, no, now that I come to think of it, I don't believe I have.'

'Well, let me tell you that meekness is her last quality. Why should she be meek? Doesn't she go in after the Groom of the Chambers?'

'Go in? Go in where?'

'Into dinner.'

She smiled at the sight of his bewildered face.

'I'm afraid you don't know much about the etiquette of the new world you have entered so rashly. Didn't you know that the rules of precedence among the servants of a big house are more rigid and complicated than in Society?'

'You're joking.'

'I'm not joking. You try going into dinner out of your proper place when we get to Blandings, and see what happens. A public rebuke from the butler is the least that you could expect.'

A bead of perspiration appeared on Ashe's forehead.

'My God!' he whispered. 'If a butler publicly rebuked me I think I should commit suicide. I couldn't survive it.'

He stared with fallen jaw into the abyss of horror into which he had leaped so light-heartedly. The Servant Problem, on this large scale, had been non-existent for him till now. In the days of his youth at Much Middleford, Salop, his needs had been ministered to by a muscular Irishwoman. Later, at Oxford, there had been his 'scout' and his bedmaker, harmless persons both, provided you locked up your whisky. And in London, his last phase, a succession of servitors of the type of the dishevelled maid at No. 7A, had tended him. That, dotted about the land, there were houses in which larger staffs of domestics were maintained, he had been vaguely aware. Indeed, in 'Gridley Quayle, Investigator, The Adventure of the Missing Marquess' (number four of the series) he had drawn a picture of the home-life of a Duke, in which a butler and two powdered footmen had played their parts. But he had had no idea that rigid and complicated rules of etiquette swayed the private lives of these individuals. If he had given the matter a thought, he had supposed that, when the dinner-hour arrived, the butler and the two footmen would troop into the kitchen and squash in at the table wherever they found room.

'Tell me,' he said, 'tell me all you know. I feel as if I had escaped a frightful disaster.'

'You probably have. I don't suppose there is anything so terrible as a snub from a butler.'

'If there is I can't think of it. When I was at Oxford, I used to go and stay with a friend of mine who had a butler who looked like a Roman emperor in swallow-tails. He terrified me. I used to grovel to the man. Please give me all the tips you can.'

'Well, as Mr. Peters' valet, I suppose you will be rather a big man.'

'I shan't feel it.'

'However large the house-party is, Mr. Peters is sure to be the principal guest, so your standing will be correspondingly magnificent. You come after the butler, the housekeeper, the groom of the chambers, Lord Emsworth's valet, Lady Ann Warblington's lady's maid——'

'Who is she?'

'Lady Ann? Lord Emsworth's sister. She has lived with him since his wife died. What was I saying? Oh yes. After them come the Hon. Frederick Threepwood's valet and myself, and then you.'

'I'm not so high up then, after all?'

'Yes, you are. There's a whole crowd who come after you. It all depends on how many other guests there are besides Mr. Peters.'

'I suppose I charge in at the head of a drove of housemaids and scullery-maids?'

'My dear Mr. Marson, if a housemaid or a scullery-maid tried to get into the Steward's Room and have her meals with us, she would be——'

'Rebuked by the butler?'

'Lynched, I should think. Kitchen-maids and scullery-maids eat in the kitchen. Chauffeurs, footmen, under-butler, pantry-boys, hall-boys, odd man, and steward's room footman take their meals in the Servant's Hall, waited on by the hall-boy. The still-room maids have breakfast and tea in the still-room and dinner and supper in the Hall. The housemaids and nursery-maids have breakfast and tea in the housemaids' sitting-room and dinner and supper in the Hall. The head-housemaid ranks next to the head still-room maid. The laundry-maids have a place of their own near the laundry, and the head laundry-maid ranks above the head housemaid. The chef has his meals in a room of his own near the kitchen.... Is there anything else I can tell you, Mr. Marson?'

Ashe was staring at her with vacant eyes. He shook his head dumbly.

'We stop at Swindon in half an hour,' said Joan softly. 'Don't you think you would be wise to get out there and go straight back to London, Mr. Marson? Think of all you would avoid.'

Ashe found speech.

'It's a nightmare.'

'You would be far happier in Arundell Street. Why don't you get out at Swindon and go back?'

Ashe shook his head.

'I can't. There's—there's a reason.'

Joan picked up her magazine again. Hostility had come out from the corner into which she had tucked it away, and was once more filling her mind. She knew that it was illogical, but she could not help it. For a moment during her revelations of servants' Etiquette she had allowed herself to hope that she had frightened her rival out of the field, and the disappointment made her feel irritable. She buried herself in a short story, and countered Ashe's attempts at renewing the conversation with cold monosyllables, till he ceased his efforts and fell into a moody silence.

He was feeling hurt and angry. Her sudden coldness, following on the friendliness with which she had talked for so long, puzzled and infuriated him. He felt as if he had been snubbed, and for no reason.

82

He resented the defensive magazine, though he had bought it for her himself. He resented her attitude of having ceased to recognize his existence. A sadness, a filmy melancholy crept over him. He brooded on the unutterable silliness of humanity, especially the female portion of it, in erecting artificial barriers to friendship.

It was so unreasonable. At their first meeting, when she might have been excused for showing defensiveness, she had treated him with unaffected ease. When that meeting had ended, there was a tacit understanding between them that all the preliminary awkwardnesses of the first stages of acquaintanceship were to be considered as having been passed, and that when they met again, if they ever did, it would be as friends. And here she was, luring him on with apparent friendliness, and then withdrawing into herself as if he had presumed.

A rebellious spirit took possession of him. *He* didn't care! Let her be cold and distant. He would show her that she had no monopoly of those qualities. He would not speak to her until she spoke to him, and when she spoke to him, he would freeze her with his courteous but bleakly aloof indifference. . . .

The train rattled on, Joan read her magazine. Silence reigned in the second-class compartment.

Swindon was reached and passed. Darkness fell on the land. The journey began to seem interminable to Ashe.

But presently there came a creaking of brakes, and the train jerked itself to another stop.

A voice on the platform made itself heard, calling, 'Market Blandings Market Blandings Station.'

II

The village of Market Blandings is one of those sleepy hamlets which modern progress has failed to touch, except by the addition of a railroad station and a room over the grocer's shop where moving-pictures are on view on Tuesdays and Fridays. The church is Norman, and the intelligence of the majority of the natives palaeozoic. To alight at Market Blandings Station in the dusk of a rather chilly Spring day, when the south-west wind has shifted to due east, and the thrifty inhabitants have not yet lit their windows, is to be smitten with the feeling that one is at the edge of the world with no friends near.

Ashe, as he stood beside Mr. Peters' luggage and raked the unsympathetic darkness with a dreary eye, gave himself up to melancholy. Above him an oil lamp shed a meagre light. Along the platform a small but sturdy porter was juggling with a milk-can. The east wind explored his system with chilly fingers.

Somewhere out in the darkness, into which Mr. Peters and Aline had already vanished in a large automobile, lay the Castle with its butler, and its fearful code of etiquette. Soon the cart which was to convey him and the trunks thither would be arriving. He shivered.

Out of the gloom and into the feeble rays of the oil-lamp came Joan Valentine. She had been away tucking Aline into the car. She looked warm and cheerful. She was smiling in the old friendly way.

If girls realized their responsibilities, they would be so careful when they smiled that they would probably abandon the practice altogether. There are moments in a man's life when a girl's smile can have as important results as an explosion of dynamite. In the course of their brief acquaintance Joan had smiled at Ashe many times, but the conditions governing those occasions had not been such as to permit him to be seriously affected. He had been pleased on such occasions; he had admired her smile in a detached and critical spirit; but he had not been overwhelmed by it. The frame of mind necessary for that result had been lacking. But now, after five minutes of solitude on the depressing platform of Market Blandings Station, he was what the spiritualists call a sensitive subject. He had reached that depth of gloom and bodily discomfort when a sudden smile has all the effect of strong liquor and good news administered simultaneously, warming the blood and comforting the soul and generally turning the world from a bleak desert into a land flowing with milk and honey.

It is not too much to say that he reeled before Joan's smile. It was so entirely unexpected. He clutched Mr. Peter's steamer-trunk in his emotion.

All his resolutions to be cold and distant were swept away. He had the feeling that in a friendless universe here was some-one who was fond of him and glad to see him.

A smile of such importance demands analysis, and in this case repays it; for many things lay behind this smile of Joan Valentine's on the platform of Market Blandings Station.

In the first place, she had had another of her swift changes of mood, and had once again tucked away hostility into its

84

corner. She had thought it over, and had come to the conclusion that as she had no logical grievance against Ashe for anything he had done, to be distant to him was the behaviour of a cat. Consequently, she resolved, when they should meet again, to resume her attitude of good-fellowship. That in itself would have been enough to make her smile.

But there was another reason, which had nothing to do with Ashe. While she had been tucking Aline into the automobile, she had met the eye of the driver of that vehicle and had perceived a curious look in it, a look of amazement and sheer terror. A moment later, when Aline called the driver Freddie, she had understood. No wonder the Hon. Freddie had looked as if he had seen a ghost. It would be a relief to the poor fellow when, as he undoubtedly would do in the course of the drive, he inquired of Aline the name of her maid and was told it was Simpson. He would mutter something about, 'Reminds me of a girl I used to know,' and would brood on the remarkable way in which Nature produces doubles. But he had had a bad moment, and it was partly at the recollection of his face that Joan smiled.

A third reason was that the sight of the Hon. Freddie had reminded her that R. Jones had said that he had written her poetry. That thought too had contributed towards the smile that so dazzled Ashe.

Ashe, not being miraculously intuitive, accepted the easier explanation that she smiled because she was glad to be in his company, and this thought, coming on top of his mood of despair and general dissatisfaction with everything mundane, acted on him like some powerful chemical.

In every man's life there is generally one moment to which in later years he can look back and say, 'In this moment I fell in love'. Such a moment came to Ashe now.

> *Betwixt the stirrup and the ground*
> *Mercy I asked, mercy I found.*

So sings the poet, and so it was with Ashe.

In the almost incredibly brief time which it took the small but sturdy porter to roll a milk-can across the platform and bump it with a clang against other milk-cans similarly treated a moment before, Ashe fell in love.

The word is so loosely used to cover a thousand varying shades of emotion—from the volcanic passion of an Anthony for a Cleopatra to the tepid preference of a grocer's assistant for the housemaid at the second house in the High Street as opposed to the cook at the first house past the post-office—that the mere statement that Ashe fell in love is not a sufficient description of his feelings as he stood grasping Mr. Peters' steamer-trunk. We must expand. We must analyse.

From his fourteenth year onward Ashe had been in love many times. His sensations in the case of Joan were neither the terrific upheaval which had caused him in his fifteenth year to collect twenty-eight photographs of the principal girl of the Theatre Royal, Birmingham, pantomime, nor the milder flame which had caused him, when at Oxford, to give up smoking for a week and try to learn by heart the Sonnets from the Portuguese. His love was something that lay between these two poles. He did not wish the station platform of Market Bland-ings to become suddenly congested with Red Indians, so that he might save Joan's life, and he did not wish to give up anything at all. But he was conscious, to the very depths of his being, that a future in which Joan did not figure would be so insupportable as not to bear considering, and in the immediate present, he very strongly favoured the idea of clasping Joan in his arms and kissing her till further notice. Mingled with these feelings was an excited gratitude to her for coming to him like this with that electric smile on her face; a stunned realization that she was a thousand times prettier than he had ever imagined: and a humility which threatened to make him loose his clutch on the steamer-trunk and roll about at her feet, yapping like a dog.

Gratitude, as far as he could dissect his tangled emotions, was the predominating ingredient of his mood. Only once in his life had he felt so passionately grateful to any human being. On that occasion, too, the object of his gratitude had been feminine.

Years before, when a boy in his father's home in distant Much Middleford, Salop, those in authority had commanded that he, in his eleventh year and shy as one can be only at that interesting age, rise in the presence of a room full of strangers, adult guests, and recite, 'The Wreck of the Hesperus.'

He had risen. He had blushed. He had stammered. He had contrived to whisper. 'It was the schooner Hesperus.' And then, in a corner of the room, a little girl, for no properly explained reason, had burst out crying. She had yelled, she had bellowed, and would not be comforted, and in the ensuing

86

confusion Ashe had escaped to the woodshed at the bottom of the garden, saved by a miracle.

All his life he had remembered the gratitude he had felt for that timely girl, and never till now had he experienced any other similar spasm.

But, as he looked at Joan, he found himself renewing that emotion of fifteen years ago.

She was about to speak. In a sort of trance he watched her lips part. He waited almost reverently for the first words which she should speak to him in her new rôle of the only authentic goddess.

'Isn't it a shame,' she said, 'I've just put a penny in the chocolate slot machine, and it's empty. I've a good mind to write to the company.'

Ashe felt as if he were listening to the strains of some grand, sweet anthem.

The small but sturdy porter, weary of his work among the milk-cans, or perhaps—let us not do him an injustice, even in thought—having finished it, approached them.

'The cart from the castle's here.'

In the gloom beyond him there gleamed a light which had not been there before. The meditative snort of a horse supported his statement. He began to deal as authoritatively with Mr. Peters' steamer-trunk as he had dealt with the milk-cans.

'At last,' said Joan. 'I hope it's a covered cart. I'm frozen. Let's go and see.'

Ashe followed her with the rigid gait of an automaton.

III

Cold is the ogre which drives all beautiful things into hiding. Below the surface of a frost-bound garden there lurk hidden bulbs which are only biding their time to burst forth in a riot of laughing colour (unless the gardener has planted them upside down) but shivering Nature dare not put forth her flowers till the ogre has gone. Not otherwise does cold suppress love. A man in an open cart on an English Spring night may continue to be in love, but love is not the emotion uppermost in his bosom. It shrinks within him and waits for better times.

For the cart was not a covered cart. It was open to the four winds of heaven, of which the one at present active proceeded from the bleak east. To this fact may be attributed Ashe's swift recovery from the exalted mood into which Joan's smile had

87

thrown him, his almost instant emergence from the trance. Deep down in him he was aware that his attitude towards Joan had not changed, but his conscious self was too fully occupied with the almost hopeless task of keeping his blood circulating to permit of thoughts of love. Before the cart had travelled twenty yards he was a mere chunk of frozen misery.

After an eternity of winding roads, darkened cottages, and black fields and hedges, the cart turned in at a massive iron gate which stood open, giving entrance to a smooth gravel drive. Here the way ran for nearly a mile through an open park of great trees, and was then swallowed in the darkness of dense shrubberies. Presently to the left appeared lights, at first in ones and twos, shining out and vanishing again, then as the shrubberies ehded and the smooth lawns and terraces began, blazing down on the travellers from a score of windows with the heartening effect of fires on a winter night. Against the pale grey sky Blandings Castle stood out like a mountain.

It was a noble pile, of early Tudor building. Its history is recorded in England's history books and Violett-le-duc has written of its architecture. It dominated the surrounding country.

The feature of it which impressed Ashe most at this moment, however, was the fact that it looked warm, and for the first time since the drive began he found himself in a mood that approximated to cheerfulness. It was a little early to begin feeling cheerful, he discovered, for the journey was by no means over. Arrived within sight of the Castle, the cart began a detour, which, ten minutes later, brought it under an arch and over cobble-stones to the rear of the buildings, where it eventually pulled up in front of a great door.

Ashe descended painfully, and beat his feet against the cobbles. He helped Joan to climb down. Joan was apparently in a gentle glow. Women seem impervious to cold.

The door opened. Warm, kitcheny scents came through it. Strong men hurried out to take down the trunks, while fair women, in the shape of two nervous, scullery-maids, approached Joan and Ashe and bobbed curtseys. This, under more normal conditions, would have been enough to unman Ashe, but in his frozen state a mere curtseying scullery-maid expended herself harmlessly upon him. He even acknowledged the greeting with a kindly nod.

The scullery-maids, it seemed were acting in much the same capacity as the *attachés* of Royalty. One was there to conduct

Joan to the presence of Mrs. Twemlow the housekeeper, the other to lead Ashe to where Beach the butler waited to do honour to the valet of the Castle's most important guest.

After a short walk down a stone-flagged passage, Joan and her escort turned to the right. Ashe's objective appeared to be located to the left. He parted from Joan with regret. Her moral support would have been welcome.

Presently his scullery-maid stopped at a door and tapped thereon. A fruity voice, like old tawny port made audible, said 'Come in.' Ashe's guide opened the door.

'The gentleman, Mr. Beach,' said she, and scuttled away to the less rarified atmosphere of the kitchen.

Ashe's first impression of Beach the butler was one of tension. Other people, confronted for the first time with Beach, had felt the same. He had that strained air of being on the very point of bursting which one sees in frogs and toy balloons. Nervous and imaginative men, meeting Beach, braced themselves involuntarily, stiffening their muscles for the explosion. Those who had the pleasure of more intimate acquaintance with him soon passed this stage, just as people whose homes are on the slopes of Mount Vesuvius become immune to fear of eruptions. As far back as they could remember, Beach had always looked as if an apoplectic fit were a matter of minutes, but he never had apoplexy, and in time they came to ignore the possibility of it. Ashe, however, approaching him with a fresh eye, had the feeling that this strain could not possibly continue, and that within a very short space of time the worst must happen. The prospect of this did much to arouse him from the coma into which he had been frozen by the rigours of the journey.

Butlers as a class seem to grow less and less like anything human in proportion to the magnificence of their surroundings. There is a type of butler, employed in the comparatively modest homes of small country gentlemen, who is practically a man and a brother, who hob-nobs with the local tradesmen, sings a good comic song at the village inn, and in times of crisis will even turn to and work the pump when the water supply suddenly fails. The greater the house, the more does the butler diverge from this type. Blandings Castle was one of the more important of England's show-places, and Beach, accordingly, had acquired a dignified inertia which almost qualified him for inclusion in the vegetable kingdom. He moved, when he moved at all, slowly. He distilled speech with the air of one

89

measuring out drops of some precious drug. His heavy-lidded eyes had the fixed expression of a statue's.

With an almost imperceptible wave of a fat white hand he conveyed to Ashe that he desired him to sit down. With a stately movement of his other hand he picked up a kettle which simmered on the hob. With an inclination of his head he called Ashe's attention to a decanter on the table.

In another moment Ashe was sipping a whisky toddy with the feeling that he had been privileged to assist at some mystic rite.

Mr. Beach, posting himself before the fire and placing his hands behind his back, permitted speech to drip from him.

'I have not the advantage of your name, Mr.——'

Ashe introduced himself. Beach acknowledged the information with a half bow.

'You must have had a cold ride, Mr. Marson. The wind is in the east.'

Ashe said yes, the ride had been cold.

'When the wind is in the east,' continued Mr. Beach, letting each syllable escape with apparent reluctance, 'I Suffer From My Feet.'

'I beg your pardon?'

'I Suffer From My Feet,' repeated the butler, measuring out the drops. 'You are a young man, Mr. Marson. Probably you do not know what it is to Suffer From Your Feet.'

He surveyed Ashe, his whisky toddy, and the wall beyond with his heavy-lidded inscrutability.

'Corns,' he said.

Ashe said that he was sorry.

'I Suffer Extremely From My Feet. Not only corns. I have but recently recovered from an Ingrowing Toe-Nail. I Suffered Greatly From My Ingrowing Toe-Nail. I Suffer From Swollen Joints.'

Ashe regarded this martyr with increasing disfavour. It is the flaw in the character of many excessively healthy young men that, while kind-hearted enough in most respects, they listen with a regrettable feeling of impatience to the confessions of those less happily situated as regards the ills of the flesh. Rightly or wrongly they hold that these statements should be reserved for the ear of the medical profession and other and more general topics selected for conversation with laymen.

'I'm sorry,' he said hastily. 'You must have a bad time. Is

90

there a large house-party here just now?'

'We are expecting,' said Mr. Beach, 'a Number of Guests. We shall in all probability sit down thirty or more to dinner.'

'A responsibility for you,' said Ashe ingratiatingly, well pleased to be quit of the feet topic.

Mr. Beach nodded.

'You are right, Mr. Marson. Few persons realize the responsibilities of a man in my position. Sometimes, I can assure you, it preys upon my mind, and I Suffer From Nervous Headaches.'

Ashe began to feel like a man trying to put out a fire which, as fast as he checks it at one point, breaks out at another.

'Sometimes, when I come off duty, everything gets Blurred. The outlines of objects grow misty. I have to sit down in a chair. The Pain Is Excruciating.'

'But it helps you to forget the pain in your feet.'

'No. No. I Suffer From My Feet simultaneously.'

Ashe gave up the struggle.

'Tell me about your feet,' he said.

Mr. Beach told him all about his feet.

The pleasantest functions must come to an end, and the moment arrived when the final word on the subject of swollen joints was spoken. Ashe, who had resigned himself to a permanent contemplation of the subject, could hardly believe that he heard correctly when, at the end of some ten minutes, his companion changed the conversation.

'You have been with Mr. Peters some time, Mr. Marson?'

'Eh? Oh! Oh no, only since last Wednesday.'

'Indeed! Might I inquire whom you assisted before that?'

For a moment Ashe did what he would not have believed himself capable of doing—regretted that the topic of feet was no longer under discussion. The question placed him in an awkward position. If he lied, and credited himself with a lengthy experience as a valet, he risked exposing himself. If he told the truth, and confessed that this was his maiden effort in the capacity of gentleman's gentleman, what would the butler think? There were objections to each course, but to tell the truth was the easier of the two, so he told it.

'Your first situation?' said Mr. Beach. 'Indeed!'

'I was—er—doing something else before I met Mr. Peters,' said Ashe.

Mr. Beach was too well bred to be inquisitive, but his eyebrows were not.

91

'Ah!' he said.

'?', cried his eyebrows. '? ? ?'

Ashe ignored the eyebrows.

'Something different,' he said.

There was an awkward silence. Ashe appreciated its awkwardness. He was conscious of a grievance against Mr. Peters. Why could not Mr. Peters have brought him down here as his secretary? To be sure, he had advanced some objection to that course in their conversation at the offices of Mainprice, Mainprice & Boole, but merely some silly, far-fetched objection. He wished that he had had the sense to fight the point while there was time; but, at the moment when they were arranging plans, he had been rather tickled by the thought of becoming a valet. The notion had a pleasing musical-comedy touch about it. Why had he not foreseen the complications which must ensue? He could tell by the look on his face that this confounded butler was waiting for him to give a full explanation. What would he think if he withheld it? He would probably suppose that Ashe had been in prison.

Well, there was nothing to be done about it. If Beach was suspicious, he must remain suspicious. Fortunately, the suspicions of a butler do not matter much.

Mr. Beach's eyebrows were still mutely urging him to reveal all, but Ashe directed his gaze at that portion of the room which Mr. Beach did not fill. He was hanged if he was going to let himself be hypnotized by a pair of eyebrows into incriminating himself. He glared stolidly at the pattern of the wall-paper, which represented a number of birds of an unknown species seated on a corresponding number of exotic shrubs.

The silence was growing oppressive. Somebody had to break it soon. And, as Mr. Beach was still confining himself to the language of the eyebrow and apparently intended to fight it out on these lines if it took all summer, Ashe broke it himself.

It seemed to him, as he reconstructed the scene in bed that night, that Providence must have suggested the subject of Mr. Peters' indigestion, for the mere mention of his employer's sufferings acted like magic on the butler.

'I might have had better luck, while I was looking for a place,' said Ashe. 'I dare say you know how bad-tempered Mr. Peters is? He is dyspeptic.'

'So,' responded Mr. Beach, 'I have been informed.' He brooded for a space. 'I, too,' he proceeded, 'Suffer From My Stomach. I have a Weak Stomach. The Lining Of My Stomach

92

is not what I could wish the Lining Of My Stomach to be.'

'Tell me,' said Ashe gratefully, 'all about the lining of your stomach.'

It was a quarter of an hour later that Mr. Beach was checked in his discourse by the chiming of the little clock on the mantelpiece. He turned round and gazed at it with surprise not unmixed with displeasure.

'So late!' he said. 'I shall have to be going about my duties. And you also, Mr. Marson, if I may make the suggestion. No doubt Mr. Peters will be wishing to have your assistance in preparing for dinner. If you go along the passage outside you will come to the door which separates our portion of the house from the other. I must beg you to excuse me. I have to go to the cellar.'

Following his directions, Ashe came, after a walk of a few yards, to a green baize door, which, swinging at his push, gave him a view of what he took correctly to be the main hall of the Castle, a wide, comfortable space, ringed with settees and warmed by a log fire burning in a mammoth fireplace. To the right a broad staircase led to upper regions.

It was at this point that Ashe realized the incompleteness of Mr. Beach's directions. Doubtless the broad staircase would take him to the floor on which were the bedrooms, but how was he to ascertain without the tedious process of knocking and inquiring at each door which was the one assigned to Mr. Peters? It was too late to go back and ask the butler for further guidance. Already he was on his way to the cellar in quest of the evening's wine.

As he stood irresolute, a door across the hall opened, and a man of his own age came out. Through the door which the young man held open for an instant while he answered a question from someone still within, Ashe had a glimpse of glass-topped cases.

Could this be the museum, his goal? The next moment the door, opening another few inches, revealed the outlying portions of an Egyptian mummy, and brought certainty.

It flashed across Ashe's mind that the sooner he explored the museum and located Mr. Peters' scarab the better. He decided to ask Beach to take him there as soon as he had leisure.

Meanwhile the young man had closed the museum door, and was crossing the hall. He was a wiry-haired, severe-looking young man, with a sharp nose and eyes that gleamed through rimless spectacles. None other, in fact, than Lord

93

Emsworth's private secretary, the Efficient Baxter.

Ashe hailed him.

'I say, old man, would you mind telling me how I get to Mr. Peters' room? I've lost my bearings.'

He did not reflect that this was hardly the way in which valets in the best society addressed the Upper Classes. That is the worst of adopting what might be called a 'character' part. One can manage the business well enough; it is the dialogue which provides the pitfalls.

Mr. Baxter would have accorded a hearty agreement to the statement that this was not the way in which a valet should have spoken to him. But at the moment he was not aware that Ashe was a valet. From his easy mode of address he assumed that he was one of the numerous guests who had been arriving at the Castle all day. As he had asked for Mr. Peters he fancied that Ashe must be the Hon. Freddie's friend, George Emerson, whom he had not yet met.

Consequently, he replied with much cordiality that Mr. Peter's room was the second to the left on the second floor.

He said that Ashe couldn't miss it. Ashe said that he was much obliged.

'Awfully good of you,' said Ashe.

'Not at all,' said Mr. Baxter.

'You lose your way in a place like this,' said Ashe

'Yes, don't you!' said Mr. Baxter.

And Ashe went on his upward path, and in a few moments was knocking at the door indicated.

And sure enough it was Mr. Peters' voice that invited him to enter.

IV

Mr. Peters, partially arrayed in the correct garb for gentlemen to dine, was standing in front of the mirror, wrestling with his evening tie. As Ashe entered, he removed his fingers and anxiously examined his handiwork. It proved unsatisfactory. With a yelp and an oath he tore the offending linen from his neck.

'Damn the thing!'

It was plain to Ashe that his employer was in no sunny mood. There are few things less calculated to engender sunniness in a naturally bad-tempered man than a dress-tie which will not let itself be pulled and twisted into the right shape. Even when things went well, Mr. Peters hated dressing for

94

dinner. Words cannot describe his feelings when they went wrong.

There is something to be said in excuse for this impatience. It is a hollow mockery to be obliged to deck one's person as for a feast, when that feast is to consist of a little asparagus and a few nuts.

His eyes met Ashe's in the mirror.

'Oh, it's you, is it? Come in then. Don't stand staring. Close that door quick. Hustle! Don't scrape your feet on the floor. Try to look intelligent. Don't gape. Where have you been all this while? Why didn't you come before? Can you tie a tie? All right then, do it.'

Somewhat calmed by the snow-white butterfly-shaped creation which grew under Ashe's fingers he permitted himself to be helped into his coat. He picked up the remnant of a black cigar from the dressing-table and relit it.

'I've been thinking about you,' he said.

'Yes?' said Ashe.

'Have you located the scarab yet?'

'No.'

'What the devil have you been doing with yourself then? You've had time to grab it a dozen times.'

'I have been talking to the butler.'

'What the devil do you waste time talking to butlers for? I suppose you haven't even located the museum yet?'

'Yes, I've done that.'

'Oh, you have, have you? Well, that's something. And how do you propose setting about the job?'

'The best plan would be to go there very late at night.'

'Well, you didn't propose to stroll in in the afternoon, did you? How are you going to find the scarab when you do get in?'

Ashe had not thought of that. The deeper he went into this business, the more things did there seem to be in it of which he had not thought.

'I don't know,' he confessed.

'You don't know! Tell me, young man, are you considered pretty bright, as Englishmen go?'

'I really couldn't say.'

'Oh, you couldn't, couldn't you, you blanked bone-headed boob!' cried Mr. Peters, frothing over quite unexpectedly and waving his arms in a sudden burst of fury. 'What's the matter with you? Why don't you show a little more enterprise? Why

95

don't you put something over? Why do you loaf about the place as if you were supposed to be an ornament? I want results, and I want them quick! I'll tell you how you can recognize my scarab when you get into the museum. That shameless old crook who sneaked it away from me has had the impudence to put it all by itself with a notice as big as a circus-poster alongside it saying that it is a Cheops of the Fourth Dynasty, presented'—Mr. Peters choked—'*presented* by J. Preston Peters, Esq. That's how you're going to recognize it.'

Ashe did not laugh, but he nearly dislocated a rib in his effort to abstain. To rob a man of his choicest possession and then thank him publicly for letting you have it appealed to Ashe as excellent comedy.

'The thing isn't even in a glass case,' continued Mr. Peters. 'It's lying on an open tray on top of a cabinet of Roman coins. Anybody who was left alone for two minutes in the place could take it. It's criminal carelessness to leave a valuable scarab lying about like that. If he was going to steal my Cheops, he might at least have had the decency to treat it as if it was worth something.'

'But it makes it easier for me to get it,' said Ashe consolingly.

'It's got to be made easy if you are to get it,' snapped Mr. Peters. 'Here's another thing. You are going to try for it late at night. Well, what are you going to say if anyone catches you prowling around at that time? Have you considered that?'

'No.'

'You would have to say something, wouldn't you? You wouldn't discuss the latest play? You would have to think up some mighty good reason for being out of bed at that time, wouldn't you?'

'I suppose so.'

'Oh, you do admit that, do you? Well, what you would say is this. You would explain that I had rung for you to come and read me to sleep. Do you understand?'

'You think that would be a satisfactory explanation of my being in the museum?'

'Idiot! I don't mean that you're to say it if you're caught actually in the museum. If you're caught in the museum, the best thing you can do is to say nothing and hope that the judge will let you off lightly because it's your first offence. You're to say it if you're found wandering about on your way there.'

'It sounds thin to me.'

96

'Does it! Well let me tell you that it isn't so thin as you suppose, for it's what you will actually have to do most nights. Two nights out of three I have to be read to sleep. My indigestion gives me insomnia.'

As if to push this fact home, Mr. Peters suddenly bent double.

'Oof!' he said. 'Wow!'

He removed the cigar from his mouth, and inserted a digestive tabloid.

'The lining of my stomach is all wrong,' he added.

It is curious how trivial are the immediate causes which produce revolutions. If Mr. Peters had worded his complaint differently, Ashe would, in all probability, have borne it without active protest. He had been growing more and more annoyed with this little person who buzzed and barked and bit at him, but the idea of definite revolt had not occurred to him. But his sufferings at the hands of Beach the butler had reduced him to a state where he could endure no further mention of stomachic linings. There comes a time when our capacity for listening to data about the linings of other people's stomachs is exhausted.

He looked at Mr. Peters sternly. He had ceased to be intimidated by the fiery little man, and regarded him simply as a hypochondriac who needed to be told a few useful facts.

'How do you expect not to have indigestion? You take no exercise and you smoke all day long.'

The novel sensation of being criticized, and by a beardless youth at that, held Mr. Peters silent. He started convulsively, but he did not speak.

Ashe, on his pet subject, became eloquent. In his opinion dyspeptics cumbered the earth. To his mind, they had the choice between health and sickness, and they deliberately chose the latter.

'Your sort of man makes me sick. I know your type inside out. You overwork and shirk exercise and let your temper run away with you and smoke strong cigars on an empty stomach, and when you get indigestion as a natural result, you look on yourself as a martyr, and make the lives of everybody you meet miserable. If you would put yourself into my hands for a month I would have you eating bricks and thriving on them. Up in the morning, Larsen exercises, cold bath, brisk rub down, sharp walk....'

'Who the devil asked your opinion, you impertinent young

97

hound?' inquired Mr. Peters.

'Don't interrupt, confound you,' shouted Ashe. 'Now you have made me forget what I was going to say.'

There was a tense silence. Then Mr. Peters began to speak.

'You—infernal—impudent——'

'Don't talk to me like that.'

'I'll talk to you just how——'

Ashe took a step towards the door.

'Very well, then,' he said. 'I resign. I give notice. You can get somebody else to do this job of yours for you.'

The sudden sagging of Mr. Peters' jaw, the look of consternation which flashed upon his face, told him that he had found the right weapon, that the game was in his hands. He continued with a feeling of confidence.

'If I had known what being your valet involved, I wouldn't have undertaken the thing for a hundred thousand pounds. Just because you had some idiotic prejudice against letting me come down here as your secretary, which would have been the simple and obvious thing, I find myself in a position where at any moment I may be publicly rebuked by the butler and have the head still-room maid looking at me as if I were something the cat had brought in.' His voice trembled with self-pity. 'Do you realize a fraction of the awful things you have let me in for? How on earth am I to remember whether I go in before the chef or after the third footman? I shan't have a peaceful minute while I'm in this place. I've got to sit and listen by the hour to a bore of a butler who seems to be a sort of walking hospital. I've got to steer my way through a complicated system of etiquette. And on top of all that you have the nerve, the insolence, to imagine that you can use me as a punching-bag to work your bad temper off! You have the immortal rind to suppose that I will stand being nagged and bullied by you whenever your suicidal way of living brings on an attack of indigestion! You have the supreme cheek to fancy that you can talk as you please to me! Very well! I've had enough of it. If you want this scarab of yours recovered, let somebody else do it. I've retired from business.'

He took another step towards the door. A shaking hand clutched at his sleeve.

'My boy, my dear boy, be reasonable!'

Ashe was intoxicated with his own oratory. The sensation of bully-ragging a genuine millionaire was new and exhilarating. He expanded his chest, and spread his feet like a Colossus.

'That's all very well,' he said, coldly disentangling himself from the hand. 'You can't get out of it like that. We have got to come to an understanding. The point is that, if I am to be subjected to your—your senile malevolence every time you have a twinge of indigestion, no amount of money could pay me to stop on.'

'My dear boy, it shall not occur again. I was hasty.'

Mr. Peters with agitated fingers relit the stump of his cigar.

'Throw away that cigar!'

'My boy!'

'Throw it away! You say you were hasty. Of course you were hasty. And as long as you abuse your digestion you will go on being hasty. I want something better than apologies. If I am to stop here, we must get to the root of things. You must put yourself in my hands as if I were your doctor. No more cigars. Every morning regular exercises.'

'No, no.'

'Very well.'

'No, stop, stop! What sort of exercises?'

'I'll show you tomorrow morning. Brisk walks.'

'I hate walking.'

'Cold baths.'

'No, no.'

'Very well.'

'No, stop. A cold bath would kill me at my age.'

'It would put new life into you. Do you consent to cold baths? No? Very well.'

'Yes, yes, yes.'

'You promise?'

'Yes, yes.'

'All right, then.'

The distant sound of the dinner-gong floated in.

'We settled that just in time,' said Ashe.

Mr. Peters regarded him fixedly.

'Young man,' he said slowly, 'if, after all this you fail to recover my Cheops for me, I'll—I'll—by George, I'll skin you.'

'Don't talk like that,' said Ashe. 'That's another thing you have got to remember. If my treatment is to be successful, you must not let yourself think in that way. You must exercise self-control mentally. You must think beautiful thoughts.'

'The idea of skinning you *is* a beautiful thought,' said Mr. Peters wistfully.

99

In order that their gaiety might not be diminished and the food turned to ashes in their mouths by the absence from the festive board of Mr. Beach, it was the custom for the upper servants at Blandings to postpone the start of their evening meal until dinner was nearly over above stairs. This enabled the butler to take his place at the head of the table, without fear of interruption except for a few moments when coffee was being served.

Every night, shortly before half past eight, at which hour Mr. Beach felt that he might safely withdraw from the dining-room and leave Lord Emsworth and his guests to the care of Merridew, the under-butler, and James and Alfred, the footmen, returning only for a few minutes to lend tone and distinction to the distribution of cigars and liqueurs, those whose rank entitled them to do so made their way to the House-keeper's Room, to pass in desultory conversation the interval before Mr. Beach should arrive and a kitchen-maid, with all the appearance of one who has been straining at the leash and has at last managed to get free, opened the door with the announcement, 'Mr. Beach, if you please, dinner is served.' Upon which Mr. Beach, extending a crooked elbow towards the housekeeper, would say, 'Mrs. Twemlow,' and lead the way high and disposedly down the passage, followed in order of rank by the rest of the company in couples, to the Steward's room. For Blandings was not one of those houses—or shall we say hovels?—where the upper servants are expected not only to feed but to congregate before feeding in the Steward's Room. Under the auspices of Mr. Beach and of Mrs. Twemlow, who saw eye to eye with him in these matters, things were done properly at the Castle, with the right solemnity. To Mr. Beach and to Mrs. Twemlow the suggestion that they and their peers should gather together in the same room in which they were to dine would have been as repellent as an announcement from Lady Ann Warblington, the chatelaine, that the house-party would eat in the drawing-room.

When Ashe, returning from his interview with Mr. Peters, was intercepted by a respectful small boy and conducted to the Housekeeper's Room, he was conscious of a sensation of shrinking inferiority akin to his emotions on his first day at school. The room was full and apparently on very cordial terms with itself. Everybody seemed to know everybody, and conversation was proceeding in the liveliest manner. As a matter of fact, the house-party at Blandings being in the main a gathering together of the Emsworth clan by way of honour and as a means of introduction to Mr. Peters and his daughter, the bride-of-the-house-to-be, most of the occupants of the Housekeeper's Room were old acquaintances, and were renewing interrupted friendships at the top of their voices.

A lull followed Ashe's arrival, and all eyes, to his great discomfort, were turned in his direction. His embarrassment was relieved by Mrs. Twemlow, who advanced to do the honours. Of Mrs. Twemlow little need be attempted in the way of pen-portraiture beyond the statement that she went as harmoniously with Mr. Beach as one of a pair of vases or one of a brace of pheasants goes with its fellow. She had the same appearance of imminent apoplexy, the same air of belonging to some dignified and haughty branch of the vegetable kingdom.

'Mr. Marson, welcome to Blandings Castle.'

Ashe had been waiting for somebody to say that, and had been a little surprised that Mr. Beach had not done so. He was also surprised at the housekeeper's ready recognition of his identity, until he saw Joan in the throng and deduced that she must have been the source of information. He envied Joan. In some amazing way she contrived to look not out of place in this gathering. He himself, he felt, had impostor stamped in large characters all over him.

Mrs. Twemlow began to make the introductions—a long and tedious process which she performed relentlessly, without haste and without scamping her work. With each member of the aristocracy of his new profession Ashe shook hands, and on each member he smiled, until his facial and dorsal muscles were like to crack under the strain. It was amazing that so many high-class domestics could be collected into one moderate-sized room.

'Miss Simpson you know,' said Mrs. Twemlow, and Ashe was about to deny the charge when he perceived that Joan was the individual referred to. 'Mr. Judson, Mr. Marson. Mr. Judson is the Honourable Frederick's gentleman.'

'You have not the pleasure of our Freddie's acquaintance as yet, I take it, Mr. Marson?' observed Mr. Judson genially, a smooth-faced, lazy-looking young man. 'Freddie repays inspection.'

'Mr. Marson, permit me to introduce you to Mr. Ferris, Lord Stockheath's gentleman.'

101

Mr. Ferris, a dark, cynical man with a high forehead, shook Ashe by the hand.

'Happy to meet you, Mr. Marson.'

'Miss Willoughby, this is Mr. Marson, who will take you in to dinner. Miss Willoughby is Lady Mildred Mant's lady. As of course you are aware, Lady Mildred, our eldest daughter married Colonel Horace Mant.'

Ashe was not aware, and he was rather surprised that Mrs. Twemlow should have a daughter whose name was Lady Mildred, but Reason, coming to his rescue, suggested that by 'our' she meant the offspring of the Earl of Emsworth and his late countess. Miss Willoughby was a light-hearted damsel with a smiling face and chestnut hair done low over her forehead. Since Etiquette forbade that he should take Joan in to dinner, Ashe was glad that at least an apparently pleasant substitute had been provided. He had just been introduced to an appallingly statuesque lady of the name of Chester, Lady Ann Warblington's own maid, and his somewhat hazy recollections of Joan's lecture on Below Stairs precedence had left him with the impression that this was his destined partner. He had frankly quailed at the prospect of being linked to so much aristocratic hauteur.

When the final introduction had been made, conversation broke out again. It dealt almost exclusively as far as Ashe could follow it, with the idiosyncrasies of the employers of those present. He took it that this happened all down the social scale below stairs. Probably the lower servants in the Servants' Hall discussed the upper servants in the Steward's Room, and the still lower servants in the housemaids' sitting-room discussed their superiors of the Servants' Hall, and the still-room gossiped about the housemaids' sitting-room. He wondered which was the bottom circle of all, and came to the conclusion that it was probably represented by the small respectful boy who had acted as his guide a short while before. This boy, having nobody to discuss anybody with, presumably sat in solitary meditation, brooding on the odd-job man.

He thought of mentioning this theory to Miss Willoughby, but decided that it was too abstruse for her, and contented himself with speaking of some of the plays he had seen before leaving London. Miss Willoughby was an enthusiast on the drama, and, Colonel Mant's devotion to his various clubs keeping him much in town, she had had wide opportunities of indulging her tastes. Miss Willoughby did not like the country.

102

She thought it dull.

'Don't you think the country dull, Mr. Marson.'

'I shan't find it dull here,' said Ashe, and was surprised to discover through the medium of a pleased giggle that he was considered to have perpetrated a compliment.

Mr. Beach appeared in due season, a little distrait as becomes a man who has just been engaged on important and responsible duties.

'Alfred spilled the 'ock!' Ashe heard him announce to Mrs. Twemlow in a bitter undertone. 'Within 'alf an inch of 'is lordship's arm he spilled it.'

Mrs. Twemlow muttered condolences. Mr. Beach's set expression was that of one who is wondering how long the strain of existence can be supported.

'Mr. Beach, if you please, dinner is served.'

The butler crushed down sad thoughts, and crooked his elbow.

'Mrs. Twemlow.'

Ashe, miscalculating degrees of rank in spite of all his caution, was within a step of leaving the room out of his proper turn, but the startled pressure of Miss Willoughby's hand on his arm warned him in time. He stopped to allow the statuesque Miss Chester to sail out under escort of a wizened little man with a horseshoe pin in his tie, whose name, in company with nearly all the others which had been spoken to him since he came into the room, had escaped Ashe's memory.

'You *were* nearly making a bloomer,' said Miss Willoughby brightly. 'You must be absent-minded, Mr. Marson, like his lordship.'

'Is Lord Emsworth absent-minded?'

Miss Willoughby laughed.

'Why, he forgets his own name sometimes. If it wasn't for Mr. Baxter, goodness knows what would happen to him.'

'I don't think I know Mr. Baxter.'

'You will if you stay here long. You can't get away from him if you're in the same house. Don't tell anyone I said so, but he's the real master here. His lordship's secretary he calls himself, but he's really everything rolled into one like the man in the play.'

Ashe, searching in his dramatic memories for such a person in a play, inquired if Miss Willoughby meant Pooh Bah in the 'Mikado', of which there had been a revival in London recently. Miss Willoughby did mean Pooh Bah.

103

'But Nosey Parker is what *I* call him,' she said. 'He minds everybody's business as well as his own.'

The last of the procession trickled into the Steward's Room. Mr. Beach said grace somewhat patronizingly. The meal began.

'You've seen Miss Peters, of course, Mr. Marson?' said Miss Willoughby, resuming conversation with the soup.

'Just for a few minutes at Paddington.'

'Oh! You haven't been with Mr. Peters long then?'

Ashe began to wonder if everybody he met was going to ask him this dangerous question.

'Only a day or so.'

'Where were you before that?'

Ashe was conscious of a prickly sensation. A little more of this and he might as well reveal his true mission at the Castle and have done with it.

'Oh, I was—that is to say——'

'How are you feeling after the journey, Mr. Marson?' said a voice from the other side of the table, and Ashe, looking up gratefully, found Joan's eyes looking into his with a curiously amused expression. He was too grateful for the interruption to try to account for this. He replied that he was feeling very well, which was not the case. Miss Willoughby's interest was diverted to a discussion of the defects of the various railroad systems of Great Britain.

At the head of the table, Mr. Beach had started an intimate conversation with Mr. Ferris, the valet of Lord Stockheath, the Hon. Freddie's 'poor old Percy'—a cousin, Ashe had gathered, of Aline Peter's husband-to-be. The butler spoke in more measured tones even than usual, for he was speaking of tragedy.

'We were all extremely sorry, Mr. Ferris, to read of your misfortune.'

Ashe wondered what had been happening to Mr. Ferris.

'Yes, Mr. Beach,' replied the valet, 'it's a fact we made a pretty poor show.' He took a sip from his glass. 'There is no concealing the fact—I have never tried to conceal it—that poor Percy is *not* bright.'

Miss Chester entered the conversation.

'I couldn't see where the girl, what's her name, was so very pretty. All the papers had pieces where it said that she was attractive and what not, but she didn't look anything special to *me* from her photograph in the *Daily Sketch*. What his lord-

104

ship could see in her I can't understand.'

'The photo didn't quite do her justice, Miss Chester. I was present in court, and I must admit she was *svelte*, decidedly *svelte*. And you must recollect that Percy, from childhood up, has always been a highly susceptible young nut. I speak as one who knows him.'

Mr. Beach turned to Joan.

'We are speaking of the Stockheath breach-of-promise case, Miss Simpson, of which you doubtless read in the newspapers. Lord Stockheath is a nephew of ours. I fancy his lordship was greatly shocked at the occurrence.'

'He was,' chimed in Mr. Judson from down the table. 'I happened to overhear him speaking of it to young Freddie. It was in the library on the morning when the judge made his final summing up and slipped into Lord Stockheath so crisp. "If ever anything of this sort happens to you, you young scallywag," he says to Freddie——'

Mr. Beach coughed.

'Mr. Judson!'

'Oh, it's all right, Mr. Beach, we're all in the family here, in a manner of speaking. It isn't as if I was telling it to a lot of outsiders. I'm sure none of these ladies or gentlemen will let it go beyond this room?'

The company murmured virtuous acquiescence.

'He says to Freddie, "You young scallywag, if ever anything of this sort happens to you, you can pack up and go off to Canada, for I'll have nothing more to do with you," or words to that effect. And Freddie says, "Oh, dash it all, guv'nor, you know, what!"'

However short Mr. Judson's imitation of his master's voice may have fallen of histrionic perfection, it pleased the company. The room shook with mirth.

Mr. Beach thought it expedient to deflect the conversation. By the unwritten laws of the room every individual had the right to speak as freely as he wished about his own personal employer, but Judson, in his opinion, sometimes went a trifle too far.

'Tell me, Mr. Ferris,' he said, 'does his lordship seem to bear it well?'

'Oh, Percy is bearing it well enough.' Ashe noted as a curious fact that while the actual valet of any person under discussion spoke of him almost affectionately by his Christian name, the rest of the company used the greatest ceremony and gave him his title with all respect. Lord Stockheath was Percy to Mr. Ferris, and the Hon. Frederick Threepwood was Freddie to Mr. Judson; but to Ferris Mr. Judson's Freddie was the Hon. Frederick, and to Judson Mr. Ferris' Percy was Lord Stockheath. It was rather a pleasant form of etiquette, and struck Ashe as somehow vaguely feudal.

'Percy,' went on Mr. Ferris, 'is bearing it like a little Briton. The damages not having come out of *his* pocket. It's his old father, who had to pay them, that's taking it to heart. You might say he's doing himself proud. He says it's brought on his gout again, and that's why he's gone to Droitwich instead of coming here. I dare say Percy isn't sorry.'

'It has been,' said Mr. Beach, summing up, 'a Most Unfortunate Occurrence. The modern tendency of the Lower Classes to get above themselves is becoming more marked every day. The young female in this case was, I understand, a barmaid. It is Deplorable that our young men should allow themselves to get into Such Entanglements.'

'The wonder to me,' said the irrepressible Mr. Judson, 'is that more of these young chaps don't get put through it. His lordship wasn't so wide of the mark when he spoke like that to Freddie in the library that time. I give you my word it's a mercy young Freddie *hasn't* been up against it. When we was in London, Freddie and I,' he went on, cutting through Mr. Beach's disapproving cough, 'before what you might call the crash, when his lordship cut off supplies and had him come back and live here, Freddie was asking for it, believe me. Fell in love with a girl in the chorus of one of the theatres. Used to send me to the stage-door with notes and flowers every night as regular as clockwork for weeks. What was her name? It's on the tip of my tongue. Funny how you forget these things. Freddie was pretty far gone. I recollect once, happening to be looking round his room in his absence, coming on a poem he had written to her. It was hot stuff, very hot. If that girl has kept those letters, it's my belief we shall see Freddie following in Lord Stockheath's footsteps.'

There was a hush of delighted horror round the table.

'Goo!' said Miss Chester's escort, with unction. 'You don't say so, Mr. Judson! It wouldn't half make them look silly if the Honourable Freddie was sued for breach just now with the wedding coming on.'

'There is no danger of that.'

It was Joan's voice, and she had spoken with such decision

that she had the ear of the table immediately. All eyes looked in her direction. Ashe was struck with her expression. Her eyes were shining, as if she were angry, and there was a flush on her face. A phrase he had used in the train came back to him. She looked like a princess in disguise.

'What makes you say that, Miss Simpson?' inquired Judson, annoyed. He had been at pains to make the company's flesh creep, and it appeared to be Joan's aim to undo his work.

It seemed to Ashe that Joan made an effort of some sort, as if she were pulling herself together and remembering where she was.

'Well,' she said, almost lamely, 'I don't think it at all likely that he proposed marriage to this girl.'

'You never can tell,' said Judson. 'My impression is that Freddie did. It's my belief that there's something on his mind these days. Before he went to London with his lordship the other day, he was behaving very strange. And since he came back it's my belief that he has been brooding. And I happen to know that he followed the affair of Lord Stockheath pretty close, for he clipped the clippings out of the paper. I found them myself one day when I happened to be going through his things.'

Beach cleared his throat—his mode of indicating that he was about to monopolize the conversation.

'And in any case, Miss Simpson,' he said solemnly, 'with things come to the pass they have come to, and with juries— drawn from the lower classes—in the Nasty Mood they're in, it don't seem hardly necessary in these affairs for there to have been any definite promise of marriage. What with all this Socialism rampant, they seem so 'appy at the idea of being able to do one of Us an injury that they give 'eavy damages without it. A few ardent Expressions, and that's enough for them. You recollect the Havant case, and when young Lord Mount Anville was sued. What it comes to is that Anarchy is getting the Upper Hand, and the Lower Classes are getting above themselves. It's all these here cheap newspapers that does it. They tempt the Lower Classes to get Above Themselves. Only this morning, I had to speak severe to that young fellow James, the footman. He was a good fellow once, and did his work well, and 'ad a proper respect for people; but now he's gone all to pieces. And why? Because six months ago he had the rheumatism, and had the audacity to send his picture and a testimonial saying that it had cured him of Awful Agonies to

107

Walkinshaw's Supreme Ointment, and they printed it in half a dozen papers, and it has been the ruin of James. He has got Above Himself and don't care for nobody.'

'Well, all I can say is,' resumed Judson, 'that I 'ope to goodness nothing won't happen to Freddie of that kind, for it's not every girl that would have him.'

There was a murmur of assent to this truth.

'Now your Miss Peters,' said Judson, tolerantly, 'she seems a nice little thing.'

'She would be pleased to hear you say so,' said Joan.

'Joan Valentine!' cried Judson, bringing his hands down on tablecloth with a bang. 'I've just remembered it. That was the name of the girl Freddie used to write the letters and poems to. And that's who it is I've been trying all along to think who you reminded me of, Miss Simpson. You're the living image of Freddie's Miss Joan Valentine.'

Ashe was not normally a young man of particularly ready wit, but on this occasion it may have been that the shock of this revelation, added to the fact that something must be done speedily if Joan's discomposure was not to become obvious to all present, quickened his intelligence. Joan, usually so sure of herself, so ready of resource, had gone temporarily to pieces. She was quite white, and her eyes met Ashe's with almost a hunted expression.

If the attention of the company was to be diverted, something drastic must be done. A mere verbal attempt to change the conversation would be useless.

Inspiration descended upon Ashe.

In the days of his childhood in Much Middlefold, Salop, he had played truant from Sunday School again and again in order to frequent the society of one Eddie Waffles, the official Bad Boy of the locality. It was not so much Eddie's charm of conversation that had attracted him—though that had been great—as the fact that Eddie, among his other accomplishments, could give a life-like imitation of two cats fighting in a backyard, and Ashe felt that he could never be happy until he had acquired this gift from the master. In course of time he had done so. It might be that his absences from Sunday School in the cause of Art had left him in later years a trifle shaky on the subject of the Kings of Judah, but his hard-won accomplishment had made him in request at every smoking-concert at Oxford, and it saved the situation now.

'Have you ever heard two cats fighting in a backyard?' he

108

inquired casually of his neighbour Miss Willoughby.

The next moment the performance was in full swing.

Young Master Waffles, who had devoted considerable study to his subject, had conceived the combat of his imaginary cats in a broad, almost a Homeric vein. The unpleasantness opened with a low gurgling sound, answered by another a shade louder and possibly a little more querulous. A momentary silence was followed by a long-drawn note like rising wind cut off abruptly and succeeded by a grumbling mutter. The response to this was a couple of sharp howls. Both parties to the contest then indulged in a discontented whining, growing louder and louder till the air was full of electric menace. And then, after another sharp silence, came War, noisy and overwhelming. Standing at Master Waffles' side, you could almost follow every movement of that intricate fray, and mark how now one, now the other of the battlers gained a short-lived advantage. It was a great fight. Shrewd blows were taken and given, and in the eye of the imagination you could see the air thick with flying fur. Louder and louder grew the din, and then, at its height, it ceased in one crescendo of tumult, and all was still save for a faint, angry moaning.

Such was the cat fight of Master Eddie Waffles, and Ashe, though falling short of the master, as a pupil must, rendered it faithfully and with energy.

To say that the attention of the company was diverted from Mr. Judson and his remarks by the extraordinary noises which proceeded from Ashe's lips would be to offer a mere shadowy suggestion of the sensation caused by his efforts. At first stunned surprise, then consternation greeted him. Beach the butler was staring as one watching a miracle, nearer apparently to apoplexy than ever. On the faces of the others every shade of emotion was to be seen. That this should be happening in the Steward's Room at Blandings Castle was scarcely less amazing than if it had taken place in a cathedral. The upper servants, rigid in their seats, looked at each other, like Cortes' soldiers, 'with a wild surmise'.

The last faint moan of feline defiance died away, and silence fell upon the room.

Ashe turned to Miss Willoughby.

'Just like that,' he said. 'I was telling Miss Willoughby,' he added apologetically to Mrs. Twemlow, 'about the cats in London. They were a great trial.'

For perhaps three seconds his social reputation swayed to

109

and fro in the balance, while the company pondered on what he had done. It was new—but was it humorous or was it vulgar? There is nothing your upper servants so abhor as vulgarity. That was what the Steward's Room was trying to make up its mind about.

And then Miss Willoughby threw her shapely head back, and the squeal of her laughter smote the ceiling. And at that the company made its decision. Everybody laughed. Everybody urged Ashe to give an encore. Everybody was his friend and admirer.

Everybody but Beach the butler. Beach the butler was shocked to his very core. His heavy-lidded eyes rested on Ashe with disapproval.

It seemed to Beach the butler that this young man Marson had Got Above Himself.

Ashe found Joan at his side. Dinner was over, and the diners were making for the Housekeeper's Room.

'Thank you, Mr. Marson. That was very good of you, and very clever.' Her eyes twinkled. 'But what a terrible chance you took. You have made yourself a popular success, but you might just as easily have become a social outcast. As it is, I am afraid Mr. Beach did not approve.'

'I'm afraid he didn't. In a minute or so I'm going to fawn upon him and make all well.'

Joan lowered her voice.

'It was quite true what that odious little man said. He did write me letters. Of course I destroyed them long ago.'

'But weren't you running the risk in coming here that he might recognize you? Wouldn't that make it rather unpleasant for you?'

'I never met him, you see. He only wrote to me. When he came to the station to meet us this evening, he looked startled to see me, so I suppose he remembers my appearance. But Aline will have told him that my name is Simpson.'

'That fellow Judson said that he was brooding. I think you ought to put him out of his misery.'

'Mr. Judson must have been letting his imagination run away with him. He is out of his misery. He sent a horrid fat man named Jones to see me in London about the letters, and I told him that I had destroyed them. He must have let him know that by this time.'

'I see.'

110

They went into the housekeeper's room. Mr. Beach was standing before the fire. Ashe went up to him.

It was not an easy matter to mollify Mr. Beach. Ashe tried the most tempting topics. He mentioned swollen feet, he dangled the lining of Mr. Beach's stomach temptingly before his eyes, but the butler was not to be softened. Only when Ashe turned the conversation to the subject of the museum did a flicker of animation stir him.

Mr. Beach was fond and proud of the Blandings Castle museum. It had been the means of getting him into print for the first and only time in his life. A year ago a representative of the *Intelligencer and Echo* from the neighbouring town of Blatchford had come to visit the Castle on behalf of his paper, and he had begun one section of his article with the words: 'Under the auspices of Mr. Beach, my genial cicerone, I then visited his lordship's museum. . . .' Mr. Beach treasured the clipping in a special writing desk.

He responded almost amiably to Ashe's questions. Yes, he had seen the scarab—he pronounced it 'scayrub'—which Mr. Peters had presented to 'is lordship. He understood that 'is lordship thought very highly of Mr. Peters' scayrub. He had overheard Mr. Baxter telling his lordship that it was extremely valuable.

'Mr. Beach,' said Ashe, 'I wonder if you would take me to see Lord Emsworth's museum?'

Mr. Beach regarded him heavily.

'I shall be pleased to take you to see 'is lordship's museum,' he replied.

VI

One can only attribute to the nervous mental condition following on the interview which he had had with Ashe in his bedroom the rash act which Mr. Peters attempted shortly after dinner.

Mr. Peters, shortly after dinner, was in a dangerous and reckless mood. He had had a wretched time all through the meal. The Blandings *chef* had extended himself in honour of the house-party, and had produced a succession of dishes which, in happier days, Mr. Peters would have devoured eagerly. To be compelled by considerations of health to pass these by was enough to damp the liveliest optimist. Mr. Peters had suffered terribly. Occasions of feasting and revelry like the

111

present were for him so many battlefields on which Greed fought with Prudence.

All through dinner he brooded upon Ashe's defiance and the horrors which were to result from that defiance. One of Mr. Peters' most painful memories was of a two weeks' visit which he had once paid to Mr. William Muldoon at his celebrated health-restoring establishment at White Plains in the State of New York. He had been persuaded to go there by a brother-millionaire whom till then he had always regarded as a friend. The memory of Mr. Muldoon's cold shower-baths and brisk system of physical exercise still lingered.

The thought that under Ashe's rule he was to go through privately very much what he had gone through in the company of a gang of other unfortunates at Muldoon's froze him with horror. He knew these health-cranks who believed that all mortal ailments could be cured by cold showers and brisk walks. They were all alike, and they nearly killed you. His worst nightmare was the one where he dreamed that he was back at Muldoon's leading his horse up that infernal hill outside the village, your only reward, when you reached the summit, being the distant prospect of Sing-Sing prison.

He wouldn't stand it. He would be hanged if he would stand it. He would defy Ashe.

But if he defied Ashe, Ashe would go away, and then whom could he find to recover his lost scarab?

Mr. Peters began to appreciate the true meaning of the phrase about the horns of a dilemma.

The horns of this dilemma occupied his attention until the end of dinner. He shifted uneasily from one to the other and back again. He rose from the table in a thoroughly over-wrought condition of mind.

And then, somehow, in the course of the evening, he found himself alone in the Hall, not a dozen feet from the unlocked museum door.

It was not immediately that he appreciated the significance of this fact. He had come to the Hall because its solitude suited his mood. It was only after he had finished a cigar—Ashe could not stop him smoking after dinner—that it suddenly flashed upon him that he had ready to hand a solution of all his troubles. A brief minutes' resolute action, and the scarab would be his again and the menace of Ashe a thing of the past.

He glanced about him. Yes, he was alone.

Not once, since the removal of the scarab had begun to exercise his mind, had Mr. Peters contemplated for an instant the possibility of recovering it for himself. The prospect of the unpleasantness which would ensue had been enough to make him regard such an action as out of the question. The risk was too great to be considered for a moment.

But here he was in a position where the risk was negligible. Like Ashe, he had always visualized the recovery of his scarab as a thing of the small hours, a daring act to be performed when sleep held the Castle in its grip. That an opportunity would be presented to him of walking in quite calmly and walking out again with the Cheops in his pocket had never occurred to him as a possibility.

Yet now this chance was presenting itself in all its simplicity, and all he had to do was to grasp it. The door of the museum was not even closed. He could see from where he stood that it was ajar.

He moved cautiously in its direction—not in a straight line, as one going to a museum, but circuitously, as one strolling without an aim. From time to time he glanced over his shoulder.

He reached the door, hesitated, and passed it. He turned, reached the door again, and again passed it. He stood for a moment darting his eyes about the Hall, then, in a burst of resolution, dashed for the door and shot in like a rabbit.

At the same moment the Efficient Baxter, who from the shelter of a pillar on the gallery that ran round two-thirds of the Hall had been eyeing the peculiar movements of the distinguished guest with considerable interest for some minutes, began to descend the stairs.

Rupert Baxter, the Earl of Emsworth's indefatigable private secretary, was one of those men whose chief characteristic is a vague suspicion of their fellow human beings. He did not suspect them of this or that definite crime: he simply suspected them. He prowled through life as we are told that the Hosts of Midian prowled. His powers in this respect were well known at Blandings Castle. The Earl of Emsworth said: 'Baxter is invaluable, positively invaluable.' The Hon. Freddie said: 'A chappie can't take a step in this bally house without stumbling over that damn feller Baxter.' The man-servant and the maid-servant within the gates, employing, like Miss Willoughby, that crisp gift for characterization which is the property of the English lower orders, described him as a Nosey Parker.

Peering over the railings of the balcony and observing the curious movements of Mr. Peters, who, as a matter of fact, while making up his mind to approach the door, had been backing and filling about the Hall in a quaint serpentine manner like a man trying to invent a new variety of the Tango, the Efficient Baxter had found himself in some way—why, he did not know—of what, he could not say—but in some nebulous way, suspicious.

He had not definitely accused Mr. Peters in his mind of any specific tort or malfeasance. He had merely felt that something fishy was toward.

He had a sixth sense in such matters.

But when Mr. Peters, making up his mind, leaped into the museum, Baxter's suspicions lost their vagueness and became crystallized. Certainty descended on him like a bolt from the skies.

On oath, before a solicitor, the Efficient Baxter would have declared that J. Preston Peters was about to try to purloin the scarab.

Lest we should seem to be attributing too miraculous powers of intuition to Lord Emsworth's secretary, it should be explained that the mystery which hung about that curio had exercised his mind not a little since his employer had given it to him to place in the museum. He knew Lord Emsworth's powers of forgetting, and he did not believe his account of the transaction. Scarab-maniacs like Mr. Peters did not give away specimens from their collections as presents. But he had not divined the truth, of what had happened in London. The conclusion at which he had arrived was that Lord Emsworth had bought the scarab, and had forgotten all about it. To support this theory was the fact that the latter had taken his chequebook to London with him. Baxter's long acquaintance with the earl had left him with the conviction that there was no saying what he might not do if let loose in London with a chequebook.

As to Mr. Peters' motive for entering the museum, that too seemed completely clear to the secretary. He was a curio enthusiast himself and he had served collectors in a secretarial capacity, and he knew both from experience and observation that strange madness which may at any moment afflict the collector, blotting out morality and the nice distinction between *meum and tuum* as with a sponge. He knew that collectors who would not steal a loaf if they were starving might, and

114

did, fall before the temptation of a coveted curio.

He descended the stairs three at a time, and entered the museum at the very instant when Mr. Peters' twitching fingers were about to close on his treasure.

He handled the delicate situation with eminent tact. Mr. Peters, at the sound of his step, had executed a backward leap which was as good as a confession of guilt, and his face was rigid with dismay, but the Efficient Baxter affected not to notice these phenomena. His manner, when he spoke, was easy and unembarrassed.

'Ah! Taking a look at our little collection, Mr. Peters? You will see that we have given the place of honour to your Cheops. It is certainly a fine specimen, a wonderfully fine specimen.'

Mr. Peters was recovering slowly. Baxter talked on to give him time. He spoke of Mut and Bubastis, of Ammon and the Book of the Dead. He directed the other's attention to the Roman coins.

He was touching on some aspects of the Princess Gilukhipa of Mitanni, in whom his hearer could scarcely fail to be interested, when the door opened and Beach the butler came in, accompanied by Ashe. In the bustle of the interruption Mr. Peters escaped, glad to be elsewhere and questioning for the first time in his life the dictum that, if you want a thing well done, you must do it yourself.

'I was not aware, sir,' said Beach the butler, 'that you were in occupation of the museum. I would not have intruded. But this young man expressed a desire to examine the exhibits, and I took the liberty of conducting him.'

'Come in, Beach, come in,' said Baxter.

The light fell on Ashe's face, and he recognized him as the cheerful young man who had inquired the way to Mr. Peter's room before dinner, and who, he had by this time discovered, was not the Hon. Freddie's friend George Emerson, nor indeed any other of the guests of the house.

He felt suspicious.

'Oh, Beach.'

'Sir.'

'Just a moment.'

He drew the butler into the Hall out of earshot.

'Beach, who is that man?'

'Mr. Peters' valet, sir.'

'Mr. Peters' valet?'

115

'Yes, sir.'

'Has he been in service long?' asked Baxter, remembering that a mere menial had addressed him as 'old man'.

Beach lowered his voice. He and the Efficient Baxter were old allies, and it seemed right to Beach to confide in him.

'He has only just joined Mr. Peters, sir, and he has never been in service before. He told me so himself, and I was unable to elicit from him any information as to his antecedents. His manner struck me, sir, as peculiar. It crossed my mind to wonder whether Mr. Peters happened to be aware of this. I should dislike to do any young man an injury, but, if you think that Mr. Peters should be informed ... It might be anyone coming to a gentleman without a character like this young man. Mr. Peters might have been Deceived, sir.'

The Efficient Baxter's manner became distrait. His mind was working rapidly.

'Should he be Informed, sir?

'Eh? Who?'

'Mr. Peters, sir. In case he should have been Deceived!'

'No, no. Mr. Peters knows his own business.'

'Far from me be it to appear officious, sir, but...'

'Mr. Peters probably knows all about him. Tell me, Beach, who was it suggested this visit to the museum? Did you?'

'It was at the young man's express desire that I conducted him, sir.'

The Efficient Baxter returned to the museum without a word. Ashe, standing in the middle of the room, was impressing the geography of the place on his memory. He was unaware of the piercing stare of suspicion which was being directed at him from behind.

He did not see Baxter. He was not even thinking of Baxter. But Baxter was on the alert. Baxter was on the war-path.

Baxter *knew*.

116

CHAPTER SIX

I

Among the compensations of advancing age is a wholesome pessimism, which, while it takes the fine edge off whatever triumphs may come to us, has the admirable effect of preventing Fate from working off on us any of those gold bricks, coins with strings attached, and unhatched chickens at which Ardent Youth snatches with such enthusiasm, to its subsequent disappointment. As we emerge from the twenties we grow into a habit of mind, which looks askance at Fate bearing gifts. We miss, perhaps the occasional prize, but we also avoid leaping light-heartedly into traps.

Ashe Marson had yet to reach the age of tranquil mistrust, and, when Fate seemed to be treating him kindly, he was still young enough to accept such kindnesses on their face value and rejoice at them.

As he sat on his bed, at the end of his first night at Blandings Castle, he was conscious to a remarkable degree that Fortune was treating him well. He had survived, not merely without discredit, but with positive triumph, the initiatory plunge into the etiquette-maelstrom of life below stairs. So far from doing the wrong thing and drawing down on himself the just scorn of the Steward's Room, he had been the life and soul of the party. Even if tomorrow in an absent-minded fit, he should anticipate the groom of the chambers in the march to the table, it would be forgiven him; for the humorist has his privileges.

So much for that. But that was only a part of Fortune's kindnesses. To have discovered on the first day of their association the correct method of handling and reducing to subjection his irascible employer was an even greater boon. A prolonged association with Mr. Peters on the lines of which their acquaintance had begun would have been extremely trying. Now, by virtue of a fortunate stand at the outset, he had spiked the millionaire's guns.

Thirdly, and most important than all, he had not only made himself familiar with the locality and surroundings of the scarab, but he had seen beyond the possibility of doubt that the removal of it and the earning of the thousand pounds would be the simplest possible task. Already he was spending the money in his mind, and to such lengths had optimism led him that, as he sat on his bed reviewing the events of the day, his only doubt was whether to get the scarab at once or to let it remain where it was until he had the opportunity of doing Mr. Peters' interior good on the lines which he had mapped out in their conversation. For, of course, directly he had restored the scarab to its rightful owner and pocketed the reward, his position as healer and trainer to the millionaire would cease automatically.

He was sorry for that, for it troubled him to think that a sick man should not be made well. But, on the whole, looking at it from every aspect, it would be best to get the scarab as soon as possible and leave Mr. Peters digestion to look after itself.

Being twenty-six and an optimist, he had no suspicion that Fate might be playing with him, that Fate might have unpleasant surprises in store, that Fate even now was preparing to smite him in his hour of joy with that powerful weapon, the Efficient Baxter.

He looked at his watch. It was five minutes to one. He had no idea whether they kept early hours at Blandings Castle or not, but he deemed it prudent to give the household another hour in which to settle down. After which he would just trot down and collect the scarab.

The novel which he had brought down with him from London fortunately proved interesting. Two o'clock came before he was ready for it. He slipped the book in his pocket, and opened the door.

All was still—still and uncommonly dark. Along the corridor in which his room was situated the snores of sleeping domestics exploded, growled, and twittered in the air. Every menial on the list seemed to be snoring, some in one key, some in another, some defiantly, some plaintively; but the main fact was that they were all snoring, somehow thus intimating that, as far as this side of the house was concerned, the coast might be considered clear and interruption of his plans a negligible risk.

Researches made at an earlier hour had familiarized him with the geography of the place. He found his way to the green baize door without difficulty, and, stepping through, was in the hall where the remains of the log fire still glowed a fitful red. This, however, was the only illumination, and it was fortunate that he did not require light to guide him to the museum.

He knew the direction and had measured the distance. It

118

was precisely seventeen steps from where he stood. Cautiously, and with avoidance of noise, he began making the seventeen steps. He was beginning the eleventh when he bumped into somebody.

Somebody soft.

Somebody whose hand, as it touched his, felt small and feminine.

The fragment of a log fell on the ashes, and the fire gave a dying spurt. Darkness succeeded the sudden glow. The fire was out. That little flame had been its last effort before expiring. But it had been enough to enable him to recognize Joan Valentine.

'Good Lord!' he gasped.

His astonishment was short-lived. Next moment the only thing that surprised him was the fact that he was not more surprised. There was something about this girl that made the most bizarre happenings seem right and natural. Ever since he had met her his life had changed from an orderly succession of uninteresting days to a strange carnival of the unexpected, and use was accustoming him to it. Life had taken on the quality of a dream in which anything might happen, and in which everything which did happen was to be accepted with the calmness natural in dreams. It was strange that she should be here in the pitch-dark hall in the middle of the night, but—after all—no stranger than that he should be. In this dream-world in which he now moved it had to be taken for granted that people did all sorts of odd things from all sorts of odd motives.

'Hallo!' he said.

'Don't be alarmed.'

'No, no.'

'I think we are both here for the same reason.'

'You don't mean to say——'

'Yes, I have come to earn the thousand pounds too, Mr. Marson. We are rivals.'

In his present frame of mind it seemed so simple and intelligible to Ashe that he wondered if he was really hearing it for the first time. He had an odd feeling that he had known this all along.

'You are here to get the scarab?'

'Exactly.'

Ashe was dimly conscious of some objection to this, but at first it eluded him. Then he pinned it down.

119

'But you aren't a young man of good appearance,' he said.

'I don't know what you mean. But Aline Peters is an old friend of mine. She told me that her father would give a large reward to whoever recovered the scarab, so I——'

'Look out!' whispered Ashe. 'Run! There's someone coming!'

There was a soft footfall on the stairs, a click, and above Ashe's head a light flashed out. He looked around. He was alone, and the green baize door was swaying gently to and fro.

'Who's that? Who's there?' said a voice.

The Efficient Baxter was coming down the broad staircase.

A general suspicion of mankind and a definite and particular suspicion of one individual made a bad opiate. For over an hour sleep had avoided the Efficient Baxter with an unconquerable coyness. He had tried all the known ways of wooing slumber, but they had failed him, from the counting of sheep downwards. The events of the night had whipped his mind to a restless activity. Try as he might to lose consciousness, the recollection of the plot which he had discovered surged up and kept him wakeful. It is the penalty of the suspicious type of mind that it suffers from its own activity. From the moment when he detected Mr. Peters in the act of rifling the museum and marked down Ashe as an accomplice, Baxter's repose was doomed. Nor poppy nor mandragora nor all the drowsy syrups of the world could ever medicine him to that sweet sleep that he owed yesterday.

But it was the recollection that, on previous occasions of wakefulness, hot whisky and water had done the trick, which had now brought him from his bed and downstairs. His objective was the decanter on the table of the smoking-room, which was one of the rooms opening off the gallery which looked down on the hall. Hot water he could achieve in his bedroom by means of his Etna stove.

So out of bed he had climbed, and downstairs he had gone, and here he was, to all appearances, just in time to foil the very plot on which he had been brooding. Mr. Peters might be in bed, but there in the hall below him stood the Accomplice, not ten paces from the museum door.

He arrived on the spot at racing speed, and confronted Ashe.

'What are you doing here?'

And then, from the Baxter view-point, things began to go

wrong. By all the rules of the game Ashe, caught as it were red-handed, should have wilted, stammered, and confessed all. But Ashe was fortified by that philosophic calm which comes to us in dreams, and moreover he had his story ready.

'Mr. Peters rang for me, sir.'

He had never expected to feel grateful to the little firebrand who employed him, but he had to admit that the millionaire, in their last conversation, had shown forethought. The thought struck him that, but for Mr. Peters' advice, he might by now be in an extremely awkward position, for his was not a swiftly inventive mind.

'Rang for you? At half past two in the morning?'

'To read to him, sir.'

'To read to him at this hour?'

'Mr. Peters suffers from insomnia, sir. He has a weak digestion, and the pain sometimes prevents him from sleeping. The lining of his stomach is not at all what it should be.'

'I don't believe a word of it.'

With that meekness which makes the good man wronged so impressive a spectacle, Ashe produced and exhibited his novel.

'Here is the book, which I was about to read to him. I think, sir, if you will excuse me, I had better be going to his room. Good night, sir.'

And he proceeded to mount the stairs. He was sorry for Mr. Peters, so shortly about to be aroused from a refreshing slumber, but these were Life's tragedies and must be borne bravely.

The Efficient Baxter dogged him the whole way, springing silently in his wake, and dodging into the shadows whenever the light of an occasional electric bulb made it inadvisable to keep in the open. Then, abruptly, he gave up the pursuit. For the first time his comparative impotence in this silent conflict on which he had embarked was made manifest to him, and he perceived that on mere suspicion, however strong, he could do nothing. To accuse Mr. Peters of theft or to accuse him of being accessory to a theft was out of the question. Yet his whole being revolted at the thought of allowing the sanctity of the museum to be violated. Officially its contents belonged to Lord Emsworth, but ever since his connexion with the Castle he had been in charge of them, and he had come to look on them as his own property. If he was only a collector by proxy, he had nevertheless the collector's devotion to his curios, be-

121

side which the lioness's attachment to her cubs is tepid, and he was prepared to do anything to retain in his possession a scarab towards which he already entertained the feelings of a life-proprietor.

No, not quite anything. He stopped short at the idea of causing unpleasantness between the father of the Hon. Freddie and the father of the Hon. Freddie's fiancée. His secretarial position at the Castle was a valuable one, and he was loth to jeopardize it.

There was only one way in which this delicate affair could be brought to a satisfactory conclusion. It was obvious, from what he had seen that night, that Mr. Peters' connexion with the attempt on the scarab was to be merely sympathetic, and that the actual theft was to be accomplished by Ashe. His only course, then, was to catch Ashe actually in the museum. Then Mr. Peters need not appear in the matter at all. Mr. Peters' position in those circumstances would be simply that of a man who had happened to employ through no fault of his own a valet who happened to be a thief.

He had made a mistake, he perceived, in locking the door of the museum. In future he must leave it open, as a trap is open. And he must stay up at nights and keep watch.

With these reflections, the Efficient Baxter returned to his room.

Ashe, meanwhile, had entered Mr. Peters' bedroom and switched on the light. Mr. Peters, who had just succeeded in dropping off to sleep, sat up with a start.

'I've come to read to you,' said Ashe.

Mr. Peters, emitted a stifled howl, in which wrath and self-pity were nicely blended.

'You fool, do you know that I have just managed to get to sleep!'

'And now you're awake again,' said Ashe soothingly. 'Such is life. A little rest, a little folding of the hands in sleep, and then, bing! off we go again. I hope you will like this novel. I dipped into it and it seems good.'

'What do you mean by coming in here at this time of night? Are you crazy?'

'It was your suggestion, and, by the way, I must thank you for it. I apologize for calling it thin. It worked like a charm. I don't think he believed it—in fact, I know he didn't—but it held him. I couldn't have thought up anything half so good in an emergency.'

Mr. Peters' wrath changed to excitement.

'Did you get it? Have you been after my Cheops?'

'I have been after your Cheops, but I didn't get it. Bad men were abroad. That fellow with the spectacles who was in the museum when I met you there this evening swooped down from nowhere, and I had to tell him that you had rung for me to read to you. Fortunately I had this novel on me. I think he followed me upstairs to see that I really did come to your room.'

Mr. Peters groaned miserably.

'Baxter,' he said. 'He's a man named Baxter, Lord Emsworth's private secretary, and he suspects us. He's the man we—I mean you—have got to look out for.'

'Well, never mind. Let's be happy while we can. Make yourself comfortable, and I'll start reading. After all, what could be pleasanter than a little literature in the small hours? Shall I begin?'

II

Ashe found Joan in the stable-yard after breakfast next morning, playing with a retriever puppy.

'Can you spare me a moment of your valuable time?'

'Certainly, Mr. Marson.'

'Shall we walk out into the open somewhere where we can't be overheard?'

'Perhaps it would be better.'

They moved off.

'Request your canine friend to withdraw,' said Ashe. 'He prevents me marshalling my thoughts.'

'I'm afraid he won't withdraw.'

'Never mind. I'll do my best in spite of him. Tell me, was I dreaming, or did I really meet you in the hall this morning at about twenty minutes after two?'

'You did.'

'And did you really tell me that you had come to the Castle to steal——'

'Recover.'

'Recover Mr. Peters' scarab?'

'I did.'

'Then it's true?'

'It is.'

Ashe scraped the ground with a meditative toe.

'This,' he said, 'seems to me to complicate matters somewhat.'

'It complicates them abominably.'

'I suppose you were surprised when you found that I was on the same game as yourself?'

'Not in the least.'

'You weren't!'

'I knew directly I saw the advertisement in the *Morning Post*. And I hunted up the *Morning Post* directly you had told me that you had become Mr. Peters' valet.'

'You have known all along?'

'I have.'

Ashe regarded her admiringly.

'You're wonderful!'

'Because I saw through you?'

'Partly that. But chiefly because you had the pluck to undertake a thing like this.'

'*You* undertook it.'

'But I'm a man.'

'And I'm a woman? And my theory is, Mr. Marson, that a woman can do nearly everything better than a man. What a splendid test-case this would make to settle the Votes for Women question once and for all! Here we are, you and I, a man and a woman, each trying for the same thing, and each starting with equal chances. Suppose I beat you? How about the inferiority of women then?'

'I never said that women were inferior.'

'You did with your eye.'

'Besides you're an exceptional woman.'

'You can't get out of it with a compliment. I'm a very ordinary woman, and I'm going to beat a real man.'

Ashe frowned.

'I don't like to think of us working against each other.'

'Why not?'

'Because I like you.'

'I like you, Mr. Marson, but we must not let sentiment interfere with business. You want Mr. Peters' thousand pounds. So do I.'

'I hate the thought of being the instrument to prevent you getting the money.'

'You won't be. I shall be the instrument to prevent you getting it. I don't like that thought either, but one has got to face it.'

124

'I makes me feel mean.'

'That's simply your old-fashioned masculine attitude towards the female, Mr. Marson. You look on a woman as a weak creature to be shielded and petted. We aren't anything of the sort. We're terrors. You mustn't let my sex interfere with your trying to get this reward. Think of me as if I were another man. We're up against each other in a fair fight, and I don't want any special privileges. If you don't do your best from now onwards, I shall never forgive you. Do you understand?'

'I suppose so.'

'And we shall need to do our best. That little man with the glasses is on his guard. I was listening to you last night from behind the door. By the way, you shouldn't have told me to run away, and then have stayed yourself to be caught. That is an example of the sort of thing I mean. It was chivalry, not business.'

'I had a story ready to account for my being there. You had not.'

'And what a capital story it was! I shall borrow it for my own use. If I am caught, I shall say that I had to read Aline to sleep because she suffers from insomnia. And I shouldn't wonder if she did, poor girl. She doesn't get enough to eat. She is being starved, poor child. I heard one of the footmen say that she refused everything at dinner last night. And though she vows it isn't, my belief is that it's all because she is afraid to make a stand against her old father. It's a shame.'

'She is a weak creature to be shielded and petted,' said Ashe solemnly.

Joan laughed.

'Well, yes, you caught me there. I admit that poor Aline is not a shining example of the formidable modern women, but——' She stopped. 'Oh, bother, I've just thought of what I ought to have said—the good repartee which would have crushed you. I suppose it's too late now?'

'Not at all. I'm like that myself. Only it is generally next day that I hit the right answer. Shall we go back? ... She is a weak creature, to be shielded and petted.'

'Thank you so much,' said Joan gratefully. 'And why is she a weak creature? Because she has *allowed* herself to be shielded and petted. Because she has permitted Man to give her special privileges and generally—No, it isn't so good as I thought it was going to be.'

125

'It should be crisper,' said Ashe critically. 'It lacks the punch.'

'But it brings me back to my point, which is that I am not going to imitate her and forfeit my independence of action in return for chivalry. Try to look at it from my point of view, Mr. Marson. I know that you need the money just as much as I do. Well, don't you think that I should feel a little mean if I thought you weren't trying your hardest to get it, simply because you didn't think it would be fair to try your hardest against a woman? It would cripple me. I should not feel as if I had the right to do anything. It's too important a matter for you to treat me like a child and let me win to avoid disappointing me. I want the money, but I don't want it handed to me.'

'Believe me,' said Ashe earnestly, 'it will not be handed to you. I have studied the Baxter question more deeply than you, and I can assure you that Baxter is a menace. What has put him so firmly on the right scent I don't know, but he seems to have divined the exact state of affairs in its entirety. As far as I am concerned, that is to say. Of course he as no idea that you are mixed up in the business, but I am afraid that his suspicion of me will hit you as well. What I mean is that for some time to come I fancy that that man proposes to camp out on the rug in front of the museum door. It would be madness for either of us to attempt to go there at present.'

'It is being made very hard for us, isn't it? And I thought it was going to be so simple!'

'I think we should give him at least a week to simmer down.'

'Fully that.'

'Let us look on the bright side. We are in no hurry. Blandings Castle is quite as comfortable as No. 7A Arundell Street, and the commissariat department is a revelation to me. I had no idea that servants did themselves so well. And as for the social side, I love it. I revel in it. For the first time in my life I feel as if I were somebody. Did you observe my manner towards the kitchen-maid who waited on us at dinner last night? A touch of the old *noblesse* about it, I fancy? Dignified, but not unkind, I think? And I can keep it up. As far as I'm concerned let this life continue indefinitely.'

'But what about Mr. Peters? Don't you think there is a danger that he may change his mind about that thousand pounds if we keep him waiting too long?'

'Not a chance of it. Being almost within touch of his scarab has had the worst effects on him. It has intensified the craving.

126

By the way, have you seen the scarab?'

'Yes, I got Mrs. Twemlow to take me to the museum while you were talking to the butler. It was dreadful to feel that it was lying there in the open, waiting for someone to take it, and not be able to do anything.'

'I felt exactly the same. It isn't much to look at, is it? If it hadn't been for the label, I wouldn't have believed that it was the thing for which Peters was offering a thousand pounds reward. But that's his affair. A thing is worth what somebody will give for it. Ours not to reason why. Ours but to elude Baxter, and gather it in.'

' "Ours," indeed! You speak as if we were partners, instead of rivals.'

Ashe uttered an exclamation.

'You've hit it! Why not? Why any cut-throat competition? Why shouldn't we form a company? It would solve everything.'

Joan looked thoughtful.

'You mean, divide the reward?'

'Exactly. Into two equal parts.'

'And the labour?'

'The labour?'

'How shall we divide that?'

Ashe hesitated.

'My idea,' he said, 'was that I should do the—what I might call the *rough* work, and——'

'You mean that you should do the actual taking of the scarab?'

'Exactly. I would look after that end of it.'

'And what would *my* duties be?'

'Well, you—you would, as it were—how shall I put it? You would, so to speak, lend moral support.'

'By lying snugly in bed, fast asleep?'

Ashe avoided her eyes.

'Well, yes—er—something on those lines.'

'While you ran all the risks.'

'No, no. The risks are practically non-existent.'

'I thought you said just now that it would be madness for either of us to attempt to go to the museum at present?'

Joan laughed.

'It won't do, Mr. Marson. You remind me of an old cat I once had. Whenever he killed a mouse, he would bring it into the drawing-room and lay it affectionately at my feet. I would reject the corpse with horror and turn him out, but back he would come with his loathsome gift. I simply couldn't make him understand that he was not doing me a kindness. He thought highly of his mouse, and it was beyond him to realize that I did not want it. You are just the same with your chivalry. It's very kind of you to keep offering me your dead mouse, but, honestly, I have no use for it. I *won't* take favours just because I happen to be a female. If we are going to form this partnership, I insist on doing my fair share of the work, and running my fair share of the risks—the "practically non-existent" risks.'

'You're very—resolute.'

'Say pig-headed. I shan't mind. Certainly I am. A girl has got to be, even nowadays, if she wants to play fair. Listen, Mr. Marson, I will not have the dead mouse. I do not like dead mice. If you attempt to work off your dead mouse on me, this partnership ceases before it has begun. If we are to work together, we are going to make alternate attempts to get the scarab. No other arrangement will satisfy me.'

'Then I claim the right to make the first one.'

'You don't do anything of the sort. We toss for a first chance like little ladies and gentlemen. Have you a coin? I will spin, and you call.'

Ashe made a last stand.

'This is perfectly——'

'Mr. Marson!'

Ashe gave in. He produced a coin, and handed it to her gloomily.

'Under protest,' he said.

'Heads or tails?' said Joan, unmoved.

Ashe watched the coin gyrating in the sunshine.

'Tails,' he cried.

The coin stopped rolling.

'Tails it is,' said Joan. 'What a nuisance! Well, never mind. I get my chance if you fail.'

'I shan't fail,' said Ashe fervently. 'If I have to pull the museum down, I won't fail. Thank Heaven there's no chance now of your doing anything foolish.'

'Don't be too sure. Well, good luck, Mr. Marson.'

'Thank you, partner.'

They shook hands.

As they parted at the door Joan made one further remark:

'There's just one thing, Mr. Marson.'

'Yes?'

'If I could have accepted the mouse from anyone, I would certainly have accepted it from you.'

CHAPTER SEVEN

I

It is worthy of record, in the light of after events, that at the beginning of their visit, it was the general opinion of the guests gathered together at Blandings Castle that the place was dull. The house-party had that air of torpor which one sees in the saloon passengers of an Atlantic liner, that appearance of resignation to an enforced idleness and a monotony only to be broken by meals. Lord Emsworth's guests gave the impression, collectively, of being just about to yawn and look at their watches.

This was partly the fault of the time of year, for most house-parties are dull if they happen to fall between the hunting and the shooting seasons, but must be attributed chiefly to Lord Emsworth's extremely sketchy notions of the duties of a host.

A host has no right to intern a regiment of his relations in his house unless he also invites lively and agreeable outsiders to meet them. If he does commit this solecism, the least he can do is to work himself to the bone in the effort to invent amusements and diversions for his victims. Lord Emsworth had failed badly in both these matters. With the exception of Mr. Peters, his daughter Aline, and George Emerson, there was nobody in the house who did not belong to the clan; and as for his exerting himself to entertain, the company was lucky if it caught a glimpse of its host at meals. Lord Emsworth belonged to the people-like-to-be-left-alone-to-amuse-themselves-when-they-come-to-a-place school of hosts. He pottered about the garden in an old coat, now uprooting a weed, now wrangling with the autocrat from Scotland who was—theoretically—in his service as head-gardener; dreamily satisfied, when he thought of them at all, that his guests were as perfectly happy as he was. Apart from his son Freddie, whom he had long since dismissed as a youth of abnormal tastes from whom

129

nothing reasonable was to be expected, he could not imagine anyone not being content merely to be at Blandings when the buds were bursting on the trees.

A resolute hostess might have saved the situation, but Lady Ann Warblington's abilities in that direction stopped short at leaving everything to Miss Twemlow and writing letters in her bedroom. When Lady Ann Warblington was not writing letters in her bedroom—which was seldom, for she had an apparently inexhaustible correspondence—she was nursing sick headaches in it. She was one of those hostesses whom a guest never sees except when he goes into the library and espies the tail of her skirt vanishing through the other door.

As for the ordinary reactions of the country-house, the guests could frequent the billiard-room, where they were sure to find Lord Stockheath playing a hundred up with his cousin, Algernon Wooster—a spectacle of the liveliest interest; or they could, if fond of the game, console themselves for the absence of a links in the neighbourhood with the exhilarating pastime of clock-golf; or they could stroll about the terraces with such of their relations as they happened to be on speaking terms with at the moment and abuse their host and the rest of their relations.

This was the favourite amusement, and after breakfast on a morning ten days after Joan and Ashe had formed their compact the terraces were full of perambulating couples. Here, Colonel Horace Mant, walking with the Bishop of Godalming, was soothing that dignitary by clothing in soldierly words thoughts which the latter had not been able to crush down but which his holy office scarcely permitted him to utter. There, Lady Mildred Mant, linked to Mrs. Jack Hale, of the collateral branch of the family, was saying things about her father in his capacity of host and entertainer which were making her companion feel another woman. Farther on, stopping occasionally to gesticulate, could be seen other Emsworth relatives and connexions. It was a typical scene of quiet, peaceful English family life.

Leaning on the broad stone balustrade of the upper terrace, Aline Peters and George Emerson surveyed the malcontents.

Aline gave a little sigh, almost inaudible. But George's hearing was good.

'I was wondering when you were going to admit it,' he said, shifting his position so that he faced her.

'Admit what?'

130

'That you couldn't stand the prospect. That the idea of being stuck for life with this crowd, like a fly on fly-paper, was too much for you. That you were ready to break off your engagement to Freddie and come away and marry me and live happily ever after.'

'George!'

'Well, wasn't that what it meant? Be honest.'

'What what meant?'

'That sigh.'

'I didn't sigh. I was just breathing.'

'Then you *can* breathe in this atmosphere? You surprise me.' He raked the terraces with hostiled eyes. 'Look at them! Look at them crawling around like doped beetles. My dear girl, it's no use your pretending that this sort of thing wouldn't kill you. You're pining away already. You're thinner and paler since you came here. Heavens! How we shall look back at this and thank our stars that we're out of it, when we're settled down happily in Hong-Kong. You'll like Hong-Kong. It's a most picturesque place. Something going on all the time.'

'George, you mustn't really!'

'Why mustn't I?'

'It's wrong. You can't talk like that when we are both enjoying the hospitality——'

A wild laugh, almost a howl, disturbed the talk of the more adjacent of the perambulating relatives. Colonel Horace Mant, checked in mid-sentence, looked up resentfully at the cause of the interruption.

'I wish someone would tell me whether it's that fellow Emerson or young Freddie who's supposed to be engaged to Miss Peters. Hanged if you ever see her and Freddie together, but she and Emerson are never to be found apart. If my respected father-in-law had any sense, I should have thought he would have had sense enough to stop that. If that girl isn't in love with Emerson I'll be—I'll eat my hat.'

'No, no,' said the Bishop. 'No, no. Surely not, Horace. What were you saying when you broke off?'

'I was saying that if a man wanted his relations never to speak to each other again for the rest of their lives, the best thing he could do would be to herd them all together in a dashed barrack of a house a hundred miles from anywhere and then go off and spend all his time prodding dashed flower-beds with a spud, dash it!'

'Just so, just so. So you were. Go on, Horace. I find a

131

curious comfort in your words.'

On the terrace above them, Aline was looking at George with startled eyes.

'George!'

'I'm sorry. But you shouldn't spring these jokes on me so suddenly. You said *enjoying*. Yes. Revelling in it, aren't we?'

'It's a lovely old place,' said Aline, defensively.

'And when you've said that, you've said everything. You can't live on scenery and architecture for the rest of your life. There's the human element to be thought of. And you're beginning——'

'There goes father,' interrupted Aline. 'How fast he is walking. George, have you noticed a sort of difference in father these last few days?'

'I haven't. My speciality is keeping an eye on the rest of the Peters family.'

'He seems better somehow. He seems to have almost stopped smoking—and I'm very glad, for those cigars were awfully bad for him. The doctor expressly told him he must stop them, but he wouldn't pay any attention to him. And he seems to take so much more exercise. My bedroom is next to his, you know, and every morning I can hear things going on through the wall. Father dancing about and puffing a good deal. And one morning I met his valet going in with a pair of Indian clubs and some boxing-gloves. I believe father is really taking himself in hand at last.'

George Emerson exploded.

'And about time, too! How much longer are you to go on starving yourself to death just to give him the resolution to stick to his dieting? It maddens me to see you at dinner. And it's killing you. You're getting pale and thin. You can't go on like this.'

A wistful look came over Aline's face.

'I do get a little hungry sometimes. Late at night generally.'

'You want someone to take care of you and look after you. I'm the man. You may think you can deceive me, but I can tell. I *know*, I tell you. You're weakening. You're beginning to see that it won't do. One of these days you're going to come to me, and say, "George you were right. Let's sneak off to the station without anybody knowing and leg it for London and get married at a registrar's." Oh, *I* know! I couldn't have loved you all this time and not know. You're weakening.'

The trouble with these Supermen is that they lack reticence.

132

They do not know how to omit. They expand their chests and whoop. And a girl, even a girl like Aline Peters, cannot help resenting the note of triumph. But Supermen despise tact. As far as one can gather, that is the chief difference between them and the ordinary man.

A little frown appeared on Aline's forehead, and she set her mouth mutinously.

'I'm not weakening at all,' she said, and her voice was, for her, quite acid. 'You—you take too much for granted.'

George was contemplating the landscape with a conqueror's eye.

'You are beginning to see that it is impossible, this Freddie foolery.'

'It is not foolery,' said Aline pettishly, tears of annoyance in her eyes. 'And I wish you wouldn't call him Freddie.'

'He asked me to. He *asked* me to.'

Aline stamped her foot.

'Well, never mind. Please don't do it.'

'Very well, little girl,' said George softly. 'I wouldn't do anything to hurt you.'

The fact that it never even occurred to George Emerson that he was being offensively patronizing shows the stern stuff of which these Supermen are made.

II

The Efficient Baxter bicycled broodingly to Market Blandings for tobacco. He brooded for several reasons. He had just seen Aline Peters and George Emerson in confidential talk on the upper terrace, and that was one thing that exercised his mind, for he suspected George Emerson. He suspected him nebulously as a snake in the grass, as an influence working against the orderly progress of events concerning the marriage which had been arranged and would shortly take place between Miss Peters and the Hon. Frederick Threepwood. It would be too much to say that he had any idea that George was putting in such hard and consistent work in his serpentine rôle, indeed, if he could have overheard the conversation just recorded, it is probable that Rupert Baxter would have had heart-failure; but he had observed the intimacy between the two, as he observed most things in his immediate neighbourhood, and he disapproved of it. He blamed the Hon. Freddie. If the Hon. Freddie had been a more ardent lover, he would have spent his

133

time with Aline, and George Emerson would have taken his proper place as one of the crowd at the back of the stage. But Freddie's view of the matter seemed to be that he had done all that could be expected of a chappie in getting engaged to the girl, and that now he might consider himself at liberty to drop her for a while.

So Baxter, as he bicycled to Market Blandings for tobacco, brooded on Freddie, Aline Peters, and George Emerson.

He also brooded on Mr. Peters and Ashe Marson.

Finally he brooded in a general way because he had had very little sleep for the past week.

The spectacle of a young man doing his duty and enduring considerable discomforts while doing it is painful, but it affords so excellent a moral picture that I cannot omit a short description of the manner in which Rupert Baxter had spent the nine nights which had elapsed since his meeting with Ashe in the small hours in the hall.

In the gallery which ran above the hall, there was a large chair, situated a few paces from the great staircase. On this, in an overcoat—for the nights were chilly—and rubber-soled shoes, the efficient Baxter had sat, without missing a single night, from one in the morning till daybreak, waiting, waiting, waiting. It had been an ordeal to try the stoutest determination. Nature had never intended Baxter for a night-bird. He loved his bed. He knew that doctors held that insufficient sleep made a man pale and sallow, and he had always aimed at the peach-bloom complexion which comes from a sensible eight hours between the sheets. One of the Georges—I forget which —once said that a certain number of hours' sleep each night—I cannot recall at the moment how many—made a man something, which for the time being has slipped my memory. Baxter agreed with him. It went against all his instincts to sit up in this fashion, but it was his duty and he did it.

It troubled him that, as night after night went by, and Ashe, the suspect, did not walk into the trap so carefully laid for him, he found an increasing difficulty in keeping awake. The first two or three of his series of vigils he had passed in an unimpeachable wakefulness, his chin resting on the rail of the gallery and his ears alert for the slightest sound. But he had not been able to maintain this standard of excellence. On several occasions he had caught imself in the act of dropping off, and last night he had actually woken with a start to find it quite light. As his last recollection before that was of an inky darkness, impenetrable to the eye, dismay gripped him with a sudden clutch, and he ran swiftly down to the museum. His relief on finding that the scarab was still there had been tempered by thoughts of what might have been.

Baxter, then, as he bicycled to Market Blandings for tobacco, had good reason to brood.

Having bought his tobacco and observed the life and thought of the town for half an hour—it was market-day and the normal stagnation of the place was temporarily relieved and brightened by pigs that eluded their keepers and a bull-calf which caught a stout farmer at the psychological moment when he was tying his shoe-lace and lifted him six feet—he made his way to the Emsworth Arms, the most respectable of the eleven inns which the citizens of Market Blandings contrived in some miraculous way to support. In most English country towns, if the public-houses do not actually outnumber the inhabitants, they all do an excellent trade. It is only when they are two to one that hard times hit them and set the innkeepers blaming the Government.

It was not the busy bar, full to overflowing with honest British yeomen, many of them in the same condition, that Baxter sought. His goal was the genteel dining-room on the first floor, where a bald and shuffling waiter, own cousin to a tortoise, served luncheon to those desiring it. Lack of sleep had reduced Baxter to a condition where the presence and chatter of the house-party were unsupportable. It was his purpose to lunch at the Emsworth Arms and take a nap in an armchair afterwards.

He had relied on having the room to himself, for Market Blandings did not lunch to a great extent; but to his annoyance and disappointment the room was already occupied by a man in brown tweeds.

Occupied is the correct word, for at first sight, this man seemed to fill the room. Never since almost forgotten days when he used to frequent circuses and side-shows had Baxter seen a fellow human being so extraordinarily obese.

He was a man about fifty years old, grey-haired, of a mauve complexion, and his general appearance suggested joviality.

To Baxter's chagrin this person engaged him in conversation directly he took his seat at the table. There was only one table in the room, and it had the disadvantage that it collected those seated at it into one party. It was impossible for Baxter to withdraw into himself and ignore this person's advances.

It is doubtful if he could have done, however, had they been separated by yards of floor, for the fat man was not only naturally talkative, but as it appeared from his opening remarks, speech had been dammed up within him for some time by lack of a suitable victim.

'Morning,' he began. 'Nice day. Good for the farmers. I'll move up to your end of the table if I may, sir. Waiter, bring my beef to this gentleman's end of the table.'

He creaked into a chair at Baxter's side, and resumed.

'Infernally quiet place, this, sir. I haven't found a soul to speak to since I arrived yesterday afternoon except deaf and dumb rustics. Are you making a long stay here?'

'I live outside the town.'

'I pity you. Wouldn't care to do it myself. Had to come here on business, and shan't be sorry when it's finished. I give you my word I couldn't sleep a wink last night because of the quiet. I was just dropping off when a beast of a bird outside the window gave a chirrup, and it brought me up with a jerk as if somebody had fired a gun off. There's a damned cat somewhere near my room which mews. I lie in bed waiting for the next mew, all worked up. Heaven save me from the country. It may be all right for you, if you've got a comfortable home and a pal or two to chat with after dinner, but you've no conception what it's like in this infernal town—I suppose it calls itself a town. A man told me there was a moving-picture place here, and I hurried off to it, and found that it was the wrong day. Only open Tuesdays and Fridays. What a hole! There's a church down the street. I'm told it's Norman or something. Anyway it's old. I'm not much of a man for churches as a rule, but I went and took a look at it. And then somebody told me that there was a fine view from the end of the High Street. So I went and took a look at that, and now, as far as I can make out, I've done the sights and exhausted every possibility of entertainment the town has to provide. Unless there's another church. I'm so reduced that I'll go and see the Methodist chapel, if there is one.'

Fresh air, want of sleep, and the closeness of the dining-room combined to make Baxter drowsy. He ate his lunch in a torpor, hardly replying to his companion's remarks, who, for his part, did not seem to wish for or to expect replies. It was enough for him to be talking.

'What do people *do* with themselves in a place like this? When they want amusement, I mean. I suppose it's different if you've been brought up to it. Like being born colour-blind or

136

something. You don't notice it. It's the visitors who suffer. They've no enterprise in this sort of place. There's a bit of land just outside here which would make a sweet steeplechase course. Natural barriers. Everything. It hasn't occurred to them to do anything with it. It makes you despair of your species, that sort of thing. Now, if I——'

Baxter dozed. With his fork still impaling a piece of cold beef he dropped into that half-awake, half-asleep state which is Nature's daytime substitute for the true slumber of the night. The fat man, either not noticing or not caring, talked on. His voice was a steady drone, lulling Baxter to rest.

Suddenly there was a break. Baxter sat up, blinking. He had a curious impression that his companion had said, 'Hallo, Freddie!' and that the door had just opened and closed again.

'Eh?' he said.

'Yes?' said the fat man.

'What did you say?'

'I was speaking of——'

'I thought you said, "Hallo, Freddie!"'

His companion eyed him indulgently.

'I thought you were dropping off when I looked at you. You've been dreaming. What should I say, "Hallo, Freddie?" for?'

The conundrum was unanswerable. Baxter did not attempt to answer it. But there remained at the back of his mind a quaint idea that he had caught sight as he woke of the Hon. Frederick Threepwood, his face warningly contorted, vanishing through the door.

Yet what would the Hon. Freddie be doing at the Emsworth Arms?

A solution of the difficulty occurred to him. He had dreamed that he had seen Freddie, and that had suggested the words which, Reason pointed out, his companion could hardly have spoken. Even if the Hon. Freddie should enter the room, this fat man, who was apparently a drummer of some kind, would certainly not know who he was, nor would he address him so familiarly. Yes, that must be the explanation. After all the quaintest things happened in dreams. Last night, when he had fallen asleep in his chair, he had dreamed that he was sitting in a glass case in the museum making faces at Lord Emsworth, Mr. Peters, and Beach, the butler, who were trying to steal him under the impression that he was a scarab of the reign of the Cheops of the Fourth Dynasty—a thing which he

137

would never have done when awake.

Yes, he must certainly have been dreaming.

In the bedroom into which he had dashed to hide himself on discovering that the dining-room was in the possession of the Efficient Baxter, the Hon. Freddie sat on a rickety chair, scowling.

He elaborated a favourite dictum of his.

'You can't take a step *anywhere* without stumbling over that damn feller Baxter!'

He wondered if Baxter had seen him. He wondered if Baxter had recognized him. He wondered if Baxter had heard R. Jones say, 'Hullo, Freddie!'

He wondered, if such should be the case, whether R. Jones' presence of mind and native resource would be equal to explaining away the remark.

CHAPTER EIGHT

I

' "Put the butter or dripping in a kettle on the range, and when hot add the onions and fry them; add the veal and cook till brown. Add the water, cover closely, and cook very slowly until the meat is tender, then add the seasonings and place the potatoes on top of the meat. Cover and cook until the potatoes are tender, but not falling to pieces." '

'Sure,' said Mr. Peters. '*Not* falling to pieces. That's right. Go on.'

' "Then add the cream and cook five minutes longer," ' read Ashe.

'Is that all?'

'That's all of that one.'

Mr. Peters settled himself more comfortable in bed.

'Read me the piece where it says about Curried Lobster.'

Ashe cleared his throat.

' "Curried Lobster," ' he read. ' "Materials: Two two-pound lobsters, two teaspoonfuls lemon juice, half teaspoonful curry powder, two tablespoonfuls butter, one tablespoonful flour, one cup scalded milk, one cup cracker crumbs, half teaspoonful salt, quarter teaspoonful pepper."'

'Go on.'

' "Way of Preparing: Cream the butter and flour and add the scalded milk, then add the lemon juice, curry powder, salt and pepper. Remove the lobster meat from the shells and cut into half-inch cubes." '

' "Half-inch cubes," ' sighed Mr. Peters wistfully. 'Yes?'

' "Add the latter to the sauce." '

'You didn't say anything about the latter. Oh, I see, it means the half-inch cubes. Yes?'

' "Refill the lobster shells, cover with buttered crumbs, and bake until the crumbs are brown. This will serve six persons." '

'And make them feel an hour afterwards as if they had swallowed a live wild-cat,' said Mr. Peters ruefully.

'Not necessarily,' said Ashe. 'I could eat two portions of that at this very minute and go off to bed and sleep like a little child.'

Mr. Peters raised himself on his elbow, and stared at him. They were in the millionaire's bedroom, the time being one in the morning, and Mr. Peters had expressed a wish that Ashe would read him to sleep. He had voted against Ashe's novel and produced from the recesses of his suit-case a much-thumbed cookery-book. He explained that since his digestive misfortune had come upon him, he had derived a certain solace from its perusal. It may be that to some men a sorrow's crown of sorrow is remembering happier things, but Mr. Peters had not found that to be the case. In his hour of affliction it soothed him to read of Hungarian Goulash and Escalloped Brains and to remember that he, too, the nut-and-grass eater of today, had once dwelt in Arcadia.

The passage of the days, which had so sapped the stamina of the Efficient Baxter, had had the opposite effect on Mr. Peters. His was one of those natures which cannot deal in half-measures. Whatever he did he did with the same driving energy. After the first passionate burst of resistance, he had settled down into a model pupil in Ashe's one-man school of physical culture. It had been the same, now that he came to look back on it, at Muldoon's. Now that he remembered, he had come away from White Plains, hoping indeed never to see the place again, but undeniably a different man physically. It is not the habit of Professor Muldoon to let his patients loaf, but Mr. Peters, after the initial plunge, had needed no driving. He had worked hard at his cure then, because it was the job in

139

hand. He worked hard now, under Ashe's guidance, because, once he had begun, the thing interested and gripped him. Ashe, who had expected continued reluctance, had been astonished and delighted at the way in which the millionaire had behaved. Nature had really intended Ashe for a trainer. He identified himself so thoroughly with his man and rejoiced at the least signs of improvement.

In Mr. Peters' case there had been distinct improvement already. Miracles do not happen nowadays, and it was too much to expect one who had maltreated his body so consistently for so many years to become whole in a day, but to an optimist like Ashe signs were not wanting that in due season Mr. Peters would rise on stepping-stones of his dead self to higher things, and while never soaring into the class which devours curried lobster and smiles after it, might yet prove himself a devil of a fellow among the mutton cutlets.

'You're a wonder,' said Mr. Peters. 'You're sassy and you have no respect for your elders and betters, but you deliver the goods. That's the point. Why, I'm beginning to feel great. Say, do you know, I felt a new muscle in the small of my back this morning! They are coming out on me like a rash.'

'That's the Larsen exercises. They develop the whole body.'

'Well, you're a pretty good advertisement for them, if they need one. What were you before you came to me—a prize-fighter?'

'That's the question everybody I have met since I arrived here has asked me. I believe it made the butler think I was some sort of a crook when I couldn't answer it. I used to write stories, detective stories.'

'What you ought to be doing is running a place over here in England like Muldoon has back home. But you will be able to write one more story out of this business here, if you want to. When are you going to have another try for my scarab?'

'Tonight.'

'Tonight? How about Baxter?'

'I shall have to risk Baxter.'

Mr. Peters hesitated. He had fallen out of the habit of being magnanimous during the past few years, for dyspepsia brooks no divided allegiance and magnanimity has to take a back seat when it has its grip on a man.

'See here,' he said awkwardly, 'I've been thinking it over lately, and what's the use? It's a queer thing, and if anybody had told me a week ago that I should be saying it I wouldn't

140

have believed them, but I am beginning to like you. I don't want to get you into trouble. Let the old scarab go. What's a scarab anyway? Forget about it, and stick on here as my private Muldoon. If it's the money that's worrying you, forget that too. I'll give it you as your fee.'

Ashe was astounded. That it could really be his peppery employer who spoke was almost unbelievable. Ashe's was a friendly nature, and he could never be long associated with anyone without trying to establish pleasant relations, but he had resigned himself in the present case to perpetual warfare.

He was touched, and if he had ever contemplated abandoning his venture, this, he felt, would have spurred him on to see it through. This sudden revelation of the human in Mr. Peters was like a trumpet-call.

'I wouldn't think of it,' he said. 'It's great of you to suggest such a thing, but I know just how you feel about the thing, and I'm going to get it for you if I have to wring Baxter's neck. Probably Baxter will have given up waiting as a bad job by now, if he has been watching all this while. We've given him ten nights to cool off. I expect he is in bed, dreaming pleasant dreams. It's nearly two o'clock. I'll wait another ten minutes and then go down.'

He picked up the cookery book.

'Lie back, and make yourself comfortable, and I'll read you to sleep first.'

'You're a good boy,' said Mr. Peters drowsily.

'Are you ready? "Pork Tenderloin Larded. Half pound fat pork." '

A faint smile curved Mr. Peters' lips. His eyes were closed and he breathed softly. Ashe went on in a low voice.

' "Four large pork tenderloins, one cup cracker crumbs, one cup boiling water, two tablespoonfuls butter, one teaspoonful salt, half teaspoonful pepper, one teaspoonful poultry seasoning." '

A little sigh came from the bed.

' "Way of Preparing: Wipe the tenderloins with a damp cloth. With a sharp knife make a deep pocket lengthwise in each tenderloin. Cut your pork into long thin strips, and with a needle lard each tenderloin. Melt the butter in the water, add the seasoning and the cracker crumbs, combining all thoroughly. Now fill each pocket in the tenderloin with this stuffing, place the tenderloins——" '

A snore sounded from the pillows, punctuating the recital

141

like a mark of exclamation. Ashe laid down the book and peered into the darkness beyond the rays of the bed-lamp. His employer slept.

Ashe switched off the light and crept to the door. Out in the passage he stopped and listened. All was still.

He stole downstairs.

II

George Emerson sat in his bedroom smoking a cigarette. A light of resolution was in his eyes. He glanced at the table beside his bed and at what was on that table, and the light of resolution flamed into a glare of fanatic determination. So might a mediaeval knight have looked on the eve of setting forth to rescue a maiden from a dragon.

His cigarette burned down. He looked at his watch, put it back, and lit another cigarette. His aspect was the aspect of one waiting for the appointed hour.

Smoking his second cigarette, he resumed his meditations. They had to do with Aline Peters.

George Emerson was troubled about Aline Peters. Watching over her as he did with a lover's eye, he had perceived that about her which distressed him. On the terrace that morning she had been abrupt to him—what, in a girl of a less angelic disposition, one might have called snappy. Yes, to be just, she had snapped at him. That meant something. It meant that Aline was not well. It meant what her pallor and tired eyes meant that the life she was leading was doing her no good.

Eleven nights had George dined at Blandings Castle, and on each of the eleven nights he had been distressed to see the manner in which Aline, declining the baked meats, had restricted herself to the miserable vegetable messes which were all that doctor's orders permitted to her suffering father. George's pity had its limits. His heart did not bleed for Mr. Peters. Mr. Peters' diet was his own affair. But that Aline should starve herself in this fashion, purely by way of moral support of her parent, was another matter.

George was perhaps a shade material. Himself a robust young man and taking what might be called an out-size in meals, he attached perhaps too much importance to food as an adjunct to the perfect life. In his survey of Aline, he took a line through his own requirements, and, believing that eleven such dinners as he had seen Aline partake of would have killed

142

him, he decided that his loved one was on the point of starvation. No human being, he held, could exist on such Barmecide feasts. That Mr. Peters continued to do so did not occur to him as a flaw in his reasoning. He looked on Mr. Peters as a sort of machine. Successful business men often give that impression to the young. If George had been told that Mr. Peters went along on petrol like a motor-car, he would not have been much surprised. But that Aline, his Aline, should have to deny herself the exercise of that mastication of rich meats which, together with the gift of speech, raises Man above the beasts of the field! That was what tortured George.

He had devoted the day to thinking out a solution of the problem. Such was the overflowing goodness of Aline's heart that not even he could persuade her to withdraw her moral support from her father and devote herself to the keeping up of her strength as she should do. It was necessary to think of some other plan.

And then a speech of hers had come back to him.

She had said—poor child!—'I do get a little hungry sometimes. Late at night, generally.'

The problem was solved. Food should be brought to her late at night.

On the table by his bed was a stout sheet of packing-paper. On this lay, like one of those pictures in still-life which one sees on suburban parlour-walls, a tongue, some bread, a knife, a fork, salt, a corkscrew, and a small bottle of white wine.

It is a pleasure, when one has been able hitherto to portray George's devotion only through the medium of his speeches, to produce these comestibles as Exhibit A to show that he loved Aline with no common love. For it had not been an easy task to get them there. In a house of smaller dimensions he would have raided the larder without shame, but at Blandings Castle there was no saying where the larder might be. All he knew was that it lay somewhere beyond that green-baize door opening on the Hall, past which he was wont to go on his way to bed. To prowl through the maze of the servants' quarters in search of it was impossible. The only thing to be done was to go to Market Blandings and buy the things.

Fortune had helped him at the start by arranging that the Hon. Freddie also should be going into Market Blandings in the little runabout which seated two. He had acquiesced in George's suggestion that he, George, should occupy the other seat, but with a certain lack, it seemed to George, of enthusiasm. He had not volunteered any reason why he was going to Market Blandings in the little runabout, and on arrival there had betrayed an unmistakable desire to get rid of George at the earliest opportunity. As this had suited George to perfection, he being desirous of getting rid of the Hon. Freddie at the earliest opportunity, he had not been inquisitive, and they had parted at the outskirts of the town without mutual confidences. George had then proceeded to the grocer's, and after that to another of the Market Blandings inns, not the Emsworth Arms, where he had bought the white wine. He did not believe in the white wine, for he was a young man with a palate and mistrusted country cellars, but he assumed that, whatever its quality, it would cheer Aline in the small hours.

He had then tramped the whole five miles back to the Castle with his purchases.

It was here that his real troubles began, and the quality of his love was wasted. The walk, to a heavily-laden man, was bad enough, but as nothing compared with the ordeal of smuggling the cargo up to his bedroom. Superman as he was, George was alive to the delicacy of the situation. One cannot convey food and drink to one's room at a strange house without, if detected, seeming to cast a slur on the table of the host. It was as one who carries despatches through an enemy's lines that George took cover, emerged from cover, dodged, ducked, and ran; and the moment when he sank down on his bed, the door locked behind him, was one of the happiest of his life.

The recollection of that ordeal made the one he proposed to embark on now seem light in comparison. All he had to do was to go to Aline's room, knock softly on the door till signs of wakefulness made themselves heard from within, and then dart away into the shadows whence he had come, and so back to bed. He gave Aline credit for the intelligence which would enable her on finding a tongue, some bread, a knife, a fork, salt, a corkscrew, and a bottle of white wine on the mat, to know what to do with them and, perhaps to guess whose was the loving hand which had laid them there.

The second clause, however, was not important, for he proposed to tell her whose was the hand next morning. Other people might hide their light under a bushel, not George Emerson.

It only remained now to allow time to pass until the hour should be sufficiently advanced to ensure safety for the expedition. He looked at his watch again. It was nearly two. By this time the house must be asleep.

He gathered up the tongue, the bread, the knife, the fork, the salt, the corkscrew, and the bottle of white wine, and left the room.

All was still. He stole downstairs.

III

On his chair on the gallery that ran round the Hall, swathed in an overcoat and wearing rubber-soled shoes, the Efficient Baxter sat and gazed into the darkness. He had lost the first fine careless rapture, as it were, which had helped him to endure these vigils, and a great weariness was upon him. He found a difficulty in keeping his eyes open, and when they were open the darkness seemed to press upon them painfully. Take him for all in all, the Efficient Baxter had had about enough of it.

Time stood still.

Baxter's thoughts began to wander. He knew that this was fatal, and exerted himself to drag them back. He tried to concentrate his mind on one definite thing. He selected the scarab as a suitable object, but it played him false. He had hardly concentrated on the scarab before his mind was straying off to ancient Egypt, to Mr. Peters' dyspepsia, and on a dozen other branch lines of thought.

He blamed the fat man at the inn for this. If the fat man had not thrust his presence and conversation upon him, he would have been able to enjoy a sound sleep in the afternoon, and would have come fresh to his nocturnal task. He began to muse upon the fat man.

And, by a curious coincidence, whom should he meet a few moments later but this same man.

It happened in a somewhat singular manner, though it all seemed perfectly logical and consecutive to Baxter. He was climbing up the outer wall of Westminster Abbey in his pyjamas and a tall hat, when the fat man, suddenly thrusting his head out of a window which Baxter had not noticed till that moment, said, 'Hallo, Freddie!' Baxter was about to explain that his name was not Freddie, when he found himself walking down Piccadilly with Ashe Marson. Ashe said to him, 'Nobody loves me!' and the pathos of it cut the Efficient Baxter like a knife. He was on the point of replying, but Ashe

145

vanished and Baxter discovered that he was not in Piccadilly, as he had supposed, but in an aeroplane with Mr. Peters, hovering over the Castle. Mr. Peters had a bomb in his hand, which he was fondling with loving care. He explained to Baxter that he had stolen it from the Earl of Emsworth's museum. 'I did it with a slice of cold beef and a pickle,' he explained, and Baxter found himself realizing that that was the only way.

'Now watch me drop it,' said Mr. Peters, closing one eye and taking aim at the Castle. 'I have to do this by the doctor's orders.' He loosed the bomb, and immediately Baxter was in bed watching it drop. He was frightened, but the idea of moving did not occur to him. The bomb fell slowly, dipping and fluttering like a feather. It came closer and closer. Then it struck with a roar and a sheet of flame. . . .

Baxter awoke to a sound of tumult and crashing. For a moment he hovered between dreaming and waking, and then sleep passed from him, and he was aware that something noisy and exciting was in progress in the Hall below.

IV

Coming down to first causes, the only reason why collisions of any kind occur is because two bodies defy Nature's law that a given spot on a given plane shall at a given moment of time be occupied by only one body. There was a certain spot near the foot of the great staircase which Ashe, coming downstairs, and George Emerson coming up, had to pass on their respective routes. George reached it at one minute and three seconds after 2 a.m., moving silently but swiftly, and Ashe, also maintaining a good rate of speed, arrived there at one minute and four seconds after the hour, when he ceased to walk and began to fly, accompanied by George Emerson, now going down. His arms were round George's neck, and George was clinging to his waist. In due season they reached the foot of the stairs and a small table covered with occasional china and photographs in frames which lay adjacent to the foot of the stairs.

That, especially the occasional china, was what Baxter had heard.

George Emerson thought it was a burglar. Ashe did not know what it was, but he knew he wanted to shake it off, so he insinuated a hand beneath George's chin and pushed upwards. George, by this time parted for ever from the tongue, the bread, the knife, the fork, the salt, the corkscrew, and the bottle of white wine, and having both hands free for the work of the moment, held Ashe with the left and punched him in the ribs with the right. Ashe, removing his left arm from George's neck, brought it up as a reinforcement to his right, and used both as a means of throttling George. This led George, now permanently underneath, to grasp Ashe's ears firmly and twist them, relieving the pressure on his throat and causing Ashe to utter the first vocal sound of the evening, other than the explosive *'Ugh'* which both had emitted at the instant of impact. Ashe dislodged George's hands from his ears, and hit George in the ribs with his elbow. George kicked Ashe on the left ankle. Ashe rediscovered George's throat and began to squeeze it afresh, and a pleasant time was being had by all, when the Efficient Baxter, whizzing down the stairs, tripped over Ashe's legs, shot forward, and cannoned into another table, also covered with occasional china and photographs in frames. The hall at Blandings Castle was more an extra drawing-room than a hall, and, when not nursing a sick headache in her bedroom, Lady Ann Warblington would dispense afternoon tea there to her guests. Consequently it was dotted pretty freely with small tables. There were indeed, no fewer than five or more in various spots waiting to be bumped into and smashed.

But the bumping into and smashing of small tables is a task that calls for plenty of time, a leisured pursuit, and neither George nor Ashe, a third party having been added to their little affair, felt a desire to stay on and do the thing properly. Ashe was strongly opposed to being discovered and called upon to account for his presence there at that hour, and George, conscious of the tongue and its adjuncts now strewn about the hall, had a similar prejudice against the tedious explanations which detection must involve. As if by mutual consent each relaxed his grip. They stood panting for an instant, then, Ashe in the direction where he supposed the green-baize door of the servant's quarters to be, George to the staircase which led to his bedroom, they went away from that place.

They had hardly done so, when Baxter, having dissociated himself from the contents of the table which he had upset, began to grope his way towards the electric light switch, the same being situated near the foot of the main staircase. He went on all fours, as a safer method of locomotion, if slower, than the one which he had attempted before.

Noises began to make themselves heard on the floors above.

Roused by the merry crackle of occasional china, the house-party was bestirring itself to investigate. Voices sounded, muffled and inquiring.

Baxter, meanwhile crawled steadily on his hands and knees towards the light switch. He was in much the same condition as one White Hope of the ring is after he has put his chin in the way of the fist of a rival member of the Truck-driver's Union. He knew that he was still alive. More he could not say. The mists of sleep which still shrouded his brain and the shaking-up he had had from his encounter with the table, a corner of which he had rammed with the top of his head, combined to produce a dream-like state.

And so the Efficient Baxter crawled on, and as he crawled his hand, advancing cautiously, fell on a Something—a some-thing that was not alive, something clammy and icy-cold, the touch of which filled him with a nameless horror.

To say that Baxter's heart stood still would be medically inexact. The heart does not stand still. Whatever the emotions of its owner, it goes on beating. It would be more accurate to say that Baxter felt like a man taking his first ride in an ex-press elevator who has outstripped his vital organs by several floors and sees no immediate prospect of their ever catching up with him again. There was a great cold void where the more intimate parts of his body should have been. His throat was dry and contracted. The flesh of his back crawled. For he knew what it was that he had touched.

Painful and absorbing as had been his encounter with the table, Baxter had never lost sight of the fact that close beside him a furious battle between unseen forces was in progress. He had heard the bumping and the thumping and the tense breath-ing even as he picked occasional china from his person. Such a combat, he had felt, could hardly fail to result in personal injury to either the party of the first part or the party of the second part, or both. He knew now that worse than mere in-jury had happened, and that he knelt in the presence of death.

There was no doubt that the man was dead. Insensibility alone could never have produced this icy chill.

He raised his head in the darkness, and cried aloud, to those approaching.

He meant to cry, 'Help! Murder!' but fear prevented clear articulation.

What he shouted was, 'Heh! Mer!'

Upon which from the neighbourhood of the staircase, someone began to fire off a revolver.

The Earl of Emsworth had been sleeping a sound and peaceful sleep when the imbroglio began downstairs. He sat up and listened. Yes, undoubtedly burglars. He switched on his light and jumped out of bed. He took a pistol from the drawer, and thus armed, went to look into the matter. The dreamy peer was no poltroon.

It was quite dark when he arrived on the scene of conflict in the van of a mixed bevy of pyjamaed and dressing-gowned relations. He was in the van because meeting those relations in the passage above, he had said to them, 'Let me go first. I have a pistol.' And they had let him go first. They were, indeed, awfully nice about it, not thrusting themselves forward or jostling or anything, but behaving in a modest and self-effacing manner which was pretty to watch. When Lord Emsworth said, 'Let me go first,' young Algernon Wooster, who was on the very point of leaping to the fore, said, 'Yes, by Jove, sound scheme, by Gad!' and withdrew into the background, and the Bishop of Godalming said, 'By all means Clarence, undoubtedly, most certainly precede us.'

When his sense of touch told him that he had reached the foot of the stairs, Lord Emsworth paused. The Hall was very dark, and the burglars seemed temporarily to have suspended activities. And then one of them, a man with a ruffianly grating voice, spoke. What it was he said, Lord Emsworth could not understand. It sounded like 'Heh! Mer!' Probably some secret signal to his confederate. Lord Emsworth raised his revolver and emptied it in the direction of the sound.

Extremely fortunate for him, the Efficient Baxter had not changed his all-fours attitude. This undoubtedly saved Lord Emsworth the worry of engaging a new secretary. The shots sang above Baxter's head, one after the other, six in all, and found themselves billets other than his person. They disposed themselves as follows. The first shot broke a window and whistled out into the night. The second shot hit the dinner-gong and made a perfectly extraordinary noise like the Last Trump. The third, fourth, and fifth shots embedded themselves in the wall. The sixth and final shot hit a life-size picture of his lordship's maternal grandmother in the face and improved it out of all knowledge. One thinks no worse of Lord Emsworth's maternal grandmother because she looked like George Robey, and had allowed herself to be painted, after the heavy Classical manner of some of the portraits of a hundred years ago, in the character of Venus (suitably draped, of course) rising from the sea; but it was beyond the possibility of denial that her grandson's bullet permanently removed one of Blandings Castle's most prominent eyesores.

Having emptied his revolver, Lord Emsworth said, 'Who is there! Speak?' in rather an aggrieved tone, as if he felt he had done his part in breaking the ice and it was now for the intruder to exert himself and bear his share of the social amenities.

The Efficient Baxter did not reply. Nothing in the world would have induced him to speak at that moment or to make any sound whatsoever that might betray his position to a dangerous maniac who might at any instant reload his pistol and resume the fusillade. Explanations, in his opinion, could be deferred till somebody had the presence of mind to switch on the lights. He flattened himself on the carpet, and hoped for better things. His cheek touched the corpse beside him, but, though he winced and shuddered, he made no outcry. After those six shots he was through with outcries.

A voice from above—the Bishop's voice—said, 'I think you have killed him, Clarence.'

Another voice—that of Colonel Horace Mant said, 'Switch on those dashed lights, why doesn't someone dash it?'

The whole strength of the company began to demand light.

When the lights came it was from the other side of the Hall. Six revolver shots, fired at a quarter-past two in the morning, will rouse even sleeping domestics. The servants' quarters were buzzing like a hive. Shrill feminine screams were puncturing the air. Mr. Beach, the butler, in a suit of pink silk pyjamas of which no one would have suspected him, was leading a party of men-servants down the stairs, not so much because he wanted to lead them as because they pushed him. The passage beyond the green-baize door became congested, and there were cries for Mr. Beach to open it, and look through and see what was the matter, but Mr. Beach was smarter than that, and wriggled back so that he no longer headed the procession.

This done, he shouted. 'Open the door there, open that door. Look and see what the matter is.'

Ashe opened the door. Since his escape from the Hall he had been lurking in the neighbourhood of the green-baize, and had been engulfed by the swirling throng. Finding himself with elbow-room for the first time, he pushed through, swung the door open, and switched on the lights.

150

They shone on a collection of semi-dressed figures, crowding the staircase, on a hall littered with china and glass, on a dented dinner-gong, on an edited and improved portrait of the late Countess of Emsworth and on the Efficient Baxter, in an overcoat and rubber-soled shoes, lying beside a cold tongue.

At no great distance lay a number of other objects—a knife, a fork, some bread, salt, a corkscrew, and a bottle of white wine.

Using the word in the sense of saying something coherent, the Earl of Emsworth was the first to speak. He peered down at his recumbent secretary and said, 'Baxter! My dear fellow, what the devil?'

The feeling of the company was one of profound disappointment. They were disgusted at the anti-climax. For an instant, when the Efficient one did not move, hope began to stir, but as soon as it was seen that he was not even injured, gloom reigned. One of two things would have satisfied them—either a burglar or a corpse. A burglar would have been welcome, dead or alive, but if Baxter proposed to fill the part adequately, it was imperative that he be dead. He had disappointed them deeply by turning out to be the object of their quest. That he should not have been even grazed was too much.

There was a cold silence as he slowly raised himself from the floor.

As his eyes fell on the tongue, he started, and remained gazing fixedly at it. Surprise paralysed him.

Lord Emsworth was also looking at the tongue, and he leaped to a not unreasonable conclusion. He spoke coldly and haughtily, for he was not only annoyed like the others at the anti-climax, but offended. He knew that he was not one of your energetic hosts who exert themselves unceasingly to supply their guests with entertainment, but there was one thing on which, as a host, he did pride himself. In the material matters of life he did his guests well. He kept an admirable table.

'My dear Baxter,' he said in the tones which usually he reserved for the correction of his son Freddie, 'if your hunger is so great that you are unable to wait for breakfast and have to raid my larder in the middle of the night, I wish to goodness you would contrive to make less noise about it. I do not grudge you the food—help yourself when you please—but do remember that people who have not such keen appetites as yourself, like to sleep during the night. A far better plan, my dear fellow, would be to have sandwiches—or buns—whatever you consider most sustaining sent up to your bedroom.'

Not even the bullets had disordered Baxter's faculties so much as this monstrous accusation. Explanations pushed and jostled one another in his fermenting brain, but he could not utter them. On every side he met gravely reproachful eyes. George Emerson was looking at him in pained disgust. Ashe Marson's face was the face of one who could never have believed this had he not seen it with his own eyes. The scrutiny of the knife-and-shoe boy was unendurable.

He stammered. Words began to proceed from him, tripping and stumbling over each other.

Lord Emsworth's frigid disapproval did not relax.

'Pray do not apologize, Baxter. The desire for food is human. It is your boisterous mode of securing and conveying it that I deprecate. Let us all go to bed.'

'But, Lord Emsworth——!'

'To bed,' repeated his lordship firmly.

The company began to stream moodily upstairs. The lights were switched off. The Efficient Baxter dragged himself away.

From the darkness in the direction of the servant's door a voice spoke.

'Greedy pig!' said the voice scornfully.

It sounded like the fresh young voice of the knife-and-shoe boy, but Baxter was too broken to investigate. He continued his retreat without pausing.

'Stuffin' of 'isself at all hours!' said the voice.

There was a murmur of approval from the unseen throng of domestics.

CHAPTER NINE

I

As we grow older and realize more clearly the limitations of human happiness, we come to see that the only real and abiding pleasure in life is to give pleasure to other people. One must assume that the Efficient Baxter had not reached the age when this comes home to a man, for the fact that he had given genuine pleasure to some dozens of his fellow-men brought him no balm.

There was no doubt about the pleasure which he had given. Once they had got over their disappointment at finding that he was not a dead burglar, the house-party rejoiced wholeheartedly at the break in the monotony of life at Blandings Castle. Relations who had not been on speaking terms for years forgot their quarrels, and strolled about the grounds in perfect harmony, abusing Baxter. The general verdict was that he was insane.

'Don't tell me that young fellow's all there,' said Colonel Horace Mant, 'because I know better. Have you noticed his eye? Furtive? Shifty! Nasty gleam in it. Besides, dash it, did you happen to take a look at the Hall last night after he had been there? It was in ruins, my dear sir, absolute dashed ruins. It was positively littered with broken china and tables which had been bowled over. Don't tell me that was just an accidental collision in the dark. My dear sir, the man must have been thrashing about, absolutely *thrashing* about, like a dashed salmon on a dashed hook. He must have had a paroxysm of some kind. Some kind of a dashed fit. A doctor could give you the name for it. It's a well-known form of insanity. Paranoia— isn't that what they call it? Rush of blood to the head, followed by a general running amuck. I've heard fellows who have been in India talk of it. Natives get it. Don't know what they're doing, and charge through the streets taking cracks at people with dashed whacking great knives. Same with this young man, probably in a modified form at present. He ought to be in a Home. One of these nights, if the thing grows on him, he will be massacring Emsworth in his bed.'

'My dear Horace!'

The Bishop of Godalming's voice was properly horror-stricken, but there was a certain unctuous relish in it.

'Take my word for it. Though, mind you, I don't say they aren't well suited. Every one knows that Emsworth has been to all practical intents and purposes a dashed lunatic for years.'

'My dear Horace! Your father-in-law. The head of the family.'

'A dashèd lunatic, my dear sir, head of the family or no head of the family. A man as absent-minded as he is has no right to call himself sane.'

The Efficient Baxter, who had just left his presence, was feeling much the same about his noble employer. After a sleepless night he had begun at an early hour to try and corner Lord

153

Emsworth in order to explain to him the true inwardness of last night's happenings. Eventually he had tracked him to the museum where he had found him happily engaged in painting a cabinet of birds' eggs. He was seated on a small stool, a large pot of red paint on the floor beside him dabbing at the cabinet with a dripping brush. He was absorbed, and made no attempt whatever to follow his secretary's remarks.

For ten minutes Baxter gave a vivid picture of his vigil and the manner in which it had been interrupted.

'Just so, just so, my dear fellow,' said the earl, when he had finished. 'I quite understand. All I say is, if you do require additional food in the night, let one of the servants bring it to your room, before bed-time, then there will be no danger of these disturbances. There is no possible objection to your eating a hundred meals a day, my good Baxter, provided you do not rouse the whole house over them. Some of us like to sleep during the night.'

'But Lord Emsworth! I have just explained ... It was not ... I was not...!'

'Never mind, my dear fellow, never mind. Why take such an important thing of it? Many people like a light snack before actually retiring. Doctors, I believe, sometimes recommend it. Tell me, Baxter, how do you think the museum looks now? A little brighter? Better for the dash of colour? I think so. Museums are generally such gloomy places.'

'Lord Emsworth, may I explain once again?'

The earl looked annoyed.

'My dear Baxter, I have told you that there is nothing to explain. You are getting a little tedious.... What a deep, rich red this is, and how clean new paint smells! Do you know, Baxter, I have been longing to mess about with paint ever since I was a boy. I recollect my old father beating me with a walking-stick. That would be before your time, of course. By the way, if you see Freddie, will you tell him I want to speak to him? He is probably in the smoking-room. Send him to me here.'

It was an overwrought Baxter, who delivered the message to the Hon. Freddie, who, as predicted, was in the smoking-room, lounging in a deep armchair.

There are times when Life presses hard upon a man, and it pressed hard on Baxter now. Fate had played him a sorry trick. It had put him in a position where he had to choose between two courses, each as disagreeable as the other. He must

154

either face a possible fiasco like that of last night, or else he must abandon his post and cease to mount guard over his threatened treasure.

His imagination quailed at the thought of a repetition of last night's horrors. He had been badly shaken by his collision with the table and even more so by the events which had followed it. Those revolver shots still rang in his ears.

It was probably the memory of those shots which turned the scale. It was unlikely that he would again become entangled with a man bearing a tongue and the other things—he had given up in despair the attempt to unravel the mystery of the tongue; it completely baffled him; but it was by no means unlikely that, if he spent another night in the gallery looking on the Hall he might again become a target for Lord Emsworth's irresponsible fire-arm. Nothing, in fact, was more likely, for in the disturbed state of the public mind the slightest sound after nightfall would be sufficient cause for a fusillade. He had actually overheard young Algernon Wooster telling Lord Stockheath that he had a jolly good mind to sit upon the stairs that night with a shot-gun, because it was his opinion that there was a jolly sight more in this business than there seemed to be, and that what he thought of the bally affair was that there was a gang of some kind at work and that that feller, what's-his-name, that feller Baxter, was some sort of an accomplice.

With these things in his mind, Baxter decided to remain that night in the security of his bedroom. He had lost his nerve.

He formed this decision with the utmost reluctance, for the thought of leaving the road to the museum clear for marauders was bitter in the extreme.

If he could have overheard a conversation between, Joan Valentine and Ashe Marson, it is probable that he would have risked Lord Emsworth's revolver and the shot-gun of the Honourable Algernon Wooster

Ashe, when he met Joan and recounted the events of the past night, at which Joan, who was a sound sleeper, had not been present, was inclined to blame himself as a failure. True, fate had been against him but the fact remained that he had achieved nothing.

Joan, however, was not of this opinion.

'You have done wonders,' she said 'You have cleared the way for me. That is my idea of real team-work. I'm so glad now that we formed our partnership. It would have been too bad if

155

I had got all the advantage of your work and had jumped in and deprived you of the reward. As it is, I shall go down and finish the thing off tonight with a clear conscience.'

'You can't mean that you dream of going down to the museum tonight?'

'Of course I do.'

'But it's madness.'

'On the contrary, tonight is the one night when there ought to be no risk at all.'

'After what happened last night?'

'Because of what happened last night. Do you imagine that Mr. Baxter will dare to stir from his bed after that? If ever there was a chance of getting this thing finished, it will be tonight.'

'You're quite right. I never looked at it in that way. Baxter wouldn't risk a second disaster. I'll certainly make a success of it this time.'

Joan raised her eyebrows.

'I don't quite understand you, Mr. Marson. Do you propose to try and get the scarab again tonight?'

'Yes. It will be as easy as——'

'Are you forgetting that, by the terms of our agreement, it is my turn?'

'You surely don't intend to hold me to that?'

'Certainly I do.'

'But good heavens, consider my position! Do you seriously expect me to lie in bed while you do all the work, and then to take a half share in the reward?'

'I do.'

'It's ridiculous.'

'It's no more ridiculous than that I should do the same. Mr. Marson, it's no use our going over all this again. We settled it long ago.'

And she refused to discuss the matter further, leaving Ashe in a condition of anxious misery comparable only to that which, as night began to draw near, gnawed the vitals of the Efficient Baxter.

II

Breakfast at Blandings Castle was an informal meal. There was food and drink in the long dining-hall for such as were energetic enough to come down and get it, but the majority of the house-party breakfasted in their rooms, Lord Emsworth, whom nothing in the world would have induced to begin the day in the company of a crowd of his relations, most of whom he disliked, setting them the example.

When, therefore, Baxter yielding to Nature after having remained awake till the early morning, fell asleep at nine o'clock, nobody came to rouse him. He did not ring his bell, so he was not disturbed, and he slept on until half past eleven, by which time, it being Sunday morning and the house party including one bishop and several of the minor clergy, most of the occupants of the place had gone off to church.

Baxter shaved and dressed hastily, for he was in a state of nervous apprehension. He blamed himself for having laid in bed so long. When every minute he was away might mean the loss of the scarab, he had passed several hours in dreamy sloth.

He had woken with a presentiment. Something told him that the scarab had been stolen in the night, and he wished now that he had risked all and kept guard.

The house was very quiet as he made his way rapidly to the Hall. As he passed a window, he perceived Lord Emsworth, in an un-Sabbatarian suit of tweeds and bearing a gardening-fork which must have pained the Bishop, bending earnestly over a flower-bed; but he was the only occupant of the grounds, and indoors there was a feeling of emptiness. The Hall had that Sunday morning air of wanting to be left to itself and disapproving of the entry of anything human till lunch time, which can only be felt by a guest in a large house who remains at home when his fellows have gone to church.

The portraits on the walls, especially the one of the late Countess of Emsworth in the character of Venus rising from the sea, stared at Baxter, as he entered, with cold reproof. The very chairs seemed distant and unfriendly. But Baxter was in no mood to appreciate their attitude. His conscience slept. His mind was occupied to the exclusion of all other things, by the scarab and its probable fate. How disastrously remiss it had been of him not to keep guard last night! Long before he opened the museum door he was feeling the absolute certainty that the worst had happened.

His premonition was correct. The museum was still there; the card announcing that here was a scarab of the reign of Cheops of the Fourth Dynasty, presented by Mr. J. Preston Peters, was still there; the mummies, birds' eggs, tapestry, mis-

157

sals, and all the rest of Lord Emsworth's treasures were still there.

But the Scarab was gone.

For all that this was precisely what he had expected, it was an appreciable time before the Efficient Baxter rallied from the blow. He stood transfixed, goggling at the empty place.

He was still goggling when the Earl of Emsworth pottered in. The Earl of Emsworth was one of the world's leading potterers, and Sunday morning was his favourite time for pottering. Since breakfast he had pottered about the garden, pottered round the stables, and pottered about the library. He now pottered into the museum.

'Lord Emsworth!'

By the time Baxter sighted him and gave tongue, the earl had pottered to within a foot or so of where the secretary stood. A whisper would have reached him, but such was the Efficient Baxter's emotion that he emitted the words in a sharp roar which would have been noticeably stentorian in a sea-captain exchanging remarks with one of his men who happened at the moment to be working in the crow's-nest. Lord Emsworth sprang six feet, and, having disentangled himself from a piece of old tapestry, put one hand to his ear and, massaging it tenderly, glared at his young assistant.

'What do you mean by barking at me like that, Baxter? Really, you exceed all bounds. You are becoming a perfect pest.'

'Lord Emsworth, it has gone. The scarab has gone.'

'You have broken my ear-drum.'

'Somebody has stolen the scarab which Mr. Peters gave you, Lord Emsworth.'

The probable fate of his ear-drum ceased to grip the earl's undivided attention. He followed the secretary's pointing finger with a startled eye, and examined the spot where the tragedy had occurred.

'Bless my soul. You're perfectly right, my dear fellow. Somebody has stolen the scarab. This is extremely annoying. Mr. Peters may be offended. I should dislike intensely to wound Mr. Peters' feelings. He may think that I ought to have taken more care of it. Now, who in the world could have stolen that scarab?'

Baxter was about to reply, when there came from the direction of the Hall, slightly muffled by the intervening door and passageway, a sound like the delivery of a ton of coal. A heavy body bumped down the stairs, and a voice which both recognized as that of the Hon. Freddie Threepwood uttered an oath that lost itself in a final crash and a musical splintering sound which Baxter for one had no difficulty in diagnosing as the dissolution of occasional china

Neither Lord Emsworth nor Baxter had any difficulty in deducing from the evidence what had happened. The Hon. Freddie had fallen downstairs.

With a little ingenuity this portion of the story of Mr. Peters' scarab could be converted into an excellent tract, driving home the perils, even in this world, of absenting oneself from church on Sunday morning. If the Hon. Freddie had gone to church, he would not have been running down the great staircase of the Castle at this hour; and, if he had not been running down the great staircase of the Castle at that hour, he would not have encountered Muriel.

Muriel was a Persian cat belonging to Lady Ann Warblington. Lady Ann had breakfasted in her room and lain in bed late, as she rather fancied that she had one of her sick headaches coming on. Muriel had left the room in the wake of the breakfast tray, being anxious to be present at the obsequies of a fried sole which had formed Lady Ann's simple meal, and had followed the maid who bore it until she had reached the hall. At this point, the maid, who disliked Muriel, stopped and made a noise like an exploding ginger-beer bottle, at the same time taking a little run in Muriel's direction and kicking at her with a menacing foot. Muriel, wounded and startled, turned in her tracks and sprinted back up the stairs, at the exact moment when the Hon. Freddie, who for some reason was in a great hurry, ran lightly down them.

There was an instant when Freddie could have saved himself at the expense of planting a number ten boot on Muriel's spine, but even in that crisis he bethought him that he hardly stood solid enough with the authorities to risk adding to his misdeeds the slaughter of his aunt's favourite cat, and he executed a rapid swerve. The scared cat proceeded on her journey upstairs, while Freddie, touching the staircase at intervals, went on down.

Having reached the bottom, he sat amidst the occasional china like Marius among the ruins of Carthage, and endeavoured to ascertain the extent of his injuries. He had a

159

growing suspicion that he was irretrievably fractured in a dozen places.

When his father and the Efficient Baxter arrived, they found him being helped to his feet by Ashe Marson.

Ashe had been near at hand when the secretary made the discovery that the museum had been robbed in the night. He had, indeed, anticipated Baxter in that discovery by a matter of minutes. For some little time he had been in waiting behind the green-baize door, hoping for an opportunity of finding whether Joan had carried out her threat of stealing the scarab, and he had contrived to pop in and out of the museum while the Hall was empty. It was not until he heard Baxter's voice raised in anguish that he realized how nearly he had been discovered. He had waited in his place of hiding during the conversation between the secretary and Lord Emsworth, and, like them, had been drawn to the stairs by the noise of Freddie's downfall.

He gave the victim a tentative pull, but Freddie sat down again with a sharp howl. He was still seated when the others arrived. He gazed up at them with silent pathos.

'It was that bally cat of Aunt Ann's, gov'nor. It came legging it up the stairs. I think I've broken my ankle.'

'You certainly have broken everything else,' said his father unsympathetically. 'Between you and Baxter I wonder there's a stick of furniture standing in the house.'

'Thanks, old chap,' said Freddie, gratefully, as Ashe once more assisted him to his feet. 'I wish you would give me a hand up to my room.'

'And, Baxter, my dear fellow,' said Lord Emsworth, 'you might telephone to Doctor Bird in Market Blandings and ask him to be good enough to drive out. I am sorry, Freddie,' he added, 'that you should have met with this accident, but—but—everything is so disturbing nowadays that I feel—I feel most disturbed.'

Ashe and Freddie began to move across the Hall, Freddie hopping, Ashe advancing with a sort of polka-step. Baxter stood looking after them wistfully. The sight of Ashe, coming on top of the discovery of the loss of the scarab, made him feel more clearly than ever that he had been out-manoeuvred. He was quite certain in his mind that Ashe was the thief, and the impossibility of denouncing him made life for the moment very bitter.

There was a sound of wheels outside, and the vanguard of the party, returned from church, entered the house.

'It's all very well to give it out officially that Freddie fell downstairs and sprained his ankle,' said Colonel Mant, discussing the affair with the Bishop of Godalming later in the day, 'but it's my firm belief that that fellow Baxter did precisely as I said he would—ran amuck and inflicted dashed frightful injuries on young Freddie. When I got into the house, there was Freddie being helped up the stairs, while Baxter was looking after him with a sort of evil glare. The whole thing is dashed fishy and mysterious, and the sooner I can get Mildred safely out of the place, the better I shall be pleased. The fellow's as mad as a hatter.'

IV

When Lord Emsworth, sighting Mr. Peters in the group of returned churchgoers, drew him aside and broke the news that the valuable scarab so kindly presented by him to the Castle museum had been stolen in the night by some person unknown, he thought that the millionaire took it exceedingly well. Although the stolen object no longer belonged to him, Mr. Peters no doubt still continued to take an affectionate interest in it, and might have been excused had he shown annoyance that his gift had been so carelessly guarded.

He was, however, thoroughly magnanimous about the matter. He deprecated the notion that the earl could possibly have prevented this unfortunate occurrence. He quite understood. He was not in the least hurt. Nobody could have foreseen such a calamity. These things happened, and one had to accept them. He himself had once suffered in much the same way, the gem of his collection having been removed almost beneath his eyes in the smoothest possible fashion. Altogether, he relieved Lord Emsworth's mind very much; and, when he had finished doing so, he departed swiftly and rang for Ashe.

When Ashe arrived he bubbled over with enthusiasm. He was lyrical in his praise. He went so far as to slap Ashe on the back. It was only when the latter disclaimed all credit for what had occurred that he checked the flow of approbation.

'It wasn't you who got it? Who was it then?'

'It was Miss Peters' maid. It's a long story, but we were working in partnership. I tried for the thing and failed, and she succeeded.'

It was with mixed feelings that Ashe listened while Mr. Peters transferred his adjectives of commendation to Joan. He

161

admired Joan's courage, he was relieved that her venture had ended without disaster, and he knew that she deserved whatever anyone could find to say in praise of her enterprise; but at first, though he tried to crush it down, he could not help feeling a certain amount of chagrin that a girl should have succeeded where he, though having the advantage of first chance, had failed. The terms of his partnership with Joan had jarred on him from the beginning. A man may be in sympathy with the modern movement for the emancipation of Woman, and yet feel aggrieved when a mere girl proves herself a more efficient thief than he. Woman is invading Man's sphere more successfully every day, but there are still certain fields in which Man may consider that he is rightfully entitled to a monopoly, and the purloining of scarabs in the watches of the night is surely one of them. Joan, in Ashe's opinion, should have played a meeker and less active part.

These unworthy emotions did not last long. Whatever his shortcomings, Ashe possessed a just mind. By the time he had found Joan, after Mr. Peters had said his say and dispatched him below stairs for that purpose, he had purged himself of petty regrets and was prepared to congratulate her wholeheartedly. He was, however, resolved that nothing should induce him to share in the reward. On that point, he resolved, he would refuse to be shaken.

'I have just left Mr. Peters,' he began. 'All is well. His cheque-book lies before him on the table, and he is trying to make his fountain-pen work long enough to write a cheque. But there is just one thing I want to say.'

She interrupted him. To his surprise, she was eyeing him coldly and with disapproval.

'And there is just one thing I want to say,' she said. 'And that is that, if you imagine that I shall consent to accept a penny of the reward——'

'Exactly what I was going to say. Of course, I couldn't dream of taking any of it.'

'I don't understand you. You are certainly going to have it all. I told you when we made our agreement that I would only take my share if you let me do my share of the work. Now that you have broken that agreement, nothing would induce me to take it. I know you meant it kindly, Mr. Marson, but I simply can't feel grateful. I told you that ours was a business contract, and that I wouldn't have any chivalry, and I thought that, after you had given me your promise——'

162

'One moment,' said Ashe bewildered. 'I can't follow this. What do you mean?'

'What do I mean? Why, that you went down to the museum last night before me and took the scarab, although you had promised to stay away and give me my chance.'

'But I didn't do anything of the sort.'

It was Joan's turn to look bewildered.

'But you have got the scarab, Mr. Marson?'

'Why, you have got it.'

'No.'

'But—but it has gone.'

'I know. I went down to the museum last night, as we had arranged, and, when I got there, there was no scarab. It had disappeared.'

They looked at each other in consternation. Ashe was the first to speak.

'It was gone when you got to the museum?'

'There wasn't a trace of it. I took it for granted that you had been down before me. I was furious.'

'But this is ridiculous,' said Ashe. 'Who can have taken it? There was nobody beside ourselves who knew that Peters was offering the reward. What exactly happened last night?'

'I waited till one o'clock. Then I slipped down, got into the museum, struck a match, and looked for the scarab. It wasn't there. I couldn't believe it at first. I struck some more matches, quite a number, but it was no good. The scarab had gone, so I went back to bed, and thought hard thoughts about you. It was silly of me. I ought to have known that you would not break your word. But there didn't seem any other solution of the thing's disappearance. Well, somebody must have taken it, and the question is, What are we to do?' She laughed. 'It seems to me that we were a little premature in quarrelling about how we were to divide that reward. It looks as if there wasn't going to be any reward.'

'Meanwhile,' said Ashe gloomily. 'I suppose I have got to go back and tell Peters. I expect it will break his heart.'

163

Blandings Castle dozed in the calm of Sunday afternoon. All was peace. Freddie was in bed, with orders from the doctor to stay there till further notice. Lord Emsworth had returned to his gardening-fork. The rest of the house-party strolled about the grounds or sat in them, for the day was one of those late Spring days which are warm with a premature suggestion of midsummer.

Aline Peters was sitting at the open window of her bedroom, which commanded an extensive view of the terraces. A pile of letters lay on the table beside her. The postman came late to the Castle on Sundays, and she had not been able to read them until lunch was over.

Aline was puzzled. She was conscious of a fit of depression, for which she could in no way account. As a rule something had to go very definitely wrong to make her depressed, for she was not a girl who brooded easily on the vague undercurrent of sadness in Life. As a rule she found nothing tragic in the fact that she was alive. She liked being alive.

But this afternoon she had a feeling that all was not well with the world, which was the more remarkable in that she was usually keenly susceptible to weather conditions and revelled in sunshine like a kitten. Yet here was a day nearly as fine as an American day and she found no solace in it.

She looked down on the terrace, and as she looked the figure of George Emerson appeared, walking swiftly. And at the sight of him something seemed to tell her that she had found the key to her gloom.

There are many kinds of walk. George Emerson's was the walk of mental unrest. His hands were clasped behind his back, his eyes stared straight in front of him from beneath lowering brows, and between his teeth was an unlighted cigar. No man holds an unlighted cigar in his mouth unless unpleasant meditations have caused him to forget that he has it there. Plainly, then, all was not well with George Emerson.

Aline had suspected as much at lunch, and, looking back, she realized that it was at lunch that her depression had begun. The discovery startled her a little. She had not been aware, or she had refused to admit to herself, that George's troubles bulked so large on her horizon. She had always told herself that she liked George, that George was a dear old friend, that George amused and stimulated her; but she would have denied that she was so wrapped up in George that the sight of him in trouble would be enough to spoil for her the finest day she had seen since she left America. There was something not only startling but shocking in the thought, for she was honest enough with herself to recognize that Freddie, her official loved one, might have paced the Castle grounds chewing an unlighted cigar by the hour without stirring any emotion in her at all.

And she was to marry Freddie next month. This was surely a matter that called for thought. She proceeded, gazing down the while to the perambulating George, to give it thought.

Aline's was not a deep nature. She had never pretended to herself that she loved the Hon. Freddie in the sense in which the word is used in books. She liked him, and she liked the idea of being connected with the Peerage, and her father liked the idea, and she liked her father, and the combination of these likings had caused her to reply, 'Yes' when, last Autumn, Freddie, swelling himself out like an embarrassed frog and gulping, had uttered that memorable speech, beginning, 'I say, you know, it's like this, don't you know,' and ending, 'What I mean is, will you marry me, what?' She had looked forward to being placidly happy as the Hon. Mrs. Frederick Threepwood. And then, George Emerson had reappeared in her life, a disturbing element.

Until today she would have resented the suggestion that she was in love with George. She liked to be with him, partly because he was so easy to talk to, and partly because it was exciting to be continually resisting the will-power which he made no secret of trying to exercise.

But today there was a difference. She had suspected it at lunch, and she realized it now. As she looked down at him from behind the curtain and marked his air of gloom, she could no longer disguise it from herself.

She felt maternal, horribly maternal. George was in trouble, and she wanted to comfort him.

Freddie too was in trouble. But did she want to comfort Freddie? No. On the contrary, she was already regretting her promise, so lightly given before lunch, to come and sit with him that afternoon. A well-marked feeling of annoyance that he should have been so silly as to tumble downstairs and sprain

165

his ankle was her chief sentiment respecting Freddie.

George Emerson continued to perambulate, and Aline continued to watch him. At last she could endure it no longer. She gathered up her letters, stacked them in a corner of the dressing-table, and left the room.

George had reached the end of the terrace and turned when she began to descend the stone steps outside the front door. He quickened his pace as he caught sight of her. He halted before her and surveyed her morosely.

'I have been looking for you, he said.

'And here I am. Cheer up, George. Whatever is the matter? I've been sitting in my room looking at you, and you have been simply prowling. What has gone wrong?'

'Everything.'

'How do you mean, everything?'

'Exactly what I say. I'm done for. Read this.'

Aline took the yellow slip of paper.

'A cable,' said George. 'I got it this morning, mailed on from my rooms in London. Read it.'

'I'm trying to. It doesn't seem to make sense.'

George laughed grimly.

'It makes sense all right.'

'I don't see how you can say that. "Meredith elephant kangaroo ..." '

'Official cypher. I was forgetting. "Elephant" means "seriously ill and unable to attend to duty". Meredith is the man who was doing my work while I was on leave.'

'Oh, I'm so sorry. Do you think he is very bad? Are you very fond of Mr. Meredith?'

'Meredith is a good fellow, and I like him, but if it was simply a matter of his being ill I'm afraid I could manage to bear up. Unfortunately "kangaroo" means "return without fail by the next boat".'

'You must return by the next boat?'

Aline looked at him, in her eyes slow-growing comprehension of the situation

'Oh,' she said at length.

'I put it stronger than that,' said George.

'But ... the next boat ... when is that?'

'Wednesday morning. I shall have to leave here tomorrow.'

Aline's eyes were fixed on the blue hills across the valley, but she did not see them. There was a mist between. She was feeling crushed and ill-treated and lonely. It was as if George was

166

already gone and she left alone in an alien land.

'But, George,' she said.

She could find no other words for her protest against the inevitable.

'It's bad luck,' said Emerson quietly. 'But I shouldn't wonder if it is not the best thing really that could have happened. It finishes me cleanly, instead of letting me drag on and make both of us miserable. If this cable hadn't come, I suppose I should have gone on bothering you up to the day of your wedding. I should have fancied to the last moment that there was a chance for me. But this ends me with one punch. Even I haven't the nerve to imagine that I can work a miracle in the few hours before the train leaves tomorrow. I must just make the best of it. If we ever meet again, and I don't see why we should, you will be married. My particular brand of mental suggestion doesn't work at long range. I shan't hope to influence you by telepathy.'

He leaned on the balustrade at her side, and spoke in a low, level voice.

'This thing,' he said, 'coming as a shock, coming out of the blue sky without warning—Meredith is the last man in the world you would expect to crack up; he looked as fit as a dray-horse last time I saw him—somehow seems to have hammered a certain amount of sense into me. Odd it never struck me before, but I suppose I have been about the most bumptious, conceited fool that ever happened. Why I should have imagined that there was a sort of irresistible fascination in me which was bound to make you break off your engagement and upset the whole universe simply to win the wonderful reward of marrying me, is more than I can understand. I suppose it takes a shock to make a fellow see exactly what he really amounts to. I couldn't think any more of you than I do, but, if I could, the way you have put up with my mouthing and swaggering and posing as a sort of superman would make me do it. You have been wonderful.'

Aline could not speak. She felt as if her whole world had been turned upside down in the last quarter of an hour. This was a new George Emerson, a George at whom it was impossible to laugh, an insidiously attractive George. Her heart beat quickly. Her mind was not clear, but dimly she realized that he had pulled down her chief barrier of defence; and that she was more open to attack than she had ever been. Obstinacy, the automatic desire to resist the pressure of a will that attempted

167

to overcome her own, had kept her cool and level-headed in the past. With masterfulness she had been able to cope. Humility was another thing altogether.

Soft-heartedness was Aline's weakness. She had never clearly recognized it, but it had been partly pity which had induced her to accept Freddie. He had seemed so downtrodden and sorry for himself during those Autumn days when they had first met. Prudence warned her that strange things might happen if once she allowed herself to pity George Emerson.

The silence lengthened. Aline could find nothing to say. In her present mood there was danger in speech.

'We have known each other so long,' said Emerson, 'and I have told you so often that I love you that we have come to make almost a joke of it, as if we were playing some game. It just happens that that is our way, to laugh at things. But I am going to say it once again, even if it has come to be a sort of catchphrase. I love you. I'm reconciled to the fact that I am done for, out of the running, and that you are going to marry somebody else; but I am not going to stop loving you. It isn't a question of whether I should be happier if I forgot you. I can't do it. It's just an impossibility, and that's all there is to it. Whatever I may be to you, you are part of me, and you always will be part of me. I might just as well try to go on living without breathing as living without loving you.'

He stopped, and straightened himself.

'That's all. I don't want to spoil a perfectly good Spring afternoon for you by pulling out the tragic stop. I had to say all that, but it's the last time. It shan't occur again. There will be no tragedy when I step into the train tomorrow. Is there any chance that you might come and see me off?'

Aline nodded.

'You will? That will be splendid. Now I'll go and pack and break it to my host that I must leave him. I expect it will be news to him to learn that I am here. I doubt if he knows me by sight.'

Aline stood where he had left her, leaning on the balustrade.

In the fullness of time there came to her the recollection that she had promised Freddie that shortly after lunch she would come and sit with him.

The Hon. Freddie, draped in purple pyjamas and propped up with many pillows, was lying in bed, reading 'Gridley Quayle, Investigator'. Aline's entrance occurred at a peculiarly poignant moment in the story, and gave him a feeling of having been brought violently to earth from a flight in the clouds. It is not often that an author has the good fortune to grip a reader as the author of Gridley Quayle gripped Freddie.

One of the results of his absorbed mood was that he greeted Aline with a stare of an even glassier quality than usual. His eyes were by nature a trifle prominent, and to Aline, in the overstrung condition in which her talk with George Emerson had left her, they seemed to bulge at her like a snail's. A man seldom looks at his best in bed, and to Aline, seeing him for the first time at this disadvantage, the Hon. Freddie seemed quite repulsive. It was with a feeling of positive panic that she wondered whether he would want her to kiss him.

Freddie made no such demand. He was not one of your demonstrative lovers. He contented himself with rolling over in bed and dropping his lower jaw.

'Hello, Aline.'

Aline sat down on the edge of the bed.

'Well, Freddie.'

Her betrothed improved his appearance a little by hitching up his lower jaw. As if feeling that that would be too extreme a measure, he did not close his mouth altogether, but he diminished the abyss. The Hon. Freddie belonged to the class of persons who move through life with their mouths always restfully open.

It seemed to Aline that on this particular afternoon a strange dumbness had descended upon her. She had been unable to speak to George, and now she could not think of anything to say to Freddie. She looked at him, and he looked at her, and the clock on the mantelpiece went on ticking.

'It was that bally cat of Aunt Ann's,' said Freddie at length, essaying light conversation. 'It came legging it up the stairs, and I took the most frightful toss. I hate cats. Do you hate cats? I knew a fellow in London who couldn't stand cats.'

Aline began to wonder if there was not something permanently wrong with her organs of speech. It should have been a simple matter to develop the cat theme, but she found herself unable to do so. Her mind was concentrated, to the exclusion of all else, on the repellent nature of the spectacle provided by her loved one in pyjamas.

Freddie resumed the conversation.

'I was just reading a corking book. Have you ever read these things? They come out every month, and they're corking. The fellow who writes them must be a corker. It beats me how he thinks of these things. They are about a detective, a chap called Gridley Quayle. Frightfully exciting.'

An obvious remedy for dumbness struck Aline.

'Shall I read to you, Freddie?'

'Right-ho! Good scheme. I've got to the top of this page.'

Aline took the paper-covered book.

'"Seven guns covered him with deadly precision." Did you get as far as that?'

'Yes, just beyond. It's a bit thick, don't you know. This chappie Quayle has been trapped in a lonely house, thinking he was going to see a pal in distress, and instead of the pal there pop out a whole squad of masked blighters with guns. I don't see how he's going to get out of it myself, but I bet he does. He's a corker.'

If anybody could have pitied Aline more than she pitied herself, as she waded through the adventures of Mr. Quayle, it would have been Ashe Marson. He had writhed as he wrote the words, and she writhed as she read them. The Hon. Freddie also writhed, but with intense excitement.

'What's the matter? Don't stop,' he cried, as Aline's voice ceased.

'I'm getting hoarse, Freddie.'

Freddie hesitated. The desire to remain on the trail with Gridley struggled with rudimentary politeness.

'How would it be.... Would you mind if I just took a look at the rest of it myself? We could talk afterwards, don't you know. I shan't be long.'

'Of course. Do read if you want to. But do you really like this sort of thing, Freddie?'

'Me! Rather. Why, don't you?'

'I don't know. It seems a little ... I don't know.'

Freddie had become absorbed in his story. Aline did not attempt further analysis of her attitude towards Mr. Quayle. She relapsed into silence.

It was a silence pregnant with thought. For the first time in their relations, she was trying to visualize to herself exactly what marriage with this young man would mean. Hitherto, it struck her, she had really seen so little of Freddie that she had scarcely had a chance of examining him. In the crowded world outside he had always seemed a tolerable enough person. To-day, somehow, he was different. Everything, was different to-day.

This, she took it, was a fair sample of what she might expect

170

after marriage. Marriage meant, to come to essentials, that two people were very often and for lengthy periods alone together, dependent on each other for mutual entertainment. What exactly would it be like being alone often for lengthy periods with Freddie?

Well, it would, she assumed, be like this.

'It's all right,' said Freddie without looking up. 'He *did* get out. He had a bomb on him, and he threatened to drop it and blow the place to pieces unless the blighters let him go. So they cheesed it. I knew he had something up his sleeve.'

Like this. . . .

Aline drew a deep breath. It would be like this—for ever and ever and ever, till she died.

She bent forward, and stared at him.

'Freddie,' she said, 'do you love me?'

There was no reply.

'Freddie, do you love me? Am I a part of you? If you hadn't me, would it be like trying to go on living without breathing?'

The Hon. Freddie raised a flushed face, and gazed at her with an absent eye.

'Eh, what?' he said. 'Do I...? Oh yes. Rather. I say, one of the blighters has just loosed a rattlesnake into Gridley Quayle's bedroom through the transom.'

Aline rose from her seat and left the room softly. The Hon. Freddie read on, unheeding.

II

Ashe had not fallen far short of the truth in his estimate of the probable effect on Mr. Peters of the information that his precious scarab had once more been removed by alien hands and was now farther from his grasp than ever. A drawback to success in life is that failure, when it does come, acquires an exaggerated importance. Success had made Mr. Peters, in certain aspects of his character, a spoiled child. At the moment when Ashe broke the news, he would have parted with half his fortune to recover the scarab. Its recovery had become a point of honour. He saw it as the prize of a contest between his will and that of whatever malignant powers there might be, ranged against him in the effort to show him that there were limits to what he could achieve. He felt as he had felt in the old days when people sneaked up behind him in Wall Street and tried to

171

loosen his grip on a railway or a pet stock. He was suffering from that form of paranoia which makes men multimillionaires. Nobody would be foolish enough to become a multimillionaire, if it were not for the desire to prove himself irresistible.

He obtained a small relief for his feelings by doubling the existing reward, and Ashe went off in search of Joan, hoping that this new stimulus, acting on their joint brains, might develop inspiration.

'Have any fresh ideas been vouchsafed to you?' he asked. 'You may look on me as baffled.'

Joan shook her head.

'Don't give it up,' she urged. 'Think again. Try to realize what this means, Mr. Marson. Between us we have lost ten thousand dollars, in a single night. I can't afford it. It is like losing a legacy. I absolutely refuse to give in without an effort and go back to writing duke-and-earl stories for *Home Gossip*.'

'The prospect of tackling Gridley Quayle again——'

'Why, I was forgetting that you were a writer of detective stories. You ought to be able to solve this mystery in a moment. Ask yourself, what would Gridley Quayle have done?'

'I can answer that. Gridley Quayle would have waited helplessly for some coincidence to happen to help him out.'

'Had he no methods?'

'He was full of methods. But they never led him anywhere without a coincidence. However, we might try to figure it out. What time did you get to the museum?'

'One o'clock.'

'And you found the scarab gone. What does that suggest to you?'

'Nothing. What does it suggest to you?'

'Absolutely nothing. Let us try again. Whoever took the scarab must have had special information that Peters was offering the reward.'

'Then why hasn't he been to Mr. Peters and claimed it?'

'True. That would seem to be a flaw in the reasoning. Once again. Whoever took it must have been in urgent and immediate need of money.'

'And how are we to find out who was in urgent and immediate need of money?'

'Exactly. How indeed?'

There was a pause.

'I should think your Mr. Quayle must have been a great

172

comfort to his clients, wasn't he?' said Joan.

'Inductive reasoning, I admit, seems to have fallen down to a certain extent,' said Ashe. 'We must wait for the coincidence. I have a feeling that it will come.' He paused. 'I am very fortunate in the way of coincidences.'

'Are you?'

Ashe looked about him, and was relieved to find that they appeared to be out of earshot of their species. It was not easy to achieve this position at the Castle, if you happened to be there as a domestic servant. The space provided for the ladies and gentlemen attached to the guests was limited, and it was rarely that you could enjoy a stroll without bumping into a maid, a valet, or a footman. But now they appeared to be alone. The drive leading to the back regions of the Castle was empty. As far as the eye could reach, there were no signs of servants, upper or lower.

Nevertheless, Ashe lowered his voice.

'Was it not a strange coincidence,' he said, 'that you should have come into my life at all?'

'Not very,' said Joan prosaically. 'It was quite likely that we should meet, sooner or later, as we lived on different floors of the same house.'

'It was a coincidence that you should have taken that room.'

'Why?'

Ashe felt damped. Logically, no doubt, she was right, but surely she might have helped him out a little in this difficult situation. Surely her woman's intuition might have told her that a man who has been speaking in a loud and cheerful voice does not lower it to a husky whisper without some reason. The hopelessness of his task began to weigh upon him. Ever since that evening at Market Blandings station, when he had realized that he had loved her, he had been trying to find an opportunity to tell her so; and every time they had met the talk had seemed to be drawn irresistibly into practical and unsentimental channels. And now, when he was doing his best to reason it out that they were twin souls who had been brought together by a destiny which it would be foolish to struggle against, when he was trying to convey the impression that fate had designed them for each other, she said, 'Why?' It was hard.

He was about to go deeper into the matter, when, from the direction of the Castle, he perceived the Hon. Freddie's valet, Mr. Judson, approaching. That it was this repellent young man's object to break in upon them and rob him of his one small chance of inducing Joan to appreciate as he did the mysterious workings of Providence as they affected herself and him was obvious. There was no mistaking the valet's desire for conversation. He had the air of one brimming over with speech. His wonted indolence was cast aside, and as he drew nearer, he positively ran. He was talking before he reached them.

'Miss Simpson, Mr. Marson, it's true. What I said that night. It's a fact.'

Ashe regarded this intruder with a malevolent eye. Never fond of Mr. Judson, he looked on him now with positive loathing. It had not been easy for him to work himself up to the point where he could discuss with Joan the mysterious ways of Providence, for there was that about her which made it hard to achieve sentiment. That indefinable something in Joan Valentine which made for nocturnal raids on other people's museums also rendered her a somewhat difficult person to talk to about twin souls and destiny. The qualities that Ashe loved in her, her strength, her capability, her valiant self-sufficingness, were the very qualities which seemed to check him when he tried to tell her that he loved them.

Mr. Judson was still babbling.

'It's true. There ain't a doubt of it now. It's been and happened just as I said that night.'

'What did you say—which night?' inquired Ashe.

'That night at dinner, the first night you two came here. Don't you remember me talking about Freddie and the girl he used to write letters to in London, the girl I said was so like you, Miss Simpson? What was her name again? Joan Valentine. That was it. The girl at the theatre that Freddie used to send me with letters to pretty nearly every evening. Well, she's been and done it, same as I told you all that night that she was jolly likely to go and do. She's sticking young Freddie up for his letters, just as he ought to have known she would do if he hadn't been a young fat-head. They're all alike these girls, every one of them.'

Mr. Judson paused, subjected the surrounding scenery to a cautious scrutiny, and resumed.

'I took a suit of Freddie's clothes away to brush just now, and happening'—Mr. Judson paused and gave a little cough—'happening to glance at the contents of his pockets, I came across a letter. I took a sort of look at it before setting it aside, and it was from a fellow named Jones, and it said that this girl

174

Valentine was sticking on to young Freddie's letters what he'd written her and would see him blowed if she parted with them under another thousand. And, as I made it out, Freddie had already given her five hundred. Where he got it is more than I can understand, but that's what the letter said. The fellow Jones said that he had passed it to her with his own hands, but she wasn't satisfied, and if she didn't get the other thousand she was going to bring an action for breach. And now Freddie has given me a note to take to this Jones, who is stopping in Market Blandings.'

Joan had listened to this remarkable speech with a stunned amazement. At this point she made her first comment.

'But that can't be true.'

'Saw the letter with my own eyes, Miss Simpson.'

'But——'

She looked at Ashe helplessly. Their eyes met, hers wide with perplexity, his bright with the light of comprehension.

'It shows,' said Ashe slowly, 'that he was in immediate and urgent need of money.'

'You bet it does,' said Mr. Judson with relish. 'It looks to me as if young Freddie had about reached the end of his tether this time. My word, there won't half be a kick-up if she does sue him for breach. I'm off to tell Mr. Beach and the rest. They'll jump out of their skins.' His face fell. 'Oh, Lord, I was forgetting this note. He told me to take it at once.'

'I'll take it for you,' said Ashe. 'I'm not doing anything.'

Mr. Judson's gratitude was effusive.

'You're a good feller, Marson,' he said. 'I'll do as much for you another time. I couldn't hardly bear not to tell a bit of news like this right away. I should burst or something.'

And Mr. Judson, with shining face, hurried off to the housekeeper's room.

'I simply can't understand it,' said Joan at length. 'My head's going round.'

'Can't understand it? Why, it's perfectly clear. This is the coincidence for which, in my capacity of Gridley Quayle, I was waiting. I can now resume inductive reasoning. Weighing the evidence, what do we find? That young sweep Freddie is the man. *He* has the scarab.'

'But it's all such a muddle. I'm not holding his letters.'

'For Jones' purposes you are. Let's get this Jones element in the affair straightened out. What do you know of him?'

'He was an enormously fat man who came to see me one

175

night and said that he had been sent to get back some letters. I told him I had destroyed them ages ago, and he went away.'

'Well, that part of it is clear, then. He is working a simple but ingenious game on Freddie. It wouldn't succeed with every one, I suppose, but, from what I have seen and heard of him, Freddie isn't strong on intellect. He seems to have accepted the story without a murmur. What does he do? He has to raise a thousand pounds immediately, and the raising of the first five hundred has exhausted his credit. He gets the idea of stealing the scarab.'

'But why? Why should he have thought of the scarab at all? That is what I can't understand. He couldn't have meant to give it to Mr. Peters and claim the reward. He couldn't have known that Mr. Peters was offering a reward. He couldn't have known that Lord Emsworth had not got the scarab quite properly. He couldn't have known—he couldn't have known anything.'

Ashe's enthusiasm was a trifle damped.

'There's something in that. But—I have it. Jones must have known about the scarab and told him.'

'But how could he have known?'

'Yes, there's something in that, too. How could Jones have known?'

'He couldn't. He had gone by the time Aline came that night.'

'I don't quite understand. What night?'

'It was the night of the day I first met you. I was wondering for a moment whether he could by any chance have overheard Aline telling me about the scarab and the reward Mr. Peters was offering for it.'

'Overheard! That word is like a bugle-blast to me. Nine out of ten of Gridley Quayle's triumphs were due to his having overheard something. I think we are now on the right track.'

'I don't. How could he have overheard us? The door was closed, and he was in the street by that time.'

'How do you know he was in the street? Did you see him out?'

'No, but he went.'

'He might have waited on the stairs—you remember how dark they were at No. 7A—and listened.'

'Why?'

Ashe reflected.

'Why? Why? What a beast of a word that is. The detective's

176

bugbear. I thought I had got it till you said—Great Scott. I'll tell you why. I see it all. I have him with the goods. His object in coming to you about the letters was because Freddie wanted them back owing to his approaching marriage with Miss Peters, wasn't it?'

'Yes.'

'You tell him you have destroyed the letters. He goes off. Am I right?'

'Yes.'

'Before he is out of the house Miss Peters is giving her name at the front door. Put yourself in Jones' place. What does he think? He is suspicious. He thinks there is some game on. He skips upstairs again, waits till Miss Peters has gone into your room, then stands outside and listens. How about that?"

'I do believe you are right. He might quite easily have done that.'

'He did do exactly that. I know it as if I had been there. In fact, it is highly probable that I was there. You say all this happened on the night of the day we first met? I remember coming downstairs that night—I was going out to a music-hall—and hearing voices in your room. I remember it distinctly. In all probability I nearly ran into Jones.'

'It does all seem to fit in, doesn't it?'

'It's a clear case. There isn't a flaw in it. The only question is, can I, on the evidence, go to young Freddie and choke the scarab out of him? On the whole I think I had better take this note to Jones, as I promised Judson, and see if I can't work something through him. Yes, that's the best plan. I'll be starting at once.'

III

Perhaps the greatest hardship in being an invalid is the fact that people come and see you and keep your spirits up. The Hon. Freddie Threepwood suffered extremely from this. His was not a gregarious nature, and it fatigued his limited brain-powers to have to find conversation for his numerous visitors. All he wanted was to be left alone to read the Adventures of Gridley Quayle and when tired of doing that, to lie on his back, and look at the ceiling and think of nothing. It is your dynamic person, your energetic World's Worker, who chafes at being laid up with a sprained ankle. The Hon. Freddie enjoyed it. From boyhood up, he had loved lying in bed, and now

177

that fate had allowed him to do this without incurring rebuke, he objected to having his reveries broken in upon by officious relatives.

He spent his rare intervals of solitude in trying to decide in his mind which of his cousins, uncles, and aunts was, all things considered, the greatest nuisance. Sometimes he would give the palm to Colonel Horace Mant, who struck the soldierly note ('I recollect in a hill campaign in the Winter of the year '93 giving my ankle the deuce of a twist'); anon the more spiritual attitude of the Bishop of Godalming seemed to annoy him more keenly. Sometimes he would head the list with the name of his cousin Percy, Lord Stockheath, who refused to talk of anything except his late breach-of-promise case and the effect the verdict had had on his old governor. Freddie was in no mood just now to be sympathetic with others on their breach-of-promise cases.

As he lay in bed reading on the Monday morning, the only flaw in his enjoyment of this unaccustomed solitude was the thought that presently the door was bound to open, and some kind inquirer insinuate himself into the room.

His apprehensions proved well-founded. Scarcely had he got well into the details of an ingenious plot on the part of a secret society to eliminate Gridley Quayle by bribing his cook (a bad lot) to sprinkle chopped-up horse-hair in his chicken fricassee, when the handle turned, and Ashe Marson came in.

Freddie was not the only person who had found the influx of visitors into the sick-room a source of irritation. The fact that the invalid seemed unable to get a moment to himself had annoyed Ashe considerably. For some little time he had hung about the passage in which Freddie's room was situated, full of enterprise but unable to make a forward move owing to the throng of sympathizers. What he had to say to the sufferer could not be said in the presence of a third party.

Freddie's sensation, on perceiving him, was one of relief. He had been half afraid that it was the Bishop. He recognized Ashe as the valet chappie who had helped him to bed on the occasion of his accident. It might be that he had come in a respectful way to make inquiries but he was not likely to stop long. He nodded, and went on reading.

And then, glancing up, he perceived Ashe standing beside the bed, fixing him with a piercing stare.

The Hon. Freddie hated piercing stares. One of the reasons why he objected to being left alone with his future father-in-law, Mr. Preston Peters, was that Nature had given the millionaire a penetrating pair of eyes, and the stress of business life in New York had developed in him a habit of boring holes in people with them. A young man had to have a stronger nerve and a clearer conscience than the Hon. Freddie to enjoy a *tête-à-tête* with Mr. Peters.

But, while he accepted Aline's father as a necessary evil and recognized that his position entitled him to look at people as sharply as he liked, whatever their feelings, he was hanged if he was going to extend this privilege to Mr. Peters' valet. This man standing beside him was giving him a look which seemed to his sensitive imagination to have been fired red-hot from a gun; and this annoyed and exasperated Freddie.

'What do you want?' he said querulously. 'What are you staring at me like that for?'

Ashe sat down, leaned his elbows on the bed, and applied the look again, from a lower elevation.

'Ah!' he said.

Whatever may have been Ashe's defects as far as the handling of the inductive-reasoning side of Gridley Quayle's character was concerned, there was one scene in each of his stories in which he never failed. That was the scene in the last chapter where Quayle, confronting his quarry, unmasked him. Quayle might have floundered in the earlier part of the story, but in his big scene he was exactly right. He was curt, brisk, and mercilessly compelling. Ashe, rehearsing this interview in the passage before his entry, had decided that he could hardly do better than model himself on the detective. So he began to be curt, crisp, and mercilessly compelling to Freddie; and after the first few sentences he had that youth gasping for air.

'I will tell you,' he said. 'If you can spare me a few moments of your valuable time, I will put the facts before you. Yes, press that bell, if you wish, and I will put them before witnesses. Lord Emsworth will no doubt be pleased to learn that his son, whom he trusted, is—a thief.'

Freddie's hand fell limply. The bell remained untouched. His mouth opened to its fullest extent. In the midst of his panic he had a curious feeling that he had heard or read that last sentence somewhere before. Then he remembered. Those very words occurred in 'Gridley Quayle, Investigator. The Adventure of the Blue Ruby.'

'What—what do you mean?' he stammered.

'I will tell you what I mean. On Saturday night a valuable

scarab was stolen from Lord Emsworth's private museum. The case was put into my hands——'

'Great Scott! Are you a detective?'

'Ah!' said Ashe.

Life, as many a worthy writer has pointed out, is full of ironies. It seemed to Freddie that here was a supreme example of this fact. All these years he had wanted to meet a detective, and now that his wish had been gratified the detective was detecting *him*.

'The case,' continued Ashe severely, 'was placed in my hands. I investigated it. I discovered that you were in urgent and immediate need of money.'

'How on earth did you do that?'

'Ah!' said Ashe. 'I further discovered that you were in communication with an individual named Jones.'

'Good lord! How?'

Ashe smiled quietly.

'Yesterday I had a talk with this man Jones, who is staying in Market Blandings. Why is he staying in Market Blandings? Because he had a reason for keeping in touch with you. Because you were about to transfer to his care something which you could get possession of but which only he could dispose of. The scarab.'

The Hon. Freddie was beyond speech. He made no comment on this statement. Ashe continued.

'I interviewed this man Jones. I said to him. "I am in the Hon. Frederick Threepwood's confidence I know everything. Have you any instructions for me?" He replied, "What do you know?" I answered, "I know that the Hon. Frederick Threepwood has something which he wishes to hand to you, but which he has been unable to hand to you owing to having had an accident and being confined to his room." He then told me to tell you to let him have the scarab by messenger.'

Freddie pulled himself together with an effort. He was in sore straits, but he saw one last chance. His researches in detective fiction had given him the knowledge that detectives occasionally relaxed their austerity when dealing with a deserving case. Even Gridley Quayle could sometimes be softened by a pathetic story. Freddie could recall half a dozen times when a detected criminal had been spared by him because he had done it all from the best motives. He determined to throw himself on Ashe's mercy.

'I say, you know,' he said ingratiatingly, 'I think it's bally

180

marvellous the way you've deduced everything and so forth.'

'Well?'

'But I believe you would chuck it, if you heard my side of the case.'

'I know your side of the case. You think you are being blackmailed by a Miss Valentine for some letters you once wrote her. You are not. Miss Valentine has destroyed the letters. She told the man Jones so when he went to see her in London. He kept your five hundred pounds, and is trying to get another thousand out of you under false pretences!'

'What! You can't be right.'

'I am always right.'

'You must be mistaken.'

'I am never mistaken.'

'But how do you know?'

'I have my sources of information.'

'She isn't going to sue me for breach?'

'She never had any intention of doing so.'

The Hon. Frederick sank back on the pillows.

'Good egg!' he said with fervour. He beamed happily. 'This,' he observed, 'is a bit of all right.'

'Never mind that,' said Ashe. 'Give me the scarab. Where is it?'

'What are you going to do with it?'

'Restore it to its rightful owner.'

'Are you going to give me away to the governor?'

'I am not.'

'It strikes me,' said Freddie gratefully, 'that you are a dashed good sort. You seem to me to have the makings of an absolute topper! It's under the mattress. I had it on me when I fell downstairs, and I had to shove it in there.'

Ashe drew it out. He stood looking at it, absorbed. He could hardly believe that his quest was at an end, and that a small fortune lay in the palm of his hand.

Freddie was eyeing him admiringly.

'You know,' he said, 'I've always wanted to meet a detective. What beats me is how you chappies find out things.'

'We have our methods.'

'I believe you. You're a blooming marvel! What first put you on my track?'

'That,' said Ashe, 'would take too long to explain. Of course I had to do some tense inductive reasoning. But I could not trace every link in the chain for you. It would be tedious.'

'Not to me.'

'Some other time.'

'I say, I wonder, if you've ever read any of these things, these Gridley Quayle stories? I know them by heart.'

With the scarab safely in his pocket, Ashe could contemplate the brightly-coloured volume which the other extended towards him without active repulsion. Already he was beginning to feel a sort of sentiment for the depressing Quayle, as for something that had once formed part of his life.

'Do you read these things?'

'I should say I did.'

'I write them.'

There are certain supreme moments which cannot be adequately described. Freddie's appreciation of the fact that such a moment had occurred in his life expressed itself in a startled cry and a convulsive movement of all his limbs. He shot up from the pillows and gaped at Ashe.

'You write them? You don't mean *write* them?'

'Yes.'

'Great Scott!'

He would have gone on, doubtless, to say more, but at this moment voices made themselves heard outside the door. There was a movement of feet. Then the door opened, and a small procession entered.

It was headed by the Earl of Emsworth. Following him, came Mr. Peters. And in the wake of the millionaire Colonel Horace Mant and the Efficient Baxter. They filed into the room, and stood by the bedside. Ashe seized the opportunity to slip out.

Freddie glanced at the deputation without interest. His mind was occupied with other matters. He supposed that they had come to inquire after his ankle, and he was mildly thankful that they had come in a body instead of one by one. The deputation grouped itself about the bed, and shuffled its feet. There was an atmosphere of awkwardness.

'Er, Frederick,' said Lord Emsworth. 'Freddie, my boy.'

Mr. Peters fiddled dumbly with the coverlet, Colonel Mant cleared his throat. The Efficient Baxter scowled.

'Er, Freddie, my dear boy, I fear that we have a painful—ah —duty to perform.'

The words struck straight home at the Hon. Freddie's guilty conscience. Had they too, tracked him down, and was he now to be accused of having stolen that infernal scarab! A

182

wave of relief swept over him as he realized that he had got rid of the thing. A decent chappie like that detective would not give him away. All he had to do was to keep his head and stick to stout denial. That was the game. Stout denial.

'I don't know what you mean,' he said defensively.

'Of course you don't, dash it,' said Colonel Mant. 'We're coming to that. And I should like to begin by saying that, though in a sense it was my fault, I fail to see how I could have acted——'

'Horace.'

'Oh, very well. I was only trying to explain.'

Lord Emsworth adjusted his pince-nez, and sought inspiration from the wallpaper.

'Freddie, my boy,' he began, 'we have a somewhat unpleasant—a somewhat—ah—disturbing.... We are compelled to break it to you.... We are all most pained and astounded and ...'

The Efficient Baxter spoke. It was plain that he was in a bad temper.

'Miss Peters,' he snapped, 'has eloped with your friend Emerson.'

Lord Emsworth breathed a sigh of relief.

'Exactly, Baxter. Precisely. You have put the thing in a nutshell. Really, my dear fellow, you are invaluable.'

All eyes searched Freddie's face for signs of uncontrollable emotion. The deputation waited anxiously for his first grief-stricken cry.

'Eh, what?' said Freddie.

'It is quite true, Freddie, my dear boy. She went to London with him on the ten-fifty.'

'And, if I had not been forcibly restrained,' said Baxter acidly, casting a vindictive look at Colonel Mant, 'I could have prevented it.'

Colonel Mant cleared his throat again, and put a hand to his moustache.

'I'm afraid that is true, Freddie. It was a most unfortunate misunderstanding. I'll tell you how it happened. I chanced to be at the station bookstall when the train came in. Mr. Baxter was also in the station. The train pulled up, and this young fellow Emerson got in. Said good-bye to us, don't you know, and got in. Just as the train was about to start, Miss Peters, exclaiming, "George, dear, I'm coming with you, dash it," or some such speech, proceeded to go hell for leather for the door of young Emerson's compartment. Upon which——'

'Upon which,' interrupted Baxter. 'I made a spring to try and catch her. Apart from any other consideration, the train was already moving, and Miss Peters ran a considerable risk of injury. I had hardly moved when I felt a violent jerk at my ankle and fell to the ground. After I had recovered from the shock, which was not immediately, I found——'

'The fact is, Freddie, my boy, I acted under a misapprehension. Nobody can be sorrier for the mistake than I, but recent events in this house had left me with the impression that Mr. Baxter here was not quite responsible for his actions. Overwork or something, I imagined. I have seen it happen so often in India, don't you know, where fellows run amuck and kick up the deuce's own delight. I am bound to admit that I have been watching Mr. Baxter rather closely lately, in the expectation that something of this very kind might happen. Of course, I now realize my mistake, and I have apologized—apologized humbly, dash it. But at the moment I was firmly under the impression that our friend here had had an attack of some kind, and was about to inflict injuries on Miss Peters. If I've seen it happen once in India, I've seen it happen a dozen times. I recollect in the hot weather of the year '92—or was it '93?—I think '93—one of my native bearers.... However, I sprang forward and caught the crook of my walking-stick in Mr. Baxter's ankle and brought him down. And by the time the explanations were made, it was too late. The train had gone, with Miss Peters in it.'

'And a telegram has just arrived,' said Lord Emsworth, 'to say that they are being married this afternoon at a registrar's. The whole occurrence is most disturbing.'

'Bear it like a man, my boy,' urged Colonel Mant.

To all appearances, Freddie was bearing it magnificently. Not a single exclamation, either of wrath or pain, had escaped his lips. One would have said that the shock had stunned him or that he had not heard, for his face expressed no emotion whatsoever.

The fact was that the story had made very little impression on the Hon. Freddie of any sort. His relief at Ashe's news about Joan Valentine, the stunning joy of having met in the flesh the author of the Adventures of Gridley Quayle, the general feeling that all was now right with the world—these things deprived him of the ability to be greatly distressed.

And there was a distinct feeling of relief, actual relief, that

184

now it would not be necessary for him to get married. He had liked Aline, but, whenever he had really thought of it, the prospect of getting married had rather appalled him. A chappie looked such an ass getting married. . . .

It appeared, however, that some verbal comment on the state of affairs was required of him. He searched in his mind for something adequate.

'You mean to say Aline has bolted with Emerson?'

The deputation nodded painful nods. Freddie searched in his mind again. The deputation held its breath.

'Well, I'm blowed,' said Freddie. 'Fancy that!'

IV

Mr. Peters walked heavily into his room. Ashe Marson was waiting for him there. He eyed Ashe dully.

'Pack,' he said.

'Pack?'

'Pack. We're getting out of here by the afternoon train.'

'Has anything happened?'

'My daughter has eloped with Emerson.'

'What!'

'Don't stand there saying "What!" Pack.'

Ashe put his hand in his pocket.

'Where shall I put this,' he asked.

For a moment Mr. Peters looked without comprehension at what he was holding out, then his whole demeanour altered. His eyes lit up. He uttered a howl of pure rapture.

'You got it!'

'I got it.'

'Where was it? Who had taken it? How did you choke it out of them? How did you find it? Who had it?'

'I don't know whether I ought to say. I don't want to start anything. You won't tell anyone?'

'Tell anyone? What do you take me for? Do you think I am going about advertising this? If I can sneak out without that fellow Baxter jumping on my back, I shall be satisfied. You can take it from me that there won't be any sensational exposures if I can help it. Who had it?'

'Young Threepwood.'

'Threepwood? What did he want it for?'

'He needed money, and he was going to raise it on this.'

Mr. Peters exploded.

185

'And I have been kicking because Aline can't marry him, and has gone off with a regular fellow like young Emerson. He's a good boy, young Emerson. He'll make a name for himself one of these days. He's got get-up in him. And I have been wanting to shoot him because he has taken Aline away from that goggle-eyed chump up in bed there. Why, if she had married Threepwood, I should have had grandchildren who would have sneaked my watch while I was dancing them on my knee. There is a taint of some sort in the whole family. Father sneaks my Cheops, and sonny sneaks it from father. What a gang! And the best blood in England. If that's England's idea of good blood, give me Kalamazoo. This settles it, I was a chump ever to come to a country like this. Property isn't safe over here. I'm going back to America on the next boat.

'Where's my cheque-book? I'm going to write you out that cheque right away. You've earned it. Listen, young man, I don't know what your ideas are, but if you aren't chained to this country, I'd make it worth your while to stay on with me. They say no one's indispensable, but you come mighty near it. If I had you at my elbow for a few years, I'd get right back into shape. I'm feeling better now than I have felt in years, and you've only just started in on me. How about it? You can call yourself what you like—secretary or trainer or whatever suits you best. What you will be is the fellow who makes me take exercise and stop smoking cigars and generally looks after me. How do you feel about it?'

It was a proposition which appealed both to Ashe's commercial and to his missionary instincts. His only regret had been that, the scarab recovered, he and Mr. Peters would now, he supposed, part company. He had not liked the idea of sending the millionaire back to the world a half-cured man. Already he had begun to look upon him in the light of a piece of creative work, to which he had just set his hand.

But the thought of Joan gave him pause. If this meant separation from Joan, it was not to be considered.

'Let me think it over,' he said.

'Well, think quick,' said Mr. Peters.

V

It is said by those who have been through fires, earthquakes, and shipwrecks, that in such times of stress the social barriers are temporarily broken down, and the spectacle may be seen of

186

persons of the highest social standing speaking quite freely to persons who are not in Society at all, and of quite nice people addressing others to whom they have never been introduced. The news of Aline Peters' elopement with George Emerson, carried beyond the green-baize door by Slingsby, the chauffeur, produced very much the same state of affairs in the servants' quarters at Blandings Castle.

It was not only that Slingsby was permitted to penetrate into the housekeeper's room and tell his story to his social superiors there, though that was an absolutely unprecedented occurrence; what was really extraordinary was that mere menials discussed the affair with the personal ladies and gentlemen of the Castle guests, and were allowed to do so uncrushed. James, the footman, that pushing individual, actually shoved his way into the Room, and was heard by witnesses to remark to no less a person than Mr. Beach that it was a bit thick. And it is on record that his fellow-footman, Alfred, meeting the Groom of the Chambers in the passage outside, positively prodded him in the lower ribs, winked, and said, 'What a day we're having.' One has to go back to the worse excesses of the French Revolution to parallel these outrages.

It was held by Mr. Beach and Mrs. Twemlow afterwards that the social fabric of the Castle never fully recovered from this upheaval. It may be that they took an extreme view of the matter, but it cannot be denied that it wrought changes. The rise of Slingsby is a case in point. Until this affair took place, the chauffeur's standing had never been satisfactorily settled. Mr. Beach and Mrs. Twemlow led the party which considered that he was merely a species of coachman, but there was another smaller group which, dazzled by Slingsby's personality, openly declared that it was not right that he should take his meals in the Servants' Hall with such admitted plebians as the odd man and the Steward's Room footman. The Aline–George elopement settled the point once and for all. Slingsby had carried George's bag to the train. Slingsby had been standing a few yards from the spot where Aline began her dash for the carriage door. Slingsby was able to exhibit the actual half-sovereign which George had tipped him, only five minutes before the great event. To send such a public man back to the Servant's Hall was impossible. By unspoken consent the chauffeur dined that night in the Steward's Room, from which he was never again dislodged.

187

Mr. Judson alone stood apart from the throng which clustered about the chauffeur. He was suffering the bitterness of the supplanted. A brief while before, and he had been the central figure with his story of the letter which he had found in the Hon. Freddie's coat pocket. Now the importance of his story had been engulfed in that of this later and greater sensation, and Mr. Judson was learning for the first time on what unstable foundations popularity stands.

Joan was nowhere to be seen. In none of the spots where she might have been expected to be at such a time was she to be found. Ashe had almost given up the search when, going to the back door and looking out as a last chance, he perceived her walking slowly on the gravel drive.'

She greeted Ashe with a smile, but something was plainly troubling her. She did not speak for a moment, and they walked side by side.

'What is it?' said Ashe at length. 'What is the matter?'

She looked at him gravely.

'Gloom,' she said. 'Despondency, Mr. Marson. A sort of flat feeling. Don't you hate things happening?'

'I don't quite understand!'

'Well, this affair of Aline, for instance. It's so big. It makes you feel as if the whole world had altered. I should like nothing to happen, ever, and life just to jog peacefully along. That's not the gospel I preached to you in Arundell Street, is it? I thought I was an advanced apostle of action. But I seem to have changed. I'm afraid I should never be able to make it clear what I do mean. I only know that I feel as if I had grown suddenly old. These things are such milestones. Already I am beginning to look on the time before Aline behaved so sensationally as terribly remote. Tomorrow it will be worse, and the day after that worse still. I can see that you don't in the least understand what I mean.'

'Yes, I do. Or I think I do. What it comes to, in a few words, is that somebody you were fond of has gone out of your life. Is that it?'

Joan nodded.

'Yes. At least, that is partly it. I didn't really know Aline particularly well, beyond having been at school with her, but you're right. It's not so much what has happened as what it represents that matters. This elopement has marked the end of a phase of my life. I think I have it now. My life has been such a series of jerks. I dash along, then something happens which

188

stops that bit of my life with a jerk, and then I have to start over again—a new bit. I think I'm getting tired of jerks. I want something stodgy and continuous. I'm like one of the old bus horses who could go on for ever if people got off without making them stop. It's the having to get the bus moving again that wears one out. This little section of my life since we came here is over, and it is finished for good. I've got to start the bus going again on a new road and with a new set of passengers. I wonder if the old horses used to be sorry when they dropped one set of passengers and took on a lot of strangers?'

A sudden dryness invaded Ashe's throat. He tried to speak, but found no words. Joan went on.

'Do you ever get moods when life seems absolutely meaningless? It's like a badly-constructed story, with all sorts of characters moving in and out who have nothing to do with the plot. And, when somebody comes along who you think really has something to do with the plot, he suddenly drops out. After a while you begin to wonder what the story is about, and you feel that it's about nothing—just a jumble.'

'There is one thing,' said Ashe, 'that knits it together.'

'What is that?'

'The love interest.'

Their eyes met, and suddenly there descended upon Ashe confidence. He felt cool and alert, sure of himself, as in the old days he had felt when he ran races and, the nerve-racking hours of waiting past, he listened for the starter's gun. Subconsciously he was aware that he had always been a little afraid of Joan, and that now he was no longer afraid.

'Joan, will you marry me?'

Her eyes wandered from his face. He waited.

'I wonder,' she said softly. 'You think that is the solution?'

'Yes.'

'How can you tell?' she broke out. 'We scarcely know each other. I shan't always be in this mood. I may get restless again. I may find that it is the jerks that I really like.'

'You won't.'

'You're very confident.'

'I am absolutely confident.'

' "She travels the fastest who travels alone," ' misquoted Joan.

'What is the good,' said Ashe, 'of travelling fast if you're going round in a circle? I know how you feel. I've felt the same myself. You are an individualist. You think that there is

189

something tremendous just round the corner, and that you can get it if you try hard enough. There isn't. Or, if there is, it isn't worth getting. Life is nothing but a mutual aid association. I am going to help old Peters; you are going to help me; I am going to help you.'

'Help me to do what?'

'Make life coherent instead of a jumble.'

'Mr. Marson——'

'Don't call me Mr. Marson.'

'Ashe, you don't know what you are doing. You don't know me. I've been knocking about the world for five years, and I'm hard—hard right through. I should make you wretched.'

'You are not in the least hard, and you know it. Listen to me, Joan. Where's your sense of fairness? You crash into my life, turn it upside down, dig me out of my quiet groove, revolutionize my whole existence, and now you propose to drop me and pay no further attention to me. Is it fair?'

'But I don't. We shall always be the best of friends.'

'We shall. But we will get married first.'

'You are determined?'

'I am.'

Joan laughed happily.

'How perfectly splendid. I was terrified lest I might have made you change your mind. I had to say all I did, to preserve my self-respect after proposing to you. Yes, I did. But strange it is that men never seem to understand a woman, however plainly she talks. You don't think I was really worrying because I had lost Aline, do you? I thought I was going to lose you, and it made me miserable. You couldn't expect me to say so in so many words, but I thought you guessed. I practically said it. Ashe! What are you doing?'

Ashe paused for a moment to reply.

'I am kissing you,' he said.

'But you mustn't. There's a scullery-maid or something looking out of the kitchen window. She will see us.'

Ashe drew her to him.

'Scullery-maids have few pleasures,' he said. 'Theirs is a dull life. Let her see us.'

190

The Earl of Emsworth sat by the sick-bed, and regarded the Hon. Freddie almost tenderly.

'Oh, what? Yes, rather. Deuce of a shock, governor.'

'I have been thinking it over, my boy, and perhaps I have been a little hard on you. When your ankle is better, I have decided to renew your allowance, and you may return to London, as you do not seem happy in the country. Though how any reasonable being can prefer——'

The Hon. Freddie started, pop-eyed, to a sitting posture.

'My word! Not really?'

His father nodded.

'Yes. But, Freddie, my boy,' he added not without pathos, 'I *do* wish that this time you would endeavour, for my sake, not to make a fool of yourself.'

He eyed his offspring wistfully.

'I'll have a jolly good stab at it, governor,' said the Hon. Freddie.

A CATALOG OF SELECTED DOVER
BOOKS IN ALL FIELDS OF INTEREST

CONCERNING THE SPIRITUAL IN ART, Wassily Kandinsky. Pioneering work by father of abstract art. Thoughts on color theory, nature of art. Analysis of earlier masters. 12 illustrations. 80pp. of text. 5⅜ x 8½.　　　　23411-8 Pa. $4.95

ANIMALS: 1,419 Copyright-Free Illustrations of Mammals, Birds, Fish, Insects, etc., Jim Harter (ed.). Clear wood engravings present, in extremely lifelike poses, over 1,000 species of animals. One of the most extensive pictorial sourcebooks of its kind. Captions. Index. 284pp. 9 x 12.　　　　23766-4 Pa. $14.95

CELTIC ART: The Methods of Construction, George Bain. Simple geometric techniques for making Celtic interlacements, spirals, Kells-type initials, animals, humans, etc. Over 500 illustrations. 160pp. 9 x 12. (Available in U.S. only.)　　　　22923-8 Pa. $9.95

AN ATLAS OF ANATOMY FOR ARTISTS, Fritz Schider. Most thorough reference work on art anatomy in the world. Hundreds of illustrations, including selections from works by Vesalius, Leonardo, Goya, Ingres, Michelangelo, others. 593 illustrations. 192pp. 7⅛ x 10¼.　　　　20241-0 Pa. $9.95

CELTIC HAND STROKE-BY-STROKE (Irish Half-Uncial from "The Book of Kells"): An Arthur Baker Calligraphy Manual, Arthur Baker. Complete guide to creating each letter of the alphabet in distinctive Celtic manner. Covers hand position, strokes, pens, inks, paper, more. Illustrated. 48pp. 8¼ x 11.　　　　24336-2 Pa. $3.95

EASY ORIGAMI, John Montroll. Charming collection of 32 projects (hat, cup, pelican, piano, swan, many more) specially designed for the novice origami hobbyist. Clearly illustrated easy-to-follow instructions insure that even beginning papercrafters will achieve successful results. 48pp. 8¼ x 11.　　　　27298-2 Pa. $3.50

THE COMPLETE BOOK OF BIRDHOUSE CONSTRUCTION FOR WOODWORKERS, Scott D. Campbell. Detailed instructions, illustrations, tables. Also data on bird habitat and instinct patterns. Bibliography. 3 tables. 63 illustrations in 15 figures. 48pp. 5¼ x 8½.　　　　24407-5 Pa. $2.50

BLOOMINGDALE'S ILLUSTRATED 1886 CATALOG: Fashions, Dry Goods and Housewares, Bloomingdale Brothers. Famed merchants' extremely rare catalog depicting about 1,700 products: clothing, housewares, firearms, dry goods, jewelry, more. Invaluable for dating, identifying vintage items. Also, copyright-free graphics for artists, designers. Co-published with Henry Ford Museum & Greenfield Village. 160pp. 8¼ x 11.　　　　25780-0 Pa. $10.95

HISTORIC COSTUME IN PICTURES, Braun & Schneider. Over 1,450 costumed figures in clearly detailed engravings—from dawn of civilization to end of 19th century. Captions. Many folk costumes. 256pp. 8⅜ x 11¾.　　　　23150-X Pa. $12.95

CATALOG OF DOVER BOOKS

STICKLEY CRAFTSMAN FURNITURE CATALOGS, Gustav Stickley and L. & J. G. Stickley. Beautiful, functional furniture in two authentic catalogs from 1910. 594 illustrations, including 277 photos, show settles, rockers, armchairs, reclining chairs, bookcases, desks, tables. 183pp. 6½ x 9¼. 23838-5 Pa. $11.95

AMERICAN LOCOMOTIVES IN HISTORIC PHOTOGRAPHS: 1858 to 1949, Ron Ziel (ed.). A rare collection of 126 meticulously detailed official photographs, called "builder portraits," of American locomotives that majestically chronicle the rise of steam locomotive power in America. Introduction. Detailed captions. xi+ 129pp. 9 x 12. 27393-8 Pa. $13.95

AMERICA'S LIGHTHOUSES: An Illustrated History, Francis Ross Holland, Jr. Delightfully written, profusely illustrated fact-filled survey of over 200 American lighthouses since 1716. History, anecdotes, technological advances, more. 240pp. 8 x 10¾. 25576-X Pa. $12.95

TOWARDS A NEW ARCHITECTURE, Le Corbusier. Pioneering manifesto by founder of "International School." Technical and aesthetic theories, views of industry, economics, relation of form to function, "mass-production split" and much more. Profusely illustrated. 320pp. 6⅛ x 9¼. (Available in U.S. only.) 25023-7 Pa. $9.95

HOW THE OTHER HALF LIVES, Jacob Riis. Famous journalistic record, exposing poverty and degradation of New York slums around 1900, by major social reformer. 100 striking and influential photographs. 233pp. 10 x 7⅞. 22012-5 Pa. $11.95

FRUIT KEY AND TWIG KEY TO TREES AND SHRUBS, William M. Harlow. One of the handiest and most widely used identification aids. Fruit key covers 120 deciduous and evergreen species; twig key 160 deciduous species. Easily used. Over 300 photographs. 126pp. 5⅜ x 8½. 20511-8 Pa. $3.95

COMMON BIRD SONGS, Dr. Donald J. Borror. Songs of 60 most common U.S. birds: robins, sparrows, cardinals, bluejays, finches, more—arranged in order of increasing complexity. Up to 9 variations of songs of each species. Cassette and manual 99911-4 $8.95

ORCHIDS AS HOUSE PLANTS, Rebecca Tyson Northen. Grow cattleyas and many other kinds of orchids—in a window, in a case, or under artificial light. 63 illustrations. 148pp. 5⅜ x 8½. 23261-1 Pa. $5.95

MONSTER MAZES, Dave Phillips. Masterful mazes at four levels of difficulty. Avoid deadly perils and evil creatures to find magical treasures. Solutions for all 32 exciting illustrated puzzles. 48pp. 8¼ x 11. 26005-4 Pa. $2.95

MOZART'S DON GIOVANNI (DOVER OPERA LIBRETTO SERIES), Wolfgang Amadeus Mozart. Introduced and translated by Ellen H. Bleiler. Standard Italian libretto, with complete English translation. Convenient and thoroughly portable—an ideal companion for reading along with a recording or the performance itself. Introduction. List of characters. Plot summary. 121pp. 5¼ x 8½. 24944-1 Pa. $3.95

TECHNICAL MANUAL AND DICTIONARY OF CLASSICAL BALLET, Gail Grant. Defines, explains, comments on steps, movements, poses and concepts. 15-page pictorial section. Basic book for student, viewer. 127pp. 5⅜ x 8½. 21843-0 Pa. $4.95

THE CLARINET AND CLARINET PLAYING, David Pino. Lively, comprehensive work features suggestions about technique, musicianship, and musical interpretation, as well as guidelines for teaching, making your own reeds, and preparing for public performance. Includes an intriguing look at clarinet history. "A godsend," *The Clarinet,* Journal of the International Clarinet Society. Appendixes. 7 illus. 320pp. 5⅜ x 8½. 40270-3 Pa. $9.95

HOLLYWOOD GLAMOR PORTRAITS, John Kobal (ed.). 145 photos from 1926-49. Harlow, Gable, Bogart, Bacall; 94 stars in all. Full background on photographers, technical aspects. 160pp. 8⅜ x 11¼. 23352-9 Pa. $12.95

THE ANNOTATED CASEY AT THE BAT: A Collection of Ballads about the Mighty Casey/Third, Revised Edition, Martin Gardner (ed.). Amusing sequels and parodies of one of America's best-loved poems: Casey's Revenge, Why Casey Whiffed, Casey's Sister at the Bat, others. 256pp. 5⅜ x 8½. 28598-7 Pa. $8.95

THE RAVEN AND OTHER FAVORITE POEMS, Edgar Allan Poe. Over 40 of the author's most memorable poems: "The Bells," "Ulalume," "Israfel," "To Helen," "The Conqueror Worm," "Eldorado," "Annabel Lee," many more. Alphabetic lists of titles and first lines. 64pp. 5$^{3}/_{16}$ x 8¼. 26685-0 Pa. $1.00

PERSONAL MEMOIRS OF U. S. GRANT, Ulysses Simpson Grant. Intelligent, deeply moving firsthand account of Civil War campaigns, considered by many the finest military memoirs ever written. Includes letters, historic photographs, maps and more. 528pp. 6⅛ x 9¼. 28587-1 Pa. $12.95

ANCIENT EGYPTIAN MATERIALS AND INDUSTRIES, A. Lucas and J. Harris. Fascinating, comprehensive, thoroughly documented text describes this ancient civilization's vast resources and the processes that incorporated them in daily life, including the use of animal products, building materials, cosmetics, perfumes and incense, fibers, glazed ware, glass and its manufacture, materials used in the mummification process, and much more. 544pp. 6⅛ x 9¼. (Available in U.S. only.) 40446-3 Pa. $16.95

RUSSIAN STORIES/PYCCKNE PACCKA3bI: A Dual-Language Book, edited by Gleb Struve. Twelve tales by such masters as Chekhov, Tolstoy, Dostoevsky, Pushkin, others. Excellent word-for-word English translations on facing pages, plus teaching and study aids, Russian/English vocabulary, biographical/critical introductions, more. 416pp. 5⅜ x 8½. 26244-8 Pa. $9.95

PHILADELPHIA THEN AND NOW: 60 Sites Photographed in the Past and Present, Kenneth Finkel and Susan Oyama. Rare photographs of City Hall, Logan Square, Independence Hall, Betsy Ross House, other landmarks juxtaposed with contemporary views. Captures changing face of historic city. Introduction. Captions. 128pp. 8¼ x 11. 25790-8 Pa. $9.95

AIA ARCHITECTURAL GUIDE TO NASSAU AND SUFFOLK COUNTIES, LONG ISLAND, The American Institute of Architects, Long Island Chapter, and the Society for the Preservation of Long Island Antiquities. Comprehensive, well-researched and generously illustrated volume brings to life over three centuries of Long Island's great architectural heritage. More than 240 photographs with authoritative, extensively detailed captions. 176pp. 8¼ x 11. 26946-9 Pa. $14.95

NORTH AMERICAN INDIAN LIFE: Customs and Traditions of 23 Tribes, Elsie Clews Parsons (ed.). 27 fictionalized essays by noted anthropologists examine religion, customs, government, additional facets of life among the Winnebago, Crow, Zuni, Eskimo, other tribes. 480pp. 6⅛ x 9¼. 27377-6 Pa. $10.95

FRANK LLOYD WRIGHT'S DANA HOUSE, Donald Hoffmann. Pictorial essay of residential masterpiece with over 160 interior and exterior photos, plans, elevations, sketches and studies. 128pp. 9¼ x 10¾. 29120-0 Pa. $12.95

THE MALE AND FEMALE FIGURE IN MOTION: 60 Classic Photographic Sequences, Eadweard Muybridge. 60 true-action photographs of men and women walking, running, climbing, bending, turning, etc., reproduced from rare 19th-century masterpiece. vi + 121pp. 9 x 12. 24745-7 Pa. $12.95

1001 QUESTIONS ANSWERED ABOUT THE SEASHORE, N. J. Berrill and Jacquelyn Berrill. Queries answered about dolphins, sea snails, sponges, starfish, fishes, shore birds, many others. Covers appearance, breeding, growth, feeding, much more. 305pp. 5¼ x 8¼. 23366-9 Pa. $9.95

ATTRACTING BIRDS TO YOUR YARD, William J. Weber. Easy-to-follow guide offers advice on how to attract the greatest diversity of birds: birdhouses, feeders, water and waterers, much more. 96pp. 5³⁄₁₆ x 8¼. 28927-3 Pa. $2.50

MEDICINAL AND OTHER USES OF NORTH AMERICAN PLANTS: A Historical Survey with Special Reference to the Eastern Indian Tribes, Charlotte Erichsen-Brown. Chronological historical citations document 500 years of usage of plants, trees, shrubs native to eastern Canada, northeastern U.S. Also complete identifying information. 343 illustrations. 544pp. 6½ x 9¼. 25951-X Pa. $12.95

STORYBOOK MAZES, Dave Phillips. 23 stories and mazes on two-page spreads: Wizard of Oz, Treasure Island, Robin Hood, etc. Solutions. 64pp. 8¼ x 11. 23628-5 Pa. $2.95

AMERICAN NEGRO SONGS: 230 Folk Songs and Spirituals, Religious and Secular, John W. Work. This authoritative study traces the African influences of songs sung and played by black Americans at work, in church, and as entertainment. The author discusses the lyric significance of such songs as "Swing Low, Sweet Chariot," "John Henry," and others and offers the words and music for 230 songs. Bibliography. Index of Song Titles. 272pp. 6½ x 9¼. 40271-1 Pa. $9.95

MOVIE-STAR PORTRAITS OF THE FORTIES, John Kobal (ed.). 163 glamor, studio photos of 106 stars of the 1940s: Rita Hayworth, Ava Gardner, Marlon Brando, Clark Gable, many more. 176pp. 8⅜ x 11¼. 23546-7 Pa. $14.95

BENCHLEY LOST AND FOUND, Robert Benchley. Finest humor from early 30s, about pet peeves, child psychologists, post office and others. Mostly unavailable elsewhere. 73 illustrations by Peter Arno and others. 183pp. 5⅜ x 8½. 22410-4 Pa. $6.95

YEKL and THE IMPORTED BRIDEGROOM AND OTHER STORIES OF YIDDISH NEW YORK, Abraham Cahan. Film Hester Street based on *Yekl* (1896). Novel, other stories among first about Jewish immigrants on N.Y.'s East Side. 240pp. 5⅜ x 8½. 22427-9 Pa. $7.95

SELECTED POEMS, Walt Whitman. Generous sampling from *Leaves of Grass*. Twenty-four poems include "I Hear America Singing," "Song of the Open Road," "I Sing the Body Electric," "When Lilacs Last in the Dooryard Bloom'd," "O Captain! My Captain!"—all reprinted from an authoritative edition. Lists of titles and first lines. 128pp. 5³⁄₁₆ x 8¼. 26878-0 Pa. $1.00

THE BEST TALES OF HOFFMANN, E. T. A. Hoffmann. 10 of Hoffmann's most important stories: "Nutcracker and the King of Mice," "The Golden Flowerpot," etc. 458pp. 5⅜ x 8½. 21793-0 Pa. $9.95

FROM FETISH TO GOD IN ANCIENT EGYPT, E. A. Wallis Budge. Rich detailed survey of Egyptian conception of "God" and gods, magic, cult of animals, Osiris, more. Also, superb English translations of hymns and legends. 240 illustrations. 545pp. 5⅜ x 8½. 25803-3 Pa. $13.95

FRENCH STORIES/CONTES FRANÇAIS: A Dual-Language Book, Wallace Fowlie. Ten stories by French masters, Voltaire to Camus: "Micromegas" by Voltaire; "The Atheist's Mass" by Balzac; "Minuet" by de Maupassant; "The Guest" by Camus, six more. Excellent English translations on facing pages. Also French-English vocabulary list, exercises, more. 352pp. 5⅜ x 8½. 26443-2 Pa. $9.95

CHICAGO AT THE TURN OF THE CENTURY IN PHOTOGRAPHS: 122 Historic Views from the Collections of the Chicago Historical Society, Larry A. Viskochil. Rare large-format prints offer detailed views of City Hall, State Street, the Loop, Hull House, Union Station, many other landmarks, circa 1904-1913. Introduction. Captions. Maps. 144pp. 9⅜ x 12¼. 24656-6 Pa. $12.95

OLD BROOKLYN IN EARLY PHOTOGRAPHS, 1865-1929, William Lee Younger. Luna Park, Gravesend race track, construction of Grand Army Plaza, moving of Hotel Brighton, etc. 157 previously unpublished photographs. 165pp. 8⅞ x 11¾. 23587-4 Pa. $13.95

THE MYTHS OF THE NORTH AMERICAN INDIANS, Lewis Spence. Rich anthology of the myths and legends of the Algonquins, Iroquois, Pawnees and Sioux, prefaced by an extensive historical and ethnological commentary. 36 illustrations. 480pp. 5⅜ x 8½. 25967-6 Pa. $10.95

AN ENCYCLOPEDIA OF BATTLES: Accounts of Over 1,560 Battles from 1479 B.C. to the Present, David Eggenberger. Essential details of every major battle in recorded history from the first battle of Megiddo in 1479 B.C. to Grenada in 1984. List of Battle Maps. New Appendix covering the years 1967-1984. Index. 99 illustrations. 544pp. 6½ x 9¼. 24913-1 Pa. $16.95

SAILING ALONE AROUND THE WORLD, Captain Joshua Slocum. First man to sail around the world, alone, in small boat. One of great feats of seamanship told in delightful manner. 67 illustrations. 294pp. 5⅜ x 8½. 20326-3 Pa. $6.95

ANARCHISM AND OTHER ESSAYS, Emma Goldman. Powerful, penetrating, prophetic essays on direct action, role of minorities, prison reform, puritan hypocrisy, violence, etc. 271pp. 5⅜ x 8½. 22484-8 Pa. $7.95

MYTHS OF THE HINDUS AND BUDDHISTS, Ananda K. Coomaraswamy and Sister Nivedita. Great stories of the epics; deeds of Krishna, Shiva, taken from puranas, Vedas, folk tales; etc. 32 illustrations. 400pp. 5⅜ x 8½. 21759-0 Pa. $12.95

THE TRAUMA OF BIRTH, Otto Rank. Rank's controversial thesis that anxiety neurosis is caused by profound psychological trauma which occurs at birth. 256pp. 5⅜ x 8½. 27974-X Pa. $7.95

A THEOLOGICO-POLITICAL TREATISE, Benedict Spinoza. Also contains unfinished Political Treatise. Great classic on religious liberty, theory of government on common consent. R. Elwes translation. Total of 421pp. 5⅜ x 8½. 20249-6 Pa. $10.95

MY BONDAGE AND MY FREEDOM, Frederick Douglass. Born a slave, Douglass became outspoken force in antislavery movement. The best of Douglass' autobiographies. Graphic description of slave life. 464pp. 5⅜ x 8½. 22457-0 Pa. $8.95

FOLLOWING THE EQUATOR: A Journey Around the World, Mark Twain. Fascinating humorous account of 1897 voyage to Hawaii, Australia, India, New Zealand, etc. Ironic, bemused reports on peoples, customs, climate, flora and fauna, politics, much more. 197 illustrations. 720pp. 5⅜ x 8½. 26113-1 Pa. $15.95

THE PEOPLE CALLED SHAKERS, Edward D. Andrews. Definitive study of Shakers: origins, beliefs, practices, dances, social organization, furniture and crafts, etc. 33 illustrations. 351pp. 5⅜ x 8½. 21081-2 Pa. $10.95

THE MYTHS OF GREECE AND ROME, H. A. Guerber. A classic of mythology, generously illustrated, long prized for its simple, graphic, accurate retelling of the principal myths of Greece and Rome, and for its commentary on their origins and significance. With 64 illustrations by Michelangelo, Raphael, Titian, Rubens, Canova, Bernini and others. 480pp. 5⅜ x 8½. 27584-1 Pa. $9.95

PSYCHOLOGY OF MUSIC, Carl E. Seashore. Classic work discusses music as a medium from psychological viewpoint. Clear treatment of physical acoustics, auditory apparatus, sound perception, development of musical skills, nature of musical feeling, host of other topics. 88 figures. 408pp. 5⅜ x 8½. 21851-1 Pa. $11.95

THE PHILOSOPHY OF HISTORY, Georg W. Hegel. Great classic of Western thought develops concept that history is not chance but rational process, the evolution of freedom. 457pp. 5⅜ x 8½. 20112-0 Pa. $9.95

THE BOOK OF TEA, Kakuzo Okakura. Minor classic of the Orient: entertaining, charming explanation, interpretation of traditional Japanese culture in terms of tea ceremony. 94pp. 5⅜ x 8½. 20070-1 Pa. $3.95

LIFE IN ANCIENT EGYPT, Adolf Erman. Fullest, most thorough, detailed older account with much not in more recent books, domestic life, religion, magic, medicine, commerce, much more. Many illustrations reproduce tomb paintings, carvings, hieroglyphs, etc. 597pp. 5⅜ x 8½. 22632-8 Pa. $12.95

SUNDIALS, Their Theory and Construction, Albert Waugh. Far and away the best, most thorough coverage of ideas, mathematics concerned, types, construction, adjusting anywhere. Simple, nontechnical treatment allows even children to build several of these dials. Over 100 illustrations. 230pp. 5⅜ x 8½. 22947-5 Pa. $8.95

THEORETICAL HYDRODYNAMICS, L. M. Milne-Thomson. Classic exposition of the mathematical theory of fluid motion, applicable to both hydrodynamics and aerodynamics. Over 600 exercises. 768pp. 6⅛ x 9¼. 68970-0 Pa. $20.95

SONGS OF EXPERIENCE: Facsimile Reproduction with 26 Plates in Full Color, William Blake. 26 full-color plates from a rare 1826 edition. Includes "TheTyger," "London," "Holy Thursday," and other poems. Printed text of poems. 48pp. 5¼ x 7. 24636-1 Pa. $4.95

OLD-TIME VIGNETTES IN FULL COLOR, Carol Belanger Grafton (ed.). Over 390 charming, often sentimental illustrations, selected from archives of Victorian graphics—pretty women posing, children playing, food, flowers, kittens and puppies, smiling cherubs, birds and butterflies, much more. All copyright-free. 48pp. 9¼ x 12¼. 27269-9 Pa. $7.95

PERSPECTIVE FOR ARTISTS, Rex Vicat Cole. Depth, perspective of sky and sea, shadows, much more, not usually covered. 391 diagrams, 81 reproductions of drawings and paintings. 279pp. 5⅜ x 8½. 22487-2 Pa. $9.95

DRAWING THE LIVING FIGURE, Joseph Sheppard. Innovative approach to artistic anatomy focuses on specifics of surface anatomy, rather than muscles and bones. Over 170 drawings of live models in front, back and side views, and in widely varying poses. Accompanying diagrams. 177 illustrations. Introduction. Index. 144pp. 8⅜ x11¼. 26723-7 Pa. $9.95

GOTHIC AND OLD ENGLISH ALPHABETS: 100 Complete Fonts, Dan X. Solo. Add power, elegance to posters, signs, other graphics with 100 stunning copyright-free alphabets: Blackstone, Dolbey, Germania, 97 more–including many lower-case, numerals, punctuation marks. 104pp. 8⅛ x 11. 24695-7 Pa. $8.95

HOW TO DO BEADWORK, Mary White. Fundamental book on craft from simple projects to five-bead chains and woven works. 106 illustrations. 142pp. 5⅜ x 8. 20697-1 Pa. $5.95

THE BOOK OF WOOD CARVING, Charles Marshall Sayers. Finest book for beginners discusses fundamentals and offers 34 designs. "Absolutely first rate . . . well thought out and well executed."–E. J. Tangerman. 118pp. 7¾ x 10⅝. 23654-4 Pa. $7.95

ILLUSTRATED CATALOG OF CIVIL WAR MILITARY GOODS: Union Army Weapons, Insignia, Uniform Accessories, and Other Equipment, Schuyler, Hartley, and Graham. Rare, profusely illustrated 1846 catalog includes Union Army uniform and dress regulations, arms and ammunition, coats, insignia, flags, swords, rifles, etc. 226 illustrations. 160pp. 9 x 12. 24939-5 Pa. $10.95

WOMEN'S FASHIONS OF THE EARLY 1900s: An Unabridged Republication of "New York Fashions, 1909," National Cloak & Suit Co. Rare catalog of mail-order fashions documents women's and children's clothing styles shortly after the turn of the century. Captions offer full descriptions, prices. Invaluable resource for fashion, costume historians. Approximately 725 illustrations. 128pp. 8⅜ x 11¼. 27276-1 Pa. $11.95

THE 1912 AND 1915 GUSTAV STICKLEY FURNITURE CATALOGS, Gustav Stickley. With over 200 detailed illustrations and descriptions, these two catalogs are essential reading and reference materials and identification guides for Stickley furniture. Captions cite materials, dimensions and prices. 112pp. 6½ x 9¼. 26676-1 Pa. $9.95

EARLY AMERICAN LOCOMOTIVES, John H. White, Jr. Finest locomotive engravings from early 19th century: historical (1804–74), main-line (after 1870), special, foreign, etc. 147 plates. 142pp. 11⅜ x 8¼. 22772-3 Pa. $12.95

THE TALL SHIPS OF TODAY IN PHOTOGRAPHS, Frank O. Braynard. Lavishly illustrated tribute to nearly 100 majestic contemporary sailing vessels: Amerigo Vespucci, Clearwater, Constitution, Eagle, Mayflower, Sea Cloud, Victory, many more. Authoritative captions provide statistics, background on each ship. 190 black-and-white photographs and illustrations. Introduction. 128pp. 8⅞ x 11¾. 27163-3 Pa. $14.95

LITTLE BOOK OF EARLY AMERICAN CRAFTS AND TRADES, Peter Stockham (ed.). 1807 children's book explains crafts and trades: baker, hatter, cooper, potter, and many others. 23 copperplate illustrations. 140pp. 4⅝ x 6.
23336-7 Pa. $4.95

VICTORIAN FASHIONS AND COSTUMES FROM HARPER'S BAZAR, 1867–1898, Stella Blum (ed.). Day costumes, evening wear, sports clothes, shoes, hats, other accessories in over 1,000 detailed engravings. 320pp. 9⅜ x 12¼.
22990-4 Pa. $16.95

GUSTAV STICKLEY, THE CRAFTSMAN, Mary Ann Smith. Superb study surveys broad scope of Stickley's achievement, especially in architecture. Design philosophy, rise and fall of the Craftsman empire, descriptions and floor plans for many Craftsman houses, more. 86 black-and-white halftones. 31 line illustrations. Introduction 208pp. 6½ x 9¼.
27210-9 Pa. $9.95

THE LONG ISLAND RAIL ROAD IN EARLY PHOTOGRAPHS, Ron Ziel. Over 220 rare photos, informative text document origin (1844) and development of rail service on Long Island. Vintage views of early trains, locomotives, stations, passengers, crews, much more. Captions. 8⅞ x 11¾.
26301-0 Pa. $14.95

VOYAGE OF THE LIBERDADE, Joshua Slocum. Great 19th-century mariner's thrilling, first-hand account of the wreck of his ship off South America, the 35-foot boat he built from the wreckage, and its remarkable voyage home. 128pp. 5⅜ x 8½.
40022-0 Pa. $5.95

TEN BOOKS ON ARCHITECTURE, Vitruvius. The most important book ever written on architecture. Early Roman aesthetics, technology, classical orders, site selection, all other aspects. Morgan translation. 331pp. 5⅜ x 8½.   20645-9 Pa. $8.95

THE HUMAN FIGURE IN MOTION, Eadweard Muybridge. More than 4,500 stopped-action photos, in action series, showing undraped men, women, children jumping, lying down, throwing, sitting, wrestling, carrying, etc. 390pp. 7⅞ x 10⅝.
20204-6 Clothbd. $27.95

TREES OF THE EASTERN AND CENTRAL UNITED STATES AND CANADA, William M. Harlow. Best one-volume guide to 140 trees. Full descriptions, woodlore, range, etc. Over 600 illustrations. Handy size. 288pp. 4½ x 6⅜.
20395-6 Pa. $6.95

SONGS OF WESTERN BIRDS, Dr. Donald J. Borror. Complete song and call repertoire of 60 western species, including flycatchers, juncoes, cactus wrens, many more—includes fully illustrated booklet.   Cassette and manual 99913-0 $8.95

GROWING AND USING HERBS AND SPICES, Milo Miloradovich. Versatile handbook provides all the information needed for cultivation and use of all the herbs and spices available in North America. 4 illustrations. Index. Glossary. 236pp. 5⅜ x 8½.
25058-X Pa. $7.95

BIG BOOK OF MAZES AND LABYRINTHS, Walter Shepherd. 50 mazes and labyrinths in all—classical, solid, ripple, and more—in one great volume. Perfect inexpensive puzzler for clever youngsters. Full solutions. 112pp. 8⅛ x 11.
22951-3 Pa. $5.95

CATALOG OF DOVER BOOKS

PIANO TUNING, J. Cree Fischer. Clearest, best book for beginner, amateur. Simple repairs, raising dropped notes, tuning by easy method of flattened fifths. No previous skills needed. 4 illustrations. 201pp. 5⅜ x 8½. 23267-0 Pa. $6.95

HINTS TO SINGERS, Lillian Nordica. Selecting the right teacher, developing confidence, overcoming stage fright, and many other important skills receive thoughtful discussion in this indispensible guide, written by a world-famous diva of four decades' experience. 96pp. 5³/₈ x 8¹/₂. 40094-8 Pa. $4.95

THE COMPLETE NONSENSE OF EDWARD LEAR, Edward Lear. All nonsense limericks, zany alphabets, Owl and Pussycat, songs, nonsense botany, etc., illustrated by Lear. Total of 320pp. 5⅜ x 8½. (AVAILABLE IN U.S. ONLY.) 20167-8 Pa. $7.95

VICTORIAN PARLOUR POETRY: An Annotated Anthology, Michael R. Turner. 117 gems by Longfellow, Tennyson, Browning, many lesser-known poets. "The Village Blacksmith," "Curfew Must Not Ring Tonight," "Only a Baby Small," dozens more, often difficult to find elsewhere. Index of poets, titles, first lines. xxiii + 325pp. 5⅜ x 8¼. 27044-0 Pa. $8.95

DUBLINERS, James Joyce. Fifteen stories offer vivid, tightly focused observations of the lives of Dublin's poorer classes. At least one, "The Dead," is considered a masterpiece. Reprinted complete and unabridged from standard edition. 160pp. 5³⁄₁₆ x 8¼. 26870-5 Pa. $1.00

GREAT WEIRD TALES: 14 Stories by Lovecraft, Blackwood, Machen and Others, S. T. Joshi (ed.). 14 spellbinding tales, including "The Sin Eater," by Fiona McLeod, "The Eye Above the Mantel," by Frank Belknap Long, as well as renowned works by R. H. Barlow, Lord Dunsany, Arthur Machen, W. C. Morrow and eight other masters of the genre. 256pp. 5⅜ x 8½. (Available in U.S. only.) 40436-6 Pa. $8.95

THE BOOK OF THE SACRED MAGIC OF ABRAMELIN THE MAGE, translated by S. MacGregor Mathers. Medieval manuscript of ceremonial magic. Basic document in Aleister Crowley, Golden Dawn groups. 268pp. 5⅜ x 8½. 23211-5 Pa. $9.95

NEW RUSSIAN-ENGLISH AND ENGLISH-RUSSIAN DICTIONARY, M. A. O'Brien. This is a remarkably handy Russian dictionary, containing a surprising amount of information, including over 70,000 entries. 366pp. 4½ x 6¼. 20208-9 Pa. $10.95

HISTORIC HOMES OF THE AMERICAN PRESIDENTS, Second, Revised Edition, Irvin Haas. A traveler's guide to American Presidential homes, most open to the public, depicting and describing homes occupied by every American President from George Washington to George Bush. With visiting hours, admission charges, travel routes. 175 photographs. Index. 160pp. 8¼ x 11. 26751-2 Pa. $11.95

NEW YORK IN THE FORTIES, Andreas Feininger. 162 brilliant photographs by the well-known photographer, formerly with *Life* magazine. Commuters, shoppers, Times Square at night, much else from city at its peak. Captions by John von Hartz. 181pp. 9¼ x 10¾. 23585-8 Pa. $13.95

INDIAN SIGN LANGUAGE, William Tomkins. Over 525 signs developed by Sioux and other tribes. Written instructions and diagrams. Also 290 pictographs. 111pp. 6⅛ x 9¼. 22029-X Pa. $3.95

ANATOMY: A Complete Guide for Artists, Joseph Sheppard. A master of figure drawing shows artists how to render human anatomy convincingly. Over 460 illustrations. 224pp. 8⅜ x 11¼. 27279-6 Pa. $11.95

MEDIEVAL CALLIGRAPHY: Its History and Technique, Marc Drogin. Spirited history, comprehensive instruction manual covers 13 styles (ca. 4th century through 15th). Excellent photographs; directions for duplicating medieval techniques with modern tools. 224pp. 8⅜ x 11¼. 26142-5 Pa. $12.95

DRIED FLOWERS: How to Prepare Them, Sarah Whitlock and Martha Rankin. Complete instructions on how to use silica gel, meal and borax, perlite aggregate, sand and borax, glycerine and water to create attractive permanent flower arrangements. 12 illustrations. 32pp. 5⅜ x 8½. 21802-3 Pa. $1.00

EASY-TO-MAKE BIRD FEEDERS FOR WOODWORKERS, Scott D. Campbell. Detailed, simple-to-use guide for designing, constructing, caring for and using feeders. Text, illustrations for 12 classic and contemporary designs. 96pp. 5⅜ x 8½. 25847-5 Pa. $3.95

SCOTTISH WONDER TALES FROM MYTH AND LEGEND, Donald A. Mackenzie. 16 lively tales tell of giants rumbling down mountainsides, of a magic wand that turns stone pillars into warriors, of gods and goddesses, evil hags, powerful forces and more. 240pp. 5⅜ x 8½. 29677-6 Pa. $6.95

THE HISTORY OF UNDERCLOTHES, C. Willett Cunnington and Phyllis Cunnington. Fascinating, well-documented survey covering six centuries of English undergarments, enhanced with over 100 illustrations: 12th-century laced-up bodice, footed long drawers (1795), 19th-century bustles, l9th-century corsets for men, Victorian "bust improvers," much more. 272pp. 5⅜ x 8¼. 27124-2 Pa. $9.95

ARTS AND CRAFTS FURNITURE: The Complete Brooks Catalog of 1912, Brooks Manufacturing Co. Photos and detailed descriptions of more than 150 now very collectible furniture designs from the Arts and Crafts movement depict davenports, settees, buffets, desks, tables, chairs, bedsteads, dressers and more, all built of solid, quarter-sawed oak. Invaluable for students and enthusiasts of antiques, Americana and the decorative arts. 80pp. 6½ x 9¼. 27471-3 Pa. $8.95

WILBUR AND ORVILLE: A Biography of the Wright Brothers, Fred Howard. Definitive, crisply written study tells the full story of the brothers' lives and work. A vividly written biography, unparalleled in scope and color, that also captures the spirit of an extraordinary era. 560pp. 6⅛ x 9¼. 40297-5 Pa. $17.95

THE ARTS OF THE SAILOR: Knotting, Splicing and Ropework, Hervey Garrett Smith. Indispensable shipboard reference covers tools, basic knots and useful hitches; handsewing and canvas work, more. Over 100 illustrations. Delightful reading for sea lovers. 256pp. 5⅜ x 8½. 26440-8 Pa. $8.95

FRANK LLOYD WRIGHT'S FALLINGWATER: The House and Its History, Second, Revised Edition, Donald Hoffmann. A total revision—both in text and illustrations—of the standard document on Fallingwater, the boldest, most personal architectural statement of Wright's mature years, updated with valuable new material from the recently opened Frank Lloyd Wright Archives. "Fascinating"—*The New York Times*. 116 illustrations. 128pp. 9¼ x 10¾. 27430-6 Pa. $12.95

PHOTOGRAPHIC SKETCHBOOK OF THE CIVIL WAR, Alexander Gardner. 100 photos taken on field during the Civil War. Famous shots of Manassas Harper's Ferry, Lincoln, Richmond, slave pens, etc. 244pp. 10⅝ x 8¼. 22731-6 Pa. $10.95

FIVE ACRES AND INDEPENDENCE, Maurice G. Kains. Great back-to-the-land classic explains basics of self-sufficient farming. The one book to get. 95 illustrations. 397pp. 5⅜ x 8½. 20974-1 Pa. $7.95

SONGS OF EASTERN BIRDS, Dr. Donald J. Borror. Songs and calls of 60 species most common to eastern U.S.: warblers, woodpeckers, flycatchers, thrushes, larks, many more in high-quality recording. Cassette and manual 99912-2 $9.95

A MODERN HERBAL, Margaret Grieve. Much the fullest, most exact, most useful compilation of herbal material. Gigantic alphabetical encyclopedia, from aconite to zedoary, gives botanical information, medical properties, folklore, economic uses, much else. Indispensable to serious reader. 161 illustrations. 888pp. 6½ x 9¼. 2-vol. set. (Available in U.S. only.) Vol. I: 22798-7 Pa. $9.95
Vol. II: 22799-5 Pa. $9.95

HIDDEN TREASURE MAZE BOOK, Dave Phillips. Solve 34 challenging mazes accompanied by heroic tales of adventure. Evil dragons, people-eating plants, blood-thirsty giants, many more dangerous adversaries lurk at every twist and turn. 34 mazes, stories, solutions. 48pp. 8¼ x 11. 24566-7 Pa. $2.95

LETTERS OF W. A. MOZART, Wolfgang A. Mozart. Remarkable letters show bawdy wit, humor, imagination, musical insights, contemporary musical world; includes some letters from Leopold Mozart. 276pp. 5⅜ x 8½. 22859-2 Pa. $7.95

BASIC PRINCIPLES OF CLASSICAL BALLET, Agrippina Vaganova. Great Russian theoretician, teacher explains methods for teaching classical ballet. 118 illustrations. 175pp. 5⅜ x 8½. 22036-2 Pa. $6.95

THE JUMPING FROG, Mark Twain. Revenge edition. The original story of The Celebrated Jumping Frog of Calaveras County, a hapless French translation, and Twain's hilarious "retranslation" from the French. 12 illustrations. 66pp. 5⅜ x 8½. 22686-7 Pa. $3.95

BEST REMEMBERED POEMS, Martin Gardner (ed.). The 126 poems in this superb collection of 19th- and 20th-century British and American verse range from Shelley's "To a Skylark" to the impassioned "Renascence" of Edna St. Vincent Millay and to Edward Lear's whimsical "The Owl and the Pussycat." 224pp. 5⅜ x 8½. 27165-X Pa. $5.95

COMPLETE SONNETS, William Shakespeare. Over 150 exquisite poems deal with love, friendship, the tyranny of time, beauty's evanescence, death and other themes in language of remarkable power, precision and beauty. Glossary of archaic terms. 80pp. 5³⁄₁₆ x 8¼. 26686-9 Pa. $1.00

BODIES IN A BOOKSHOP, R. T. Campbell. Challenging mystery of blackmail and murder with ingenious plot and superbly drawn characters. In the best tradition of British suspense fiction. 192pp. 5⅜ x 8½. 24720-1 Pa. $6.95

THE WIT AND HUMOR OF OSCAR WILDE, Alvin Redman (ed.). More than 1,000 ripostes, paradoxes, wisecracks: Work is the curse of the drinking classes; I can resist everything except temptation; etc. 258pp. 5⅜ x 8½. 20602-5 Pa. $6.95

SHAKESPEARE LEXICON AND QUOTATION DICTIONARY, Alexander Schmidt. Full definitions, locations, shades of meaning in every word in plays and poems. More than 50,000 exact quotations. 1,485pp. 6½ x 9¼. 2-vol. set.
Vol. 1: 22726-X Pa. $17.95
Vol. 2: 22727-8 Pa. $17.95

SELECTED POEMS, Emily Dickinson. Over 100 best-known, best-loved poems by one of America's foremost poets, reprinted from authoritative early editions. No comparable edition at this price. Index of first lines. 64pp. 5³⁄₁₆ x 8¼.
26466-1 Pa. $1.00

THE INSIDIOUS DR. FU-MANCHU, Sax Rohmer. The first of the popular mystery series introduces a pair of English detectives to their archnemesis, the diabolical Dr. Fu-Manchu. Flavorful atmosphere, fast-paced action, and colorful characters enliven this classic of the genre. 208pp. 5³⁄₁₆ x 8¼. 29898-1 Pa. $2.00

THE MALLEUS MALEFICARUM OF KRAMER AND SPRENGER, translated by Montague Summers. Full text of most important witchhunter's "bible," used by both Catholics and Protestants. 278pp. 6⅝ x 10. 22802-9 Pa. $12.95

SPANISH STORIES/CUENTOS ESPAÑOLES: A Dual-Language Book, Angel Flores (ed.). Unique format offers 13 great stories in Spanish by Cervantes, Borges, others. Faithful English translations on facing pages. 352pp. 5⅜ x 8½.
25399-6 Pa. $8.95

GARDEN CITY, LONG ISLAND, IN EARLY PHOTOGRAPHS, 1869–1919, Mildred H. Smith. Handsome treasury of 118 vintage pictures, accompanied by carefully researched captions, document the Garden City Hotel fire (1899), the Vanderbilt Cup Race (1908), the first airmail flight departing from the Nassau Boulevard Aerodrome (1911), and much more. 96pp. 8⅞ x 11¾. 40669-5 Pa. $12.95

OLD QUEENS, N.Y., IN EARLY PHOTOGRAPHS, Vincent F. Seyfried and William Asadorian. Over 160 rare photographs of Maspeth, Jamaica, Jackson Heights, and other areas. Vintage views of DeWitt Clinton mansion, 1939 World's Fair and more. Captions. 192pp. 8⅞ x 11. 26358-4 Pa. $12.95

CAPTURED BY THE INDIANS: 15 Firsthand Accounts, 1750-1870, Frederick Drimmer. Astounding true historical accounts of grisly torture, bloody conflicts, relentless pursuits, miraculous escapes and more, by people who lived to tell the tale. 384pp. 5⅜ x 8½. 24901-8 Pa. $8.95

THE WORLD'S GREAT SPEECHES (Fourth Enlarged Edition), Lewis Copeland, Lawrence W. Lamm, and Stephen J. McKenna. Nearly 300 speeches provide public speakers with a wealth of updated quotes and inspiration–from Pericles' funeral oration and William Jennings Bryan's "Cross of Gold Speech" to Malcolm X's powerful words on the Black Revolution and Earl of Spenser's tribute to his sister, Diana, Princess of Wales. 944pp. 5⅜ x 8⅜. 40903-1 Pa. $15.95

THE BOOK OF THE SWORD, Sir Richard F. Burton. Great Victorian scholar/adventurer's eloquent, erudite history of the "queen of weapons"–from prehistory to early Roman Empire. Evolution and development of early swords, variations (sabre, broadsword, cutlass, scimitar, etc.), much more. 336pp. 6⅛ x 9¼.
25434-8 Pa. $9.95

AUTOBIOGRAPHY: The Story of My Experiments with Truth, Mohandas K. Gandhi. Boyhood, legal studies, purification, the growth of the Satyagraha (nonviolent protest) movement. Critical, inspiring work of the man responsible for the freedom of India. 480pp. 5⅜ x 8½. (Available in U.S. only.)   24593-4 Pa. $8.95

CELTIC MYTHS AND LEGENDS, T. W. Rolleston. Masterful retelling of Irish and Welsh stories and tales. Cuchulain, King Arthur, Deirdre, the Grail, many more. First paperback edition. 58 full-page illustrations. 512pp. 5⅜ x 8½.   26507-2 Pa. $9.95

THE PRINCIPLES OF PSYCHOLOGY, William James. Famous long course complete, unabridged. Stream of thought, time perception, memory, experimental methods; great work decades ahead of its time. 94 figures. 1,391pp. 5⅜ x 8½. 2-vol. set.
Vol. I: 20381-6 Pa. $14.95
Vol. II: 20382-4 Pa. $14.95

THE WORLD AS WILL AND REPRESENTATION, Arthur Schopenhauer. Definitive English translation of Schopenhauer's life work, correcting more than 1,000 errors, omissions in earlier translations. Translated by E. F. J. Payne. Total of 1,269pp. 5⅜ x 8½. 2-vol. set.
Vol. 1: 21761-2 Pa. $12.95
Vol. 2: 21762-0 Pa. $12.95

MAGIC AND MYSTERY IN TIBET, Madame Alexandra David-Neel. Experiences among lamas, magicians, sages, sorcerers, Bonpa wizards. A true psychic discovery. 32 illustrations. 321pp. 5⅜ x 8½. (Available in U.S. only.)   22682-4 Pa. $9.95

THE EGYPTIAN BOOK OF THE DEAD, E. A. Wallis Budge. Complete reproduction of Ani's papyrus, finest ever found. Full hieroglyphic text, interlinear transliteration, word-for-word translation, smooth translation. 533pp. 6½ x 9¼.
21866-X Pa. $12.95

MATHEMATICS FOR THE NONMATHEMATICIAN, Morris Kline. Detailed, college-level treatment of mathematics in cultural and historical context, with numerous exercises. Recommended Reading Lists. Tables. Numerous figures. 641pp. 5⅜ x 8½.
24823-2 Pa. $11.95

PROBABILISTIC METHODS IN THE THEORY OF STRUCTURES, Isaac Elishakoff. Well-written introduction covers the elements of the theory of probability from two or more random variables, the reliability of such multivariable structures, the theory of random function, Monte Carlo methods of treating problems incapable of exact solution, and more. Examples. 502pp. 5³⁄₈ x 8¹⁄₂.   40691-1 Pa. $16.95

THE RIME OF THE ANCIENT MARINER, Gustave Doré, S. T. Coleridge. Doré's finest work; 34 plates capture moods, subtleties of poem. Flawless full-size reproductions printed on facing pages with authoritative text of poem. "Beautiful. Simply beautiful."–*Publisher's Weekly.* 77pp. 9¼ x 12.   22305-1 Pa. $7.95

NORTH AMERICAN INDIAN DESIGNS FOR ARTISTS AND CRAFTSPEOPLE, Eva Wilson. Over 360 authentic copyright-free designs adapted from Navajo blankets, Hopi pottery, Sioux buffalo hides, more. Geometrics, symbolic figures, plant and animal motifs, etc. 128pp. 8⅜ x 11. (Not for sale in the United Kingdom.)   25341-4 Pa. $9.95

SCULPTURE: Principles and Practice, Louis Slobodkin. Step-by-step approach to clay, plaster, metals, stone; classical and modern. 253 drawings, photos. 255pp. 8⅛ x 11.
22960-2 Pa. $11.95

THE INFLUENCE OF SEA POWER UPON HISTORY, 1660–1783, A. T. Mahan. Influential classic of naval history and tactics still used as text in war colleges. First paperback edition. 4 maps. 24 battle plans. 640pp. 5⅜ x 8½.   25509-3 Pa. $14.95

THE STORY OF THE TITANIC AS TOLD BY ITS SURVIVORS, Jack Winocour (ed.). What it was really like. Panic, despair, shocking inefficiency, and a little heroism. More thrilling than any fictional account. 26 illustrations. 320pp. 5⅜ x 8½.
20610-6 Pa. $8.95

FAIRY AND FOLK TALES OF THE IRISH PEASANTRY, William Butler Yeats (ed.). Treasury of 64 tales from the twilight world of Celtic myth and legend: "The Soul Cages," "The Kildare Pooka," "King O'Toole and his Goose," many more. Introduction and Notes by W. B. Yeats. 352pp. 5⅜ x 8½.   26941-8 Pa. $8.95

BUDDHIST MAHAYANA TEXTS, E. B. Cowell and others (eds.). Superb, accurate translations of basic documents in Mahayana Buddhism, highly important in history of religions. The Buddha-karita of Asvaghosha, Larger Sukhavativyuha, more. 448pp. 5⅜ x 8½.   25552-2 Pa. $12.95

ONE TWO THREE . . . INFINITY: Facts and Speculations of Science, George Gamow. Great physicist's fascinating, readable overview of contemporary science: number theory, relativity, fourth dimension, entropy, genes, atomic structure, much more. 128 illustrations. Index. 352pp. 5⅜ x 8½.   25664-2 Pa. $9.95

EXPERIMENTATION AND MEASUREMENT, W. J. Youden. Introductory manual explains laws of measurement in simple terms and offers tips for achieving accuracy and minimizing errors. Mathematics of measurement, use of instruments, experimenting with machines. 1994 edition. Foreword. Preface. Introduction. Epilogue. Selected Readings. Glossary. Index. Tables and figures. 128pp. 5³⁄₈ x 8¹⁄₂.
40451-X Pa. $6.95

DALÍ ON MODERN ART: The Cuckolds of Antiquated Modern Art, Salvador Dalí. Influential painter skewers modern art and its practitioners. Outrageous evaluations of Picasso, Cézanne, Turner, more. 15 renderings of paintings discussed. 44 calligraphic decorations by Dalí. 96pp. 5⅜ x 8½. (Available in U.S. only.)   29220-7 Pa. $5.95

ANTIQUE PLAYING CARDS: A Pictorial History, Henry René D'Allemagne. Over 900 elaborate, decorative images from rare playing cards (14th–20th centuries): Bacchus, death, dancing dogs, hunting scenes, royal coats of arms, players cheating, much more. 96pp. 9¼ x 12¼.   29265-7 Pa. $12.95

MAKING FURNITURE MASTERPIECES: 30 Projects with Measured Drawings, Franklin H. Gottshall. Step-by-step instructions, illustrations for constructing handsome, useful pieces, among them a Sheraton desk, Chippendale chair, Spanish desk, Queen Anne table and a William and Mary dressing mirror. 224pp. 8⅛ x 11¼.
29338-6 Pa. $13.95

THE FOSSIL BOOK: A Record of Prehistoric Life, Patricia V. Rich et al. Profusely illustrated definitive guide covers everything from single-celled organisms and dinosaurs to birds and mammals and the interplay between climate and man. Over 1,500 illustrations. 760pp. 7½ x 10¼.   29371-8 Pa. $29.95

Prices subject to change without notice.

Available at your book dealer or write for free catalog to Dept. GI, Dover Publications, Inc., 31 East 2nd St., Mineola, N.Y. 11501. Dover publishes more than 500 books each year on science, elementary and advanced mathematics, biology, music, art, literary history, social sciences and other areas.